POLICE

IN

COMMUNITY

RELATIONS

Third Edition

POLICE

IN

COMMUNITY

RELATIONS

Critical Issues

Steven M. Cox
Western Illinois University

Jack D. Fitzgerald
Knox College

Brown & Benchmark
PUBLISHERS

Madison   Dubuque, IA   Guilford, CT   Chicago   Toronto London
Caracas   Mexico City   Buenos Aires   Madrid   Bogota   Sydney

Book Team

Publisher *Bevan O'Callaghan*
Publisher (Guilford) *Irv Rockwood*
Acquisitions Editor *Michael Alread*
Managing Editor *Sue Pulvermacher-Alt*
Production Editor *Kristine Queck*
Proofreading Coordinator *Carrie Barker*
Art Editor *Rachel Imsland*
Photo Editor *Leslie Dague*
Production Manager *Beth Kundert*
Production/Costing Manager *Sherry Padden*
Visuals/Design Freelance Specialist *Mary L. Christianson*

Basal Text *10/12 Times Roman*
Display Type *Bembo*
Typesetting System *Aviion*
Paper Stock *50# Solutions*

President and Chief Executive Officer *Thomas E. Doran*
Vice President of Production and Business Development *Vickie Putman*
Vice President of Sales and Marketing *Bob McLaughlin*
Director of Marketing *John Finn*

A Times Mirror Company

Cover design by *Kay Fulton Design*

Cover image © Brian Seed/Tony Stone Images

Copyedited by *Rose R. Kramer;* Proofread by *Paula Gieseman*

Library of Congress Catalog Card Number: 94–73759

ISBN 0–697–25119–5

Printed in the United States of America by Times Mirror Higher Education Group, Inc.,
2460 Kerper Boulevard, Dubuque, IA 52001

10 9 8 7 6 5 4 3 2 1

Contents

Human Relations and the Police 41

Police Public Relations 60

Youth and the Police 76

Crowds and the Police   98

 Community Policing and Police Community
Relations   119

Policing Diversity   136

Diversity in Policing   157

Training the Police in Community Relations, and Types of Police-Sponsored Community Relations Programs   171

11 The Role of the Community in Police Community Relations   188

12 The Role of the Police in Community Relations: Summary   204

Critical Issues

Preface

*T*here have been several interesting developments on the beat as well as in theory and research concerning police community relations since the second edition of this book was published in 1991. Nevertheless, in our judgment the basic themes of the book remain quite current. The fundamental challenges facing municipal or county police officers in free, open, democratic, extraordinarily diverse, and rapidly changing communities are essentially the same. If anything, the mutual dependence of the police and residents of the communities they serve has become more apparent with the widespread transition to community policing: clearly, neither can perform well without the cooperation and support of the other. As we approach the twenty-first century, cultivating positive relations with the community should be a top priority for police personnel.

The decidedly conservative political ethos of the 1980s has abated little. The public's fear of crime has grown, especially in inner-city neighborhoods, and demands on criminal justice personnel and politicians to ''get tough'' on crime and criminals persist. Legislators have passed more restrictive laws with more certain and longer incarcerations. Much of the fervor of public concern has been generated by the still-present drug crisis, involving crack cocaine, the rebirth of LSD, and heroin use. Another in the recent series of wars on drugs has been declared, this time involving the professional military, albeit in a limited role. Urban gangs continue to capture the headlines and the attention of the police as well as researchers. Yet, as the public worries, the politicians legislate, the police arrest, more prisons are built, and prisons and jails overflow, there are nagging doubts in many quarters (certainly among police officials) about the short-term viability as well as long-term efficacy of these efforts to deal with crime and order maintenance. There is no doubt about the importance of the police in managing aspects of some social problems. But, increasingly, questions are being raised about which problems are more (or less) amenable to a "get tough" approach. Recognition of the limitations of the police in changing people's behavior is growing, especially when the police attempt to do it all by themselves.

All of this, in turn, has led to a renewed interest in the dynamics of police community relations. The "community policing" initiative, which has taken hold in at least some jurisdictions, is one manifestation. So also are the gradually rising standards for police recruits, and the increasing number of police agencies seeking accreditation. It is too soon to tell whether these developments will suffer the dismal fate of previous reform efforts, but at least the debates continue. We have incorporated these and other developments in this new edition.

Among the more important changes in the third edition:

Chapter 7 has been rewritten to include an expanded discussion of community policing.

Information on the Americans with Disabilities Act and the Civil Rights Act of 1991 has been added in Chapter 9.

References have been updated and expanded throughout the book in order to provide more resources for instructors and students.

Material concerning recent events involving police brutality and public response has been added.

Several new "Critical Issues" have been included.

The "Critical Issues" proved popular in the first two editions and we hope they will continue to stimulate critical thought and vigorous debate.

Review and discussion questions are included at the end of each chapter, as is a list of suggested readings.

While there have been substantial revisions for this edition, we have not significantly expanded the length of the book in order to keep costs down for students. For those instructors who wish to do so, a book of readings or other sources of information may be added to a course syllabus without overwhelming students with material.

To facilitate instructor's course preparation, we have written an instructor's manual. Also, for any instructors who want to incorporate a reader into their course, Brown & Benchmark publishes *Annual Editions in Criminal Justice*. Any instructor can call the local Brown & Benchmark Sales Representative for more details.

We want to thank the reviewers for their in-depth comments:

Rick Michelson Grossmont College
Jay Lee Rochester Community College
Richard Anson Albany State College

As always, we welcome readers' comments.

Finally, thanks to the editorial staff at Brown & Benchmark Publishers.

S. M. C.
J. D. F.

Police in Community Relations:
An Introduction

I n a recent assessment of the problems and prospects of policing in the United States, Joseph Ryan (1994) asserts: ''Police are now realizing that they do not exist in a vacuum. The actions they take, the strategies they employ to deal with crime, suggest that the community needs to be part of their efforts.''[1] At first glance, Ryan's statement may seem puzzling. Surely, you might say, police have always been aware that their fate (both individual and collective) and that of the community in which they work are closely related. After all, police officers clearly do recognize that they are empowered by the community to act on its behalf, that they carry out their sworn missions of service and protection within the community, and that their salaries are paid by citizens of the community.

But in the long history of police community relations, it is equally clear that many of the expressions and images employed both inside and outside the police profession suggest separation of the police from the community, either as a whole or in part. Consider, for example, the portrayal of the police department as a ''closed,'' secretive society, whose members demand the unwavering loyalty of their ''own'' and vigorously resist outside (i.e., civilian citizen) ''interference'' in police affairs. Consider, also, the frequency with which we encounter the phrase: ''the thin blue line.'' This metaphor implies the crucial but precarious task of the police in preventing a community's descent into social chaos and the Hobbesian war of all against all. Often associated with this image is the idea that citizens can be divided easily into two groups, with the police acting ''for'' the good people and ''against'' the bad people, the determination of who belongs in which category being made by the police. In addition, some have argued that technology, beginning with the widespread use of the patrol car, has served to isolate police from other citizens. So also, some say, has been the modern propensity to define the police mission more or less exclusively as crime fighting, downplaying their peacekeeping, problem solving, and other public service functions.

No doubt, some tension between the police and the community is inherent in the police role, especially in a democracy with a commitment to individualism, personal liberty, and human rights. Occasionally, though, relations between police and community become the object of intense scrutiny, often as a result of media exposure and citizen outrage arising from the police use of coercive or lethal physical force. The Rodney King-Los Angeles Police Department videotape, portions of which were shown literally hundreds of times on TV over the period of about a year, is one recent and prominent example of the power of the media in focusing police and public attention on their relationships.

As with so much that pertains to the police and policing, however, media perspectives and portraits often contrast sharply with each other. Alongside the images of flailing nightsticks and feet pressed hard against the necks of prostrate suspects are the pictures of police officers risking their lives to rescue children from kidnappers or capturing a mass murderer.

The extent to which the police and citizens see each other as engaged in a common enterprise has clearly varied over time and across situations. The police can be (and have been) perceived as an occupying force acting as agents of a small but powerful and oppressive political elite; as partners with other citizens in building safe, free, and humane communities; and as almost everything in between—sometimes all at the same time. In these contrasting images and points of view may be found some of the sources of the ambivalence and tension inherent in police community relations in a diverse, democratic society.

Dramatic, widely publicized events like the Rodney King-LAPD encounter often not only stimulate discussions about police community relations, but also trigger or add impetus to reform efforts. As a society, we seem now to be at another of those potential turning points, with an opportunity as well as some incentive to examine closely and perhaps to take steps that may alter at least some aspects of police community relations in a significant way.

At the forefront of the current re-examination is the "community policing" movement. Strong support for community policing, both rhetorical and budgetary, has come from the highest ranks of civilian authority, including President Clinton, and Attorney General Janet Reno. Many police administrators and practitioners have also given strong endorsements and several communities have implemented some aspects of the community policing philosophy. Willie Williams succeeded Daryl Gates as Chief of the Los Angeles Police Department, in part at least on the basis of his earlier success in Philadelphia at building better police community relations through community policing initiatives.[2] Discussing and critically examining this movement will, therefore, be part of our task in the following chapters.

In later chapters we shall also explore some aspects of the changes in society as a whole and in policing which have played an important part in generating the current preoccupation with the nature of police community relations. Among these are rapid demographic changes, including the aging of the population and accelerating ethnic and racial diversification. Crime rates have risen dramatically (compared with the mid-century decades) and **fear** of crime has risen even more consistently and dramatically, the latter apparently fueled in part by the more national scope of the media (especially television) coverage of local crime events and by the "aging" of the population. Social movements, including the civil and human rights movements of various ethnic and racial minorities (e.g., African, Hispanic, and Native Americans) and persons with disabilities, as well as feminism, have highlighted some of the inherent tensions between the police and citizens and profoundly complicated the police image, role, and function. In spite of all the tensions and ambiguities of contemporary police community relations, as well as the limitations inherent in formal law enforcement, however, almost everyone agrees that the impact of policing activities on the quality of community life is substantial. As O'Brien (1978) suggests: "The central position of the police in the community critically affects all sections of society. The multiple duties of the police at all times and in all areas of the community dictate that they must influence the daily life of each citizen."[3] Policing communities in a democratic society poses very difficult dilemmas both for the police and for other citizens. But events of the past few decades suggest some general principles that should inform our analysis of these problems. As Trojanowicz and Bucqueroux (1990) indicate: "When people feel the police do not understand or respond to their wants and needs, the result is either vigilantism or apathy or both. History proves that safety and order are not commodities the police impose on communities from the outside; instead they are hallmarks of communities where people accept responsibility for improving the overall quality of life."[4] And, according to Wasserman and Moore (1988), "When a police agency has lost its community authority, a range of response always occurs, from widespread dissatisfaction with the department to substantial disorder when the police apply the law in the neighborhood."[5]

These concerns have rarely been given the priority they deserve by students or practitioners of policing. One implication that may be drawn from them is that police department priorities should be closely attuned to the needs and sentiments of the community. That, in turn, means accepting general community service functions as core, rather than peripheral, components of the police mission. Langworthy and Travis (1994), for example, contend that: "The number and types of services the police render to civilians varies by community and department. Some police agencies define themselves as service providers, while others prefer to emphasize crime control. Still, all local police agencies provide some noncrime services to their communities. These services may include emergency aid, licensing, provision of information, dispute resolution, lost and found, and general safety functions."[6]

Most Americans would agree that the policing function, justly and sensitively applied, is vital to community well-being. Most would also acknowledge the limitations on the capacity of the police, by themselves, to ensure high quality community life. Clearly, citizens and their police need each other.

As a result of continuing tensions between the police and some segments of the community (especially minority groups), together with the growing recognition of the hopelessness of relying solely (or even mainly) on a law enforcement approach to serious community problems (e.g., drug abuse), there has been a renewed interest in examining closely the dynamics of police community relations. Recent proposals for reform in law enforcement tactics and strategies, including team policing and foot patrol, as well as problem- and community-oriented policing, reflect this interest. The task is undeniably daunting.[7] Many previous efforts to improve police community relations have fallen victim to the reluctance of police administrators to take the issue seriously, the inertia of ponderous police department bureaucracies and individual line officers, resistance to change, and inadequate budgetary resources.

But perhaps the most important difficulty is that problems in police community relations are rooted in the basic structure and values of our society. Structurally, our society is characterized by a highly complex division of labor. Different people perform different and increasingly specialized occupational roles, often with the consequence that one person has little understanding or appreciation of another person's job, problems, or responsibilities. Police often assert, for example, that few citizens understand the difficulties they must confront on a regular basis or why they employ certain basic arrest strategies and tactics; citizens sometimes accuse the police of using unnecessary and excessive force in accomplishing their task.

Exacerbating the problems associated with occupational specialization is the fact that our society is also extraordinarily diverse ethnically, religiously, and ideologically. Stereotyping, bigotry, prejudice, discrimination, and conflict are common. Ours is a society stratified by social class, with a substantial and growing gap between the "haves" and "have nots." The social and political strains that accompany race and class differences are made more acute by urban residential patterns. People of similar class, ethnicity, and often religious beliefs are congregated in the same neighborhood, creating densely populated ghettos on the one hand and spacious, ritzy suburbs on the other.

All of these differences, of course, make understanding and communication among citizens from different segments of a community difficult. They also make identification with and genuine commitment to the welfare of the larger community for both police and citizens problematic. Furthermore, nuclear families are geographically mobile and extended family members are scattered, making communities and neighborhoods at least somewhat unstable. In such a society, some police community tensions are inevitable.

Our sometimes conflicting values, too, present some difficult challenges for improving police community relations. On the one hand, we recognize the need for "law and order" and we want to be rid of crime and criminals. We want very much to be safe in our homes and on public streets. We want our property to be secure. We want our voice and vote to be heard in community affairs. We revere the democratic principle of majority rule. On the other hand, we are very wary of governmental power. We dislike authority and authoritarianism in almost any form. We pay taxes with little enthusiasm. We resent mightily almost any governmental intrusion in our day-to-day affairs. We value highly our freedom of speech, assembly, religion, and the press. We adhere stoutly to the principle of innocent until proven guilty. We also believe strongly in protecting minorities from the tyranny of the majority. Obviously, such values are not always or easily reconciled.

In some circumstances, and to some extent, then, the structure of our society and the values we espouse may produce conflicts. When they do, they are often manifested in police community relations problems. Since at least some of the problems are deeply rooted in our society, it is unlikely that perfect, permanent solutions will be found for them. In fact, this probably should not even be our goal; living with some of the current problems in this area is undoubtedly preferable to some "solutions" that might be devised. Nevertheless, there are some community relations problems that certainly deserve our attention and ameliorative efforts. And, there is a good deal to be gained from even partial solutions to these problems for both the police and the other citizens they serve. More public approval of police efforts, less cynicism and despair and higher morale among police officers, more effective crime prevention programs, better crime clearance rates, less public fear of both crime and the police, and safer communities are among the more important benefits that are clearly possible.

In the remainder of this chapter, three closely related concepts central to the examination of police community relations will be introduced, distinguished from each other, and discussed. These three concepts are human relations, public relations, and community relations.

Human Relations

The concept of **human relations** refers to the nature and quality of the many interpersonal interactions that take place between police officers and citizens. It may be useful to distinguish between direct and indirect human relations. Direct human relations refers to what happens during those situations where citizens and police officers encounter each other in person or in other ways (e.g., over the phone or by mail) communicate directly with each other. Indirect human relations refers to the inferences about or implications for potential "in person" encounters that arise from witnessing (personally or via secondhand or media accounts) direct encounters between police and other citizens. In a sense, indirect human relations are the impressions generated when a citizen says to her or himself: "What if I were the person engaged in this encounter with the police?"

Many police officers and others who are in one way or another associated with policing think of police community relations as consisting entirely of organized programs (like DARE or Neighborhood Watch) that involve police-citizen cooperation. Without denying the potential significance of such programs, which we shall discuss later, we think such a conception of police community relations is seriously incomplete. In our view, in fact, human relations as we have defined them above, are the more fundamental and important component of police community relations.

Focusing on human relations invites attention to the consequences and implications of those qualities and attributes humans have in common.

Whatever the differences may be in the gender, ethnic heritage, age, or the particular roles people play as they interact with each other, they are alike in at least two fundamental respects. First, they are, with some notable exceptions (e.g., illegal immigrants), citizens of the same bodies politic (nation, state, county, or city). As such, they are entitled to the rights and may avail themselves of the privileges their common citizenship entails. And, they are bound by the responsibilities of and obligations imposed on all citizens. Second, they are members of the same species; they share a common humanity. As such, they have a right to expect from, and an obligation to extend to other human beings with whom they interact, a basic respect. Using common manners (politeness and other basic rules of social etiquette), for example, indicates our willingness to acknowledge the other as a fellow human being, with individuality, value, and dignity equivalent to our own, whatever other differences might exist.

In the most general sense, the concept of human relations refers to everything we do with, for, and to each other as citizens and as human beings. Positive human relations consist of those relations which are sensitive to differences as well as similarities between ourselves and others and which preserve as much of the others' dignity as possible; negative human relations deprive the other of the dignity and respect to which they are entitled.

Perhaps a brief review of the purposes and contents of ''human relations training programs'' implemented by many police departments will help clarify the concept. These programs arose during the 1960s, a period of general social unrest and considerable tension between the police and minority citizens. In somewhat modified form, they are re-emerging in some police training institutes.[8] Typical features of these programs are courses in cultural and social differences and simulated encounters and/or confrontations between police officers and members of cultural minority groups. In some of these minidramas, there were role reversals—i.e., police officers played the role of minorities and vice versa. The purpose was to help participants understand and relate to each other better, not just as police officers and minorities, but as fellow citizens and human beings. Among other things, the role-playing exercises were designed to make participants consciously aware of: (1) differences between police officers' and citizens' interpretations of the same interactions in terms of both citizen and human rights; (2) the human tendency to see and respond to others different from ourselves through the use of stereotypes, thereby denying their individuality and often relegating them to inferior status that diminishes their human value and dignity; (3) the difficulties we all have in putting ourselves in the shoes of others and in being sensitive to their needs, desires, and points of view; and (4) the changes in feelings and behavior that occur when humans assume positions of authority over or subordination to others. These are fundamental and perceived problems that may emerge in any human relationship. In the context of police community relations, then, human relations consist of person-to-person interactions between police officers and other citizens, based on the shared citizenship and humanity of the participants. Only when police officers and other citizens show respect for each other as human beings and

In Search of the Perfect Cop

By Andy Rooney

The perfect policeman?

He'd know law like a lawyer and have a judge's ability to tell right from wrong.

He'd have a doctor's knowledge of medicine, and the tenderness and compassion of a nurse.

The perfect cop would have the speed and strength of an Olympic athlete, the manners of a Japanese diplomat and the intelligence of a college professor.

On any occasion the officer would risk his life to protect the worldly goods of the rich while at the same time being content with a salary that precluded his having many worldly goods of his own.

The perfect policeman could be man or woman.

If a human being had all the attributes he needed to be the perfect cop, he'd probably be something else. And so would she. It might be easier to be president.

This summer at the political conventions, I watched with interest the behavior of the police in San Francisco and Dallas. The character of the police force in any city is as different from that of another city as its skyline. You'd think that, like the city itself, the San Francisco police force would be more liberal, more relaxed than the police in Dallas, but that didn't seem to be so.

Unfortunately for its national image, several television news cameramen were in attendance when a handful of demonstrators were administered a brutal beating by a special forces unit of the San Francisco Police. A demonstrator was seen not only being beaten with nightsticks but being speared in the stomach and kidneys by one cop while his arms were pinned by three others.

It was the sort of action that must make the good cops everywhere cringe.

On the second day in San Francisco, I walked up to one of three officers standing on a barricaded corner and asked where Folsom Street was. I had a car parked in a lot there and had lost my bearings. The officer shrugged indifferently and said he didn't know. I could see he didn't care, either.

Fifteen minutes later, after a lot of wandering and some better advice, I ended up on the same corner with the three cops.

"If anyone else asks you where Folsom Street is," I said, "you're standing on it."

He shrugged again in a why-don't-you-go-back-where-you-came-from manner. The people trying to enhance San Francisco's image as a friendly convention city, which it generally is, would have cringed.

Later that same week, I asked another cop for directions. He thought for a minute, then took out a pencil and, placing an envelope on the hood of a nearby car, proceeded to give me detailed, accurate and friendly directions. It was hard to believe the two cops belonged to the same police force.

In Dallas, the police were on their best behavior, but you had the nervous feeling it didn't come easily to them. Wednesday of that week, I pulled up near the Convention Center in a car with a camera crew. The cameraman started to get out when a nearby policeman yelled, "Hey, you. Get back in that car."

"Just going to take some pictures of the demonstrators, Officer," the cameraman said in a conciliatory voice.

"You get out of that car, you're going to jail," the Dallas cop said quite finally.

In New York, where I spend a lot of time, the police have been so consistently put down that they've lost interest in law and order. They've given up. If a New

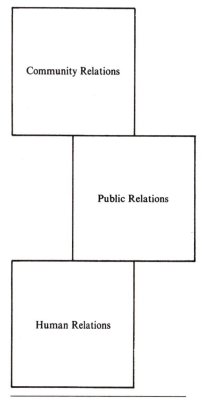

Figure 1.1 Human relations and public relations—the building blocks of community relations.

York policeman had to choose between interrupting a murder in progress in a nearby apartment or ticketing a car parked four minutes overtime at a meter, he'd probably give the ticket and ignore the murder. They've had too many bitter experiences.

I can't decide which style of police work I like least.

Reprinted with permission of the author, ANDREW A. ROONEY.

demonstrate sensitivity and understanding of each other's roles, problems, and points of view, can good relationships exist between the two groups. We will discuss this issue in greater detail in Chapter Three.

Public Relations

Virtually every organization that provides a product or service finds it necessary to communicate with the public about what it does. Typically these communications have two distinguishable but related aims. One is to inform the public about the availability of (and sometimes to increase the demand for) its products or services. In the for-profit business world, this activity is called advertising or marketing and the operating assumption is that higher demand is good. In the not-for-profit, public sector world things are a bit more complex. There are occasions, for example, when police agencies clearly do want to advertise their services and/or persuade the public that the demand for their services is growing (by touting increasing crime rates or warning the community about an impending threat, such as the appearance of a new drug, for example). At other times, though, the demand for police services is larger than can be met and efforts must be made to manage the overload through public education. In any event, providing useful and accurate information to the public, especially during times of crisis, is an important function of police **public relations** efforts.

The other aim of an agency's communication with its public is to establish and maintain a good corporate or organizational image or reputation. The quality of the product or service is, of course, the most crucial factor in the long run for accomplishing this goal. But, in the media age, organizations can seldom rely solely upon product or service quality alone to bolster their public image. Others critical of police activities may be engaged in an effort to create their own image of the police and influence public or political opinion. As a result, police agencies plan and implement a variety of activities with the express intent of creating a favorable image of themselves and/or defending their image when it is attacked.

Both of these communication activities, sponsored and paid for by the organization as an organization, are referred to as public relations. Public relations efforts of police organizations come in several different varieties. Forming good working relationships with community organizations (churches, neighborhood citizen groups, etc.) can produce major benefits in times of crisis and otherwise. Helping organize new groups that help citizens police themselves, such as neighborhood watch groups, is a useful strategy, as are public information and education programs (e.g., speakers bureaus, drug awareness, and home security presentations). Establishing good liaison with the media, often through the creation of special departments or the appointment of specially designated officers, is important. Calling the media's attention to positive incidents involving police interactions with other citizens (e.g., human interest stories) is often effective. And, of course, controlling the damage arising from "bad press"—media coverage of controversial or discrediting events involving

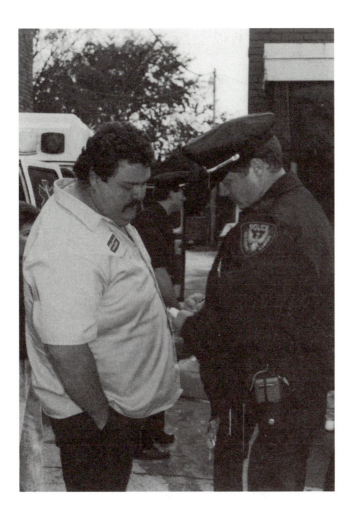

the police—is also a vital aspect of a police agency's public relations functions. We will discuss these activities in greater detail in Chapter Four.

Community Relations

Community relations are comprised of the combined effects of human and public relations. Police community relations, then, encompass the sum total of human and public relations, whether initiated by the police or other members of the community. As such, police community relations involve the police department as a whole and all individual personnel at all levels of the department, as well as other individuals and groups in the community. Police community relations may be either positive or negative, depending upon the quality of police officer interactions with other citizens (human relations) and the collective images each holds of the other (which are derived from public relations as well as human relations).

The quality of police community relations is an important concern for both the police and their communities. Among the potential benefits for police that may flow from improving community relations are: greater personal safety; increased citizen cooperation during investigations and adjudication (leading to higher crime clearance rates); more credibility in addressing community issues and problems; enhanced respect from citizens; job satisfaction and self-esteem; reduced job-related stress; and more budgetary and moral support from the communities they serve. For citizens, safer communities in which to live, raise families, earn their living, and enjoy themselves, among other things, are at stake.

In the following chapters we will examine various aspects of police community relationships in some detail, pointing out some of the reasons for poor police community relations and some actions which may be, or are already being, undertaken to improve the quality of these relationships.

Police Community Relations in Context

Although our focus in this book is on police community relations at the city and county level, it is clear that neither the local police nor the community function in a vacuum. Both may influence, and be influenced by, other actors and institutions at the local, state, national, and even international levels. Legislative bodies enact laws that the police are expected to enforce; courts determine the ultimate fate of those whom the police arrest and establish procedural rules by which the police are expected to abide; the economy may prosper or fall into recession; demographic and other social trends alter the composition and character of the populations in cities (and neighborhoods within them) in which the police serve; and national social reform movements may have advocates in the local community, for example. Media coverage of police actions in other nations may also influence the local police image, especially when the viewer identifies with those involved—as, for example, when an African American witnesses white South African security forces beating black South African citizens.

At the local level, police are employees of the community, and, hence, a part of its political structure. However, in performing some of their duties they act as officers of the court. The conduct and image of police officers are inevitably influenced by the actions and reputations of local city councils, police commissioners, prosecutors, defense attorneys, and judges. Skillful defense attorneys may undermine public confidence in the competence of the police. Careful arrest procedures and handling of evidence by the police can make the police and prosecutors look good; police foul-ups may cast the whole criminal justice network in a bad light. Even the best prepared cases in the hands of incompetent or corrupt prosecutors or judges may make the police look bad. The public may blame the police when judges grant probation or parole boards grant parole to someone who then commits another serious crime. Legislative,

Bouza Assails Plan to Hire More Police

Proposal Is An Overreaction, He Says

By Cheryl Johnson

Staff Writer

Minneapolis Police Chief Tony Bouza said Saturday that a proposal to hire 100 additional police officers for his department is "demagogic and simple-minded."

At a time when the Minneapolis school officials have talked about laying off 100 teachers, hiring that many police officers demonstrates a lack of understanding of social issues and an overreaction to recent, highly publicized murders and rapes, Bouza said.

Several proposals for improving law enforcement are being batted around City Hall, including one from Council member Walt Dziedzic to beef up the force of 722 with an additional 100 officers.

Last week, the Minneapolis Charter Commission voted to put Dziedzic's proposal before the voters in November. The plan would require a tax increase. . . .

The emphasis on police comes as the public's perception grows that Minneapolis is becoming a more dangerous place. Bouza said that crime rates go up and down so much it's hard to gauge, but that he doesn't think the city has become more dangerous. . . .

Bouza said he has been careful not to state that he is opposed to the Dziedzic proposal. "I never said I was opposed to it and nobody has been able to quote me as saying that," he said. "You can infer anything you want."

If the size of the police department is increased, he said, so should the size of the prosecutor and public-defender offices, prison and jails and other areas. "It strikes me as unwise to strengthen one link in the chain and not the others," he said. . . .

"What's unique about this controversy is that nowhere else in the county are the City Fathers and Mothers trying to force more resources on the chief," he said.

If government did a better job in social areas, Bouza is convinced crime would decrease. "When you talk social issues everyone's eyes glaze over with boredom. It's unsexy," said Bouza.

But he said if more "upstream questions" were addressed, such as birth weights, child birth, sex education, teen pregnancy, head start, abortion, hopes, and jobs, "the criminal class" would decline.

Councilwoman Sharon Sayles Belton said she agreed with Bouza about the social issues, but today in her district the problem also needs a "band-aid" and that means more police.

"I don't think it's one or the other, it's both," she said. "I think we can benefit from hiring more police."

Reprinted with permission of The Minneapolis Star Tribune.

---

judicial, correctional, and police agencies at the state and federal levels may also impact directly or indirectly, on local police and community affairs. Miranda requirements, prison overcrowding, and the consequent diversion or early release of convicts; the lack of truly effective rehabilitation programs in the correctional system; budgetary allocations for police training, equipment, and research; and the effectiveness of other police and social service agencies are just a few examples of such impact.

It is worth noting, too, that good community relations are as vital to the other local, state, and federal agencies and institutions as they are to municipal police. Without good community relations, prosecutors and judges may not be reelected or retained, for example. And, probation and parole officers cannot maintain probationers or parolees in the community unless they develop good working relations with employers, schools, and the local police.

Other contextual factors influence local police community relations as well. First, as we shall see in Chapter Two, history has changed the role of the police and their connections to the community. Second, the dominance of political parties and philosophies shifts over time. Liberalism held sway during the 1960s and, to a lesser extent, the 1970s; conservatism achieved prominence in the 1980s and carried over into the early 1990s. Such swings in philosophical orientation often change the political support for the law enforcement approach to social problems as well as the budgetary resources available to police agencies. Third, the demography of the U.S. population has undergone significant changes over the past few decades. Overall population growth has slowed, but the relative proportion represented by minority groups has grown dramatically. Among the most rapidly growing populations are the Hispanic, African, and Asian Americans. By the end of the next century, a majority of the U.S. population will be comprised of ethnic ''minorities.'' The American population is also aging rapidly and by the turn of the century roughly 30 percent of the population will be over fifty-five years of age. Population migrations from one region of the country to another, and from one part of the city or county to another also affect police community relations. Rapid population growth in the South and Southwest, the creation and dismantling of mammoth housing projects, the escape of middle-class whites to the suburbs and the ''gentrification'' of inner-city neighborhoods are just a few examples of the many demographic shifts occurring.

Finally, social reform movements have changed the American political and social landscape. The passage of the Americans with Disabilities Act as well as the civil rights movement, the gay liberation movement, and the feminist movement, among others, have produced significant new forces with which the entire society, including the police, must contend.

Even though the quality of police community relations at the local level is clearly not entirely within local control, we would suggest that the local arena is where most of the important ''action'' in police community relations occurs. Because the city and county police are typically the most visible and the most intimately involved of the criminal justice agencies affecting the community, they are in the best position to exert a positive influence over their own image and the quality of local community life.

Community Policing and Police Community Relations

In many respects, the ''community policing'' reform initiative in law enforcement (and increasingly in other aspects of the criminal justice system as well) emphasizes the importance of building partnerships between law enforcement agents and agencies on the one hand and citizens of neighborhoods and other small scale communities on the other. The principles and practices associated with ''community policing'' are quite varied, giving rise to some ambiguity about what the term means. In almost all versions, however, community policing clearly has implications for both human and public relations; it deserves careful consideration in any discussion of police community relations and we shall have more to say about it in later chapters. Given that the rhetoric of community policing has begun to dominate much of the contemporary discourse about policing, however, it is worth bearing in mind that even the late Robert Trojanowicz, generally acknowledged as the founder of the community policing movement, has observed that there is a great deal more to police community relations than community policing.[9]

Discussion Questions

1. What are some of the more important rights we all have as citizens and as humans? What are the implications of these rights for police community relations?
2. How would you distinguish between human and public relations? Why are public relations efforts sometimes viewed with skepticism by the public?
3. Reread Andy Rooney's article, "In Search of the Perfect Cop." Is Rooney concerned mostly with human relations or public relations? What do you think are the qualities of an excellent police officer? Of a really bad police officer? What are the implications of the qualities you have listed for police community relations?
4. Do citizens expect too much of the police? What should be the basic goals of the police? What are the most appropriate standards for judging whether the police are doing a good job for their community?
5. What are the implications for police community relations of local and national media coverage of police activities in your area? (Bring some examples to class for discussion.) What are the best ways for the police to build better community relations?

Endnotes

1. Joseph F. Ryan. "Community Policing: Trends, Policies, Programs and Definitions" in Albert R. Roberts, ed. 1994. *Critical Issues In Crime And Justice.* Thousand Oaks, CA: Sage Publications Inc.: 143.
2. Sally A. Stewart. 1992. "A Welcome 'Challenge' in L.A." *USA Today.* (June 29): 4A.
3. John T. O'Brien. 1978. "Public Attitudes Toward the Police." *Journal of Police Science and Administration* 6(3): 304.
4. Robert C. Trojanowicz and Bonnie Bucqueroux. 1990. *Community Policing.* Cincinnati, OH: Anderson Publishing Co.
5. Robert Wasserman and Mark H. Moore. 1988. "Values in Policing." *Perspectives on Policing.* National Institute of Justice. Washington, D.C.: U.S. Government Printing Office (November): 6.
6. Robert H. Langworthy and Lawrence F. Travis, III. 1994. *Policing in America.* New York: Macmillan: 269.
7. For discussions of previous reform efforts and difficulties they have encountered, see Chapter Two of this book and Erik Monkkonen. 1981. *Police in Urban America, 1860–1920.* New York: Cambridge University Press; Samuel J. Walker. 1977. *A Critical History*

of *Police Reform.* Lexington, MA: Lexington Books; Michael K. Brown. 1988. *Working the Street.* New York: Russell Sage Foundation; and George L. Kelling and Mark H. Moore. 1988. ''The Evolving Strategy of Policing.'' *Perspectives on Policing.* National Institute of Justice. Washington, D.C.: U.S. Government Printing Office (November); Malcolm K. Sparrow, Mark Moore, and David M. Kennedy. 1990. *Beyond 911: A New Strategy for Policing.* New York: Basic Books; Roy R. Roberg and Jack Kuykendall. 1993. *Police and Society.* Belmont, CA: Wadsworth: 106–123.

8. Joyce St. George. 1991. '' 'Sensitivity' Training Needs Rethinking.'' *Law Enforcement News* (November 30): 8–9.

9. Robert C. Trojanowicz. 1990. ''Community Policing is Not Police Community Relations.'' *FBI Law Enforcement Bulletin:* 59: 6–10.

Suggested Readings

Banton, Michael. 1961. *The Policeman in the Community.* New York: Basic Books.

Black, Donald. 1968. *The People and the Police.* New York: McGraw-Hill.

Gaines, Larry K., Victor E. Kappeler and Joseph B. Vaughn. 1994. *Policing in America.* Cincinnati, OH: Anderson Publishing Co.

Goldstein, Herman. 1979. ''Improving Policing: A Problem Oriented Approach.'' *Crime and Delinquency* 25: 236–258.

Tonry, Michael and Norval Morris, eds. 1992. *Modern Policing, Vol. 15.* Chicago: The University of Chicago Press.

Trojanowicz, Robert C. 1988. ''Serious Threats to the Future of Policing.'' *Footprints: The Community Policing Newsletter* 1(3).

Trojanowicz, Robert C. and Bonnie Bucqueroux. 1990. *Community Policing.* Cincinnati, OH: Anderson Publishing Co.

Chapter 2

Police Community Relations— Yesterday and Today

G aining an appreciation of some of the problems and prospects that characterize current police community relations depends in part on understanding the role of the police in social control and the evolution of the police as specialized social control agents in the nation state. Let us begin by making three observations which are basic to this understanding. First, human communities survived and prospered long before the law, the police, or other components of the criminal justice network as we know them existed. Second, all of the basic processes of social integration and control that bound historical communities together and maintained a reasonably stable social order not only remain with us but continue to be very significant forces in our day-to-day lives. Third, while laws and their enforcement are important, their capacity to alter established moral or social patterns or to create order from chaos is distinctly limited. In close-knit communities where informal social norms are shared and informally enforced, formal laws are unnecessary; when social order collapses, laws and law enforcement, by themselves, are not very effective remedies.[1]

The earliest human communities were comprised of small, culturally homogeneous, mobile groups sustained by hunting and gathering. These groups were bound together by ties of kinship and the advantages group life provided for obtaining food and defending against human enemies and animal predators. While hunting and gathering are no longer universal subsistence strategies, we continue to live our lives in small ''communities'' (families, neighborhoods, work groups, gangs) and these affiliations still constitute very powerful influences on our lives.

Every human group develops goals or values (which express what its members believe is ultimately important in life) and norms (which specify what people are supposed to do and not do in particular situations). These values and norms consist of both spoken guidelines for behavior transmitted by those with whom we interact in small groups and written guidelines promulgated by community leaders. Further, some of the values and norms are considered very important (mores), while others are regarded as less important (folkways). Violations of the former may threaten the existence of the community, while violations of the latter may cause inconvenience but do not constitute the same level of threat to the community.

Different groups develop different, sometimes conflicting sets of values and norms, and group members occasionally test the limits of acceptable conduct. Group members develop various ways of responding to violations of values and norms, referred to as social control strategies, in order to hold the group together. These social control strategies involve sanctions of three basic types. "Good" behavior can be rewarded with overt signs of social approval and honor or the bestowal of material rewards (positive reinforcement). "Bad" behavior can be dealt with in two ways. Rewards can be withheld by simply ignoring the disapproved conduct or it can be punished (negative reinforcement). Punishment might be either physical (e.g., spanking or flogging) or social (insulting or ridiculing or, worst of all, banishment from the group) or both.

In early human groups, values and norms were informal as were the social control processes employed. That is, there were spoken rules whose contents were defined and redefined in the course of ordinary interaction and whose upholding or violation was responded to by ordinary members of the group or community. These informal values, norms, and sanctions remain pervasive and powerful influences on our behavior. In fact, they are far more influential than the formal norms (written codes such as laws), which are formally sanctioned (enforced by specially designated agents in officially approved ways).

The first formal norms may have arisen when farming and herding replaced hunting and gathering as basic modes of subsistence. The horticultural life-style allowed for the development of larger groups, the establishment of more or less permanent settlements, and an increasingly complex division of labor in which different people devoted their energies to specialized tasks. Trading of goods and services emerged as a way of obtaining what others produced. As communities grew in size, the basic ties of kinship were supplemented by other means of holding the group together, giving rise to alliances among kinship groups and more centralized community leadership—tribal chiefs and, later, in some societies, monarchs. These community leaders ruled through a combination of religious and secular power and their wishes became law. Secular rewards and punishments were combined with promises of divine favor and divine retribution. From these societies emerged the modern, secular state.

As new sources of energy were harnessed (animal power and the use of fossil fuels) agriculture and industrialization developed, creating the possibility of much larger communities while requiring a more complex division of labor. Together with population migrations, these developments eventually gave rise to the huge concentrations of culturally diverse communities we know as the modern city. The state became the predominant form of political organization, separation between church and state authority became more pronounced, and societies became more secular.

With the emergence of the secular state came the police. The word *police* is derived from the Greek word *polis* (city) and refers to the exercise of civic or collective authority. Thus the police are best viewed not as an instrument of the law, but as a product of the form of governance known as the state. As Manning (1979) points out, "It has been a recent development that has seen the police as an appendage of law rather than as an extension of the power of the state: THE STATE AND THE LAW ARE NOT ISOMORPHIC, as much as legal historians would have us make that faulty equation. It should be emphasized that the legitimation of the police in terms of legal authority flows from the power of the state and citizens' deference to it rather than from the law as an independent entity."[2]

There are two views of the relation between the law and the state and the nature and role of law. In one view, the law reflects or embodies a broadly shared consensus among citizens about appropriate conduct. The other view holds that the law reflects the views of a small but powerful group and serves largely to protect the interests of this dominant group, including preserving their advantaged position within the society. Both of these views have merit. The conflict between them helps define many of the tensions between the police and the public in most industrialized societies, including the United States. In any event, western societies became increasingly culturally diverse. That is, different segments of the community came to hold values and expectations which were dissimilar. Behavior accepted as normal by one segment of the community was perhaps seen as deviant by another. Enforcement of norms based upon community consensus and group pressure was no longer possible in all cases. Yet there were clearly some behaviors which could not be tolerated if the members of the community were to remain secure and relatively happy. Prohibitions of these types of behavior were eventually formalized into law, and in order to ensure that these laws would not be violated, certain persons were designated to watch for violations and to apprehend or make known those who transgressed these laws. The number and variety of laws increased with growth in the size and diversity of the community. Since different segments of the community had distinct needs and expectations, some wanted certain types of laws enforced which others did not deem important. Pressures were exerted upon the individuals designated to enforce laws. These, together with the values and expectations of the enforcers themselves, led them to enforce the laws selectively (depending upon time, place, situation, etc.). It became virtually impossible for law enforcers to satisfy all segments of the community at the same time with respect to some laws (e.g., those involving services demanded by some segments of the community, such as prostitution, or gambling), while other laws retained considerable community support (e.g., predatory crimes such as murder and rape).

Laws and law enforcement, then, arose through the process of human interaction and political struggle. The relationships existing between the police and various segments of the community ultimately depend upon this same interaction (human relations). As O' Brien (1978) points out: "[human relations] is the least formalized area of all and yet it is the basis of the community relations program. Each officer should be made aware that the success of the police mission is dependent on a solid community relations program permeated by the positive community relations of each officer."[3]

Satisfactory human relations are difficult to develop and maintain when dealing with diverse segments of a community. The fact that enforcing the law has become a lesser part of what most police officers do, combined with the community's demands for a wide variety of services from the police, makes consistently good human relations a critical but fragile aspect of community relations efforts.

Police Community Relations in Historical Perspective

Thousands of encounters between municipal and county police officers and members of the public occur daily in the United States. Most of these encounters are completed without violence or major difficulty, but there is considerable disagreement among citizens in the United States as to the quality of police services. Some of these encounters clearly leave members of the public and/or police officers angry, resentful, frustrated, and dissatisfied. In addition, some sectors of the population appear to be constantly dissatisfied with police services, and many, perhaps most, citizens are critical of the police at one time or another.[4] Public dissatisfaction with the police has a number of significant consequences, such as failure to report suspicious persons, and unwillingness to testify or to aid a police officer in distress. These consequences and their significance are discussed in the chapters which follow. In this chapter, we will briefly review the development of the police in the Western world, with a view to discovering the origins of some of the problems to be discussed later.

As is the case with many customs, traditions, and institutions in the United States, our system of policing has its origins in Great Britain. The development of municipal police in Britain took place over a number of centuries, and the origins of many contemporary problems in police community relations can be traced to the early British watch-and-ward system and its American counterpart. As Rubinstein (1973) points out, the obligation of a property owner to serve as a watchman or a constable had been customary in Britain since before the Norman invasion, but it began to weaken as cities grew larger.[5] Wealthy property owners shunned the task and hired substitutes, often aged, poor, unemployed, and uneducated to serve in their place. As a result, by the mid-seventeenth century, ". . . watchmen were generally considered to be incompetent and cowardly."[6] At that time watchmen in America were held in low regard for the same reasons.

Here, then, are the origins of a major problem in police community relations: the reputation for being generally inefficient and untrustworthy in times of need, an attitude which British police were generally able to change in the 1800s through the efforts of Robert Peel, founder of the London Metropolitan Police, and others. Peel and Colonel Charles Rowan, first Commissioner of the

London Police, were convinced that public support was a requirement for effective police operations. They called for a "dignified and restrained demeanor" on behalf of police officers and they developed recruitment procedures to select officers who understood community norms.

Unfortunately, the negative image which characterized early law enforcement personnel in the United States has continued in many areas until the present time. Tradition has it that one of the major reasons for citizen failure to call the police when a crime has been committed is the belief that the police are often ineffective in apprehending offenders. However, only about 3 percent of those failing to report crimes to the police in 1991 gave police ineffectiveness as the reason,[7] thus it appears progress has been made in this area. Still, most crimes are not reported to the police making it impossible for the police to apprehend the offender(s) and thereby make the community a safer place. In addition, the fact that private security guards are being hired in increasing numbers may well be an indicator that the public feels the police are not adequate to the task of crime control/prevention.[8]

Two additional and closely related problems emerged from the watch-and-ward systems in England and colonial North America. First, we might expect that if watchmen were hired by wealthy property owners, they could also be fired by the same wealthy individuals. We might further speculate that one reason for removing a watchman might be that he enforced the law in a way which displeased his employer (e.g., against the "wrong" people). It is likely, then, that watchmen who wanted to continue to serve would enforce the law inequitably or "play political favorites." Thus the element of political corruption was introduced into policing and led to even less respect for watchmen, at least among those against whom the law was enforced. In fact, the power of "politics" to influence the police was so important that it was built into the police department in New York City at its inception. As Richardson points out: "In New York, policemen of all ranks were appointed for limited tenure by elected officials. It is not surprising that to secure appointment policemen had to be politically active for the officials who appointed them. Furthermore, they could not enforce the law too strenuously against the supporters of those responsible for their appointments."[9]

As might be expected, those who had little or no political backing resented this type of favoritism and have continued until the present time to protest this unequal enforcement of the law. The scope of the problem becomes evident when we recognize that there are still police departments in the United States which are politically manipulated in obvious ways.

A second and closely related problem stemming from the watch-and-ward system is that of economic corruption or bribery. Watchmen in both Britain and America were not well-paid and often supplemented their salary by overlooking violations of law in return for payoffs.[10] Once again, the rich and the poor received different treatment from the police, not on the basis of the offenses committed, but rather because of socioeconomic status. The police officer might now be defined as incompetent, cowardly, politically corrupt, and "on the take." Scandals in a number of cities in the United States in recent years indicate

<table>
<tr><td>*Critical
Issue*</td><td># Cops 'n' Pols—A History of Clout</td></tr>
</table>

"I know of no instance of a connection between politics and the police. I take no orders from anyone but the mayor."

—*Timothy J. O'Connor,*
police commissioner, 1950

By Zay N. Smith

The link between politics and police in Chicago, illustrated by the Sun-Times in the 1950s.

The only surprise in Chicago's latest cop-clout controversy is that anybody's surprised.

Politics and the police first got connected in this city a hundred or more years ago, when the streets were made of dirt and hotels were named after whores. That was how the system worked.

And how it still does.

"Boss" style was set by Long John Wentworth, Chicago's first strongman mayor, who fashioned the police in his own image, even if he had to fill them with whiskey to do it.

It was on June 18, 1857, that he decided the business district was too cluttered. All the low awnings, especially, bothered the mayor who was 6 feet 6 inches. So it was bourbon all around for the police and then a strange set of late-night orders.

The next morning, Chicago shopkeepers found that their city was missing all its awnings and overhanging signs. Wentworth later denied he had got his coppers drunk. He knew this to be true, he said, because he had poured the drinks himself.

Even in the 1860s, Allan Pinkerton, the city's first detective, found the Police Department a hopeless mix of politicians, crooks and cops. He said the only chance was to create a private agency that would be "independent of political

Long John Wentworth knew his cops weren't drunk—he poured the drinks. Allan Pinkerton suggested a private agency "independent of political influence." O. W. Wilson didn't outsmart the bosses when he cut the number of police districts.

influence, and by whose efforts the criminal could be punished without fear or personal favor."

It was a nice idea that didn't work. The law was the law, but Chicago was Chicago.

It stayed that way for the next century: through the glory days of John J. "Bathhouse John" Coughlin and Michael "Hinky Dink" Kenna, bosses from the 1st Ward; through Democrats and Republicans, rascals and reformers.

Police uniforms have changed since 1903. Reformers haven't changed the clout system much.

This was a city built on clout. You had to own people to get things done. Cops were especially useful, almost as good as judges.

The police districts usually followed the ward lines. The ward bosses got to pick the captains and their helpers. If mobsters owned the ward boss, they were glad to offer advice. The profitable districts were the ones heavy with saloons, gambling and friendly women.

The cops? They were there for putting in the fix, opening up the rackets, shaking down whatever moved and helping to keep the precincts in line at election time. Nobody was shy about it.

Bruce Smith, who led a 1930 reformers' survey of the department, saw enough when he visited the police commissioner's office: "An alderman appears in behalf of a suspended policemen. A ward leader enters with traffic tickets to be fixed. The anteroom is crowded [with] aldermen, ward heelers, bail bondsmen. . . ."

He noted that many had pass keys.

Tests were rigged so a cop could be promoted according to his clout. Most of the clout cops in 1927 were so dumb that officials had to grab 10 percentage points out of the air to get them a pass.

As for the honest cops? They kept the cemeteries safe and the desks dusted.

Chicago's reformers raised intermittent screams as new scandals happened, most often involving the 1st Ward and the Near North Side's only honky-tonk district.

Now and then cops were fired (Lt. Anthony De Grazio never should have taken that 39-day European vacation with mobster Tony Accardo), but most landed on their feet. There were a few prison sentences. There were reforms, many with lifespans of butterflies.

It took a babbling burglar to make something happen.

In 1960, Richard Morrison talked about how the Summerdale District police were playing cops-and-robbers the wrong way. The scandal wasn't the worst Chicago had ever known, but it caused a politically dangerous uproar. The late Mayor Richard J. Daley was forced to bring in a new chief.

O. W. Wilson, "The Professor," came in with a reputation to give any ward boss the willies, and he lived up to it. He was a chainsmoker who liked to set all the right pants on fire.

Some of his moves were symbolic. He changed his title to police superintendent. He moved his office from City Hall to police headquarters at 1121 S. State.

Other moves were more to the point. Wilson reduced the number of police districts from 38 to 21. He said this was for efficiency. The ward bosses knew better. It was to break up the borders of their ward-district domains.

What was worse, Wilson ordered new promotion examinations for the first time since 1948, tossing out the rigged lists and making merit the new measure. Good cops who had languished without sponsors suddenly were leapfrogging through the ranks.

But this was Chicago. And it had been Chicago for some time. As Wilson said when he left seven years later, "I leave many great designs unattempted and many great attempts unfinished."

Which remains ok with the ward bosses, and anybody else who enjoys being a boss. The clout is more subtle these days, but the buddy system still works.

When James M. Rochford resigned as police superintendent in late 1977, he said it was mostly for financial reasons. "I have a lump in my throat and a heavy heart," he said. "But leave I must."

Another reason was the reported heavy pestering from Mayor Michael A. Bilandic, patronage chief Tom Donovan and others. Rochford, who had lost his political protection when Mayor Daley died, now was being hit from every direction for appointments and favors.

It was said that he wanted to run his own department—or no department at all.

He got no department at all.

Welcome to Chicago.

Police in the 1930s.

Photo courtesy of Galesburg Police Department, Galesburg, Illinois.

that police officers in at least some departments can still be ''bought,'' and the image of the police is further tarnished in the eyes of both those who cannot afford to ''pay off'' the police and those who detest the necessity of doing so. Perhaps equally important is the belief in many communities that police officers routinely accept gratuities (free coffee, free or discounted meals, free access to movies, or discounts in department stores) that are unavailable to other citizens. In New York City alone, 101 police officers were arrested in 1992 for criminal conduct and large scale corruption was uncovered.[11]

Another source of conflict between the police and the public can be traced to concerns of both British and United States citizens contemplating the development of municipal police departments. In both countries, it was eventually agreed that the police were to be responsible for two major functions—enforcing the law and maintaining order. In order to accomplish the latter, municipal police had to be granted the authority to intervene in the day-to-day affairs (human relations) of private citizens.[12] Such intervention is necessary if the police are to regulate morals, break up domestic disputes, and regulate traffic. In both Britain and America, there was considerable fear that the rights of citizens would be seriously threatened by such intervention. One could hardly be certain of being secure to pursue one's happiness in one's ''castle'' if the police had the authority to intervene in these sectors. In fact, many citizens had come to America to avoid this kind of intervention, and these individuals were understandably hesitant to renounce some of their newfound freedom in the interest of public order. The realization that a number of court decisions concerning search and seizure, stop and frisk, and ''no-knock'' entry have been handed down in this century, and the fact that intervention in domestic disputes remains one of the more problematic police activities, indicate that the issue of police interference in the daily activities of citizens in their homes and vehicles remains controversial.

Chapter 2

Another area of misunderstanding between the police and the public arose partly as the result of technological advances in police work. As Rubinstein (1973) indicates: "The introduction of the patrol car and the development of the wireless radio were heralded as the way to resolve all the problems created by the territorial strategy of the New Police."[13] Since virtually all departments in the United States had adopted the territorial or "beat" strategy, police administrators in the 1930s felt that urban crime could be virtually eliminated as a result of these developments, and said so (public relations). Citizens' expectations concerning response time, apprehension of offenders, and prevention of crime were thus raised to high levels. In their initial enthusiasm, it appears that police administrators failed to anticipate, first, the tremendous number of requests for service that were to follow, and, second, the extent to which offenders would avail themselves of the same technological devices as the police. Needless to say, the expectations developed as a result of police promises to solve the crime problem have gone largely unfulfilled, creating still another area of controversy between the police and the public.

We have said little about problems in police/public encounters occasioned by our failure to eliminate from police personnel those individuals whose approach and attitudes are offensive to citizens. While there is no doubt that both past and current selection procedures leave a great deal to be desired, this situation persists because of a far more complex issue. A great deal of conflict between the police and the public results from society's inability to decide clearly, and more or less permanently, what the police are supposed to do and how they are to proceed. Although we can generally agree that the police should enforce the law when predatory crimes against the person occur, we are far less certain about what the police ought to do in the case of far more frequently occurring, less serious crimes, to say nothing of noncriminal matters such as traffic enforcement. On the one hand, we empower the police to enforce laws concerning morality, prostitution, adultery, gambling, and drugs; on the other hand, we seek and participate in the very activities we have asked the police to curb (since none of these activities would continue to exist if there was no demand). How many of us have never exceeded the speed limit, or taken an illegal drink, or placed a small wager? However, when the police take action in these matters, at least when we are personally involved, we become resentful and indignant at their intervention. After all, which of us involved in activities such as these is really a criminal? When such activities become too pronounced, however, and "the other guy" is involved, we often feel justified in demanding police action. The police, then, often find themselves in a "no win" situation where either intervention or lack of it may be severely criticized.

Similarly, we expect the police to maintain public order, but we have been and still are unable to specify how much public order is desirable. Clearly it would be possible to maintain a much higher degree of public order by granting the police powers such as those graphically described by Solzhenitsyn:

> In a night arrest the State Security men have a superiority in numbers; there are many of them, armed, against one person who hasn't even finished buttoning his trousers; the unhurried, step-by-step visits, first to one apartment, then to

another, tomorrow to a third and a fourth, provide an opportunity for the Security operations personnel to be deployed with the maximum efficiency and to imprison many more citizens of a given town than the police force itself numbers.[14]

The crime involved? Public or private dissent from official Soviet policy. This is too much public order for most of us. Contrast this description with the results of the Kerner Commission Report concerning protests in the middle 1960s in the United States, a document which indicates that one of the major complaints of black ghetto residents is failure of the police to respond and investigate cases even when murder, aggravated battery, or rape are involved.[15] This is too little public order for most of us. What we want is something in between, but people's wants vary from time to time, place to place, and group to group. And we expect the police to use "common sense," to know how much public order to maintain at different times, even though we ourselves have not been able to formulate common standards from which to develop a general understanding and to form a common sense. Again, lack of public consensus leads inevitably to tensions in police community relations.

Another source of difficulties in police community relations stems from the process by which the laws the police are expected to enforce come into existence. Contrary to what we once believed, most laws are more the result of conflict and change than of consensus or the "will of the majority." At one extreme, the targets of the law have neither legitimate voice nor vote in the political process that produces the law. People who lose military contests or who are coerced into servitude typically fall into this category. In these circumstances, the law is almost always an instrument of the extension of domination and oppression. Included here would be laws pertaining to Native Americans, African slaves and women in early U.S. history. The forceful relocation of Native American tribes and their confinement to reservations, the suppression of slave revolts and the vigorous pursuit of runaway slaves, and the denial of full political participation to women are examples of the uses of law and the actions of law enforcement agents that cast both in a very problematic light.

In the more routine political process, two or more legitimate parties or groups have a conflict of interest which is eventually resolved by the courts or the legislature. The decision handed down by the court or the statute passed by the legislature creates a winner and a loser (or partial winners and partial losers). It is to be expected that the losers will not be overjoyed at losing. Similarly, when the police enforce laws, they very frequently create a winner and a loser (who also probably is not content to lose). Thus, even in a simple two-party dispute, at least one party is likely to be dissatisfied with the outcome of police intervention. To express it another way, much law and much police law enforcement activity creates "trouble" for an individual or a group.[16] It is unlikely that the police will be able to satisfy completely both parties to a dispute, regardless of the action taken. Intervention in public disputes involving large segments of the population is especially problematic for the police. After vigorous political debate, for example, the legislature may enact laws that outlaw workers' unions and labor strikes. When an illegal strike occurs and the police are called upon to enforce the law, as they often were in the early days of union organization in the United States, violent confrontations may ensue. The image of the police that emerges for many citizens is as the brutal instruments of an oppressive and exploitative economic and political elite. Similarly, forceful police intervention in large scale political protests and demonstrations, as in the 1968 Democratic Party convention in Chicago, may influence the publics' view of police for decades.

In less consequential but far more frequent situations, such as traffic stops, the citizen involved is highly unlikely to be happy if the police officer takes any official action and may be unhappy simply because he was stopped even if no official action is taken. Similarly, during Prohibition, the police were regarded as "morally corrupt" or "on the take" by some segments of the public if they overlooked liquor violations and as "nuisances" or "do-gooders" by others if they failed to overlook such violations. Thus, a certain amount of conflict between citizens and the police is to be expected in most encounters, a fact which we often overlook in attempting to improve police community relations.

A final source of conflict in police community relations stems from the increasing educational level and awareness of personal and civil rights among the public. Encounters which were once accepted as "the way things are" are now subject to questioning. More and more citizens "know" or think they know "their rights" and say so to police officers. To some police officers this constitutes a challenge to authority to which they feel compelled to respond by exerting more authority, at times through the use of force.[17] As a result, the encounter may change from routine to one which is dangerous for all participants and which may add to the scope of police community relations problems. While many citizen participants in such confrontations come from groups who see themselves as victims of political and socioeconomic favoritism on the part of the police, many other persons so involved are also members of the middle class. These latter see the primary job of the police as enforcing the law against the "bad guys" and not harassing "decent citizens." Thus, police community relations problems are not limited to particular racial or economic groups, but cut across ethnic and class lines.

It is noteworthy that while the problems just discussed have continued to hamper police community relations in the United States, some of them have in the past been less problematic in Great Britain. In 1977, Sir Robert Mark was able to say that police in Great Britain "enjoy a rather unfair advantage" over their counterparts in the United States.

> We (in Great Britain) are a small island, able to exercise a reasonably effective control over the entry of people, firearms and drugs. During this century at least we have enjoyed a reasonable degree of prosperity, universal education and, an increasing avoidance of poverty of the kind experienced in the thirties. This has

encouraged general acceptance of our social system and of the law even by minorities . . . the legalization and improved control of betting and gaming, and changing attitudes to prostitution, homosexuality and victimless crime have to a great extent eliminated the aura of corruption which inevitably affected police involved in those matters. This has contributed significantly to an improved police image.[18]

More specifically, Mark indicated that:

. . . the reputation of a police force basically depends on its acceptability and this can only be achieved by a carefully balanced limitation of its powers which allows it to be effective but subject coincidentally to a high degree of accountability to the courts, to its police authority and to the public.[19]

In contrast, Rudovsky (1992), commenting on the situation in the United States, concludes that a law and order mentality has, along with rising racism, led many to believe that the police should have a free hand. He believes the police culture must be changed and police must be held politically and legally accountable.[20]

Recent events in Great Britain indicate that British police are now confronted by many of the difficulties their American counterparts face. Racial protests and demonstrations, increases in violent crime, and the use of firearms in the commission of crimes, as well as armed assaults on unarmed police officers, have called into question the effectiveness of the controls mentioned and raised questions regarding the role of the police. Recently, in fact, the British have decided to arm bobbies who are assigned to selected high crime/high violence areas—typically ethnic ghettos in large urban areas. As we shall see in succeeding chapters, many of these same difficulties continue to plague us in the United States. Some, to be sure, may be impossible to correct, while others may be at least partially resolved.

The Changing Role of the Police in Contemporary Society

To the extent that we were able to find a positive image of police work it was the policeman as a free, independent, active, masculine, autonomous man. In this romantic vision, the policeman is free from the burden of a fixed routine. He can express his self-image and is backed up by the power of his own manhood, of the state, and of his weapon. His self-image suggests a hope for overcoming a sense of alienation, of impersonality, of anonymity, and loss of identity under the pressures and confusions of modern urban life undergoing radical change. The reality of police work is far removed from these images. Any urban police department is necessarily a bureaucracy. The policeman is hedged in with a vast number of legal and administrative controls subordinating him to bureaucratic law and to those rules that will enable his commanders to supervise, control, and evaluate him on a regular basis and be able to separate him from the force if he does not measure up. Paperwork is central to this system of control.[21]

Or, as Bouza (1990) puts it:

> Entering cops are shocked by the contrast between their expectations of the job and the reality. They focus initially on fighting crime but soon discover that policing is mostly a service industry.[22]

As the above quotes clearly indicate, there is a great discrepancy between the ideal of police work and what a majority of police officers actually do most of the time. In this section, we will explore in some detail the reasons for, and consequences of, this discrepancy. In order to achieve these ends, we need to look first at the nature and functions of police work in contemporary society.

There are a number of problems inherent in our criminal justice network which have considerable impact both on the self-image of the police and on citizens' perceptions of the police. We place police officers in situations which require that they exercise considerable discretion. It is ironic that we place in the position of ''gatekeeper'' to the criminal justice network, one of the poorest-paid and often the least educated practitioner in the entire network, then ask him to make instantaneous decisions as important as arrest/non-arrest or life and death. Then we allow the rest of the network practitioners (prosecutors, judges, and juries) to take as much time as necessary to review the police officer's decision and reverse it if need be. If the police officer makes a mistake in ascertaining either legal or factual guilt, the defendant may be set free by the prosecutor or judge. This is as it should be according to our philosophy of justice. And the police officer should suffer the consequences (e.g., public criticism) for errors in either substance or form, provided the "ground rules" by which he or she must abide are reasonably clear. In our network, however, these ground rules are often ambiguous and receive varying emphasis at different times, making the police officer's job even more difficult. In addition, the prosecutor in our network may for political reasons dismiss cases which have been properly prepared by the police. Similarly, the judge, or judge and jury, may, from time to time, fail to convict a guilty party. Furthermore, plea bargaining arrangements may lead to reduced charges, which result in the defendant being placed on probation or receiving a minimum sentence. While it is technically true that none of these decisions reached by those "higher" in the network should have great impact on the police officer, unless she has contributed to such decisions by preparing cases badly, we might ask ourselves who is likely to be blamed if the defendant then commits another crime. In many cases, the police are held responsible by citizens because they are the only visible representatives of authority. Thus, if probation officers or correctional officers fail to rehabilitate their charges, the public may view the police as culprits. "Why do the police end up arresting the same people time after time?" is a much more frequent question than "Why do prosecutors grant political concessions?" or "Why don't probation and corrections personnel do a better job at rehabilitation?" or "What is it about our society which leads some people to repeat crimes time after time?"

By virtue of their position as "rank and file" workers in the criminal justice network, then, and because they in many ways mediate between citizens and others in that network, the police are often viewed as ineffective, because of actions over which they have little or no control. Part of the dilemma in police community relations has more to do with dissatisfaction with the criminal justice network than with the police themselves.

It has been suggested by a number of students of the police that their two basic functions in the United States are law enforcement and the maintenance of order.[23] Both are simply specific categories of what has increasingly become the most important function of the police: responding to requests for services. Our observations indicate that 80 to 90 percent of the patrol officer's time is spent responding to service requests which frequently have little or nothing to do with law enforcement. Because the police are available to the public twenty-four hours a day, every day, and because they have historically provided a wide range of services upon public request, the number and variety of requests for services has continued to increase. A good example is the preparation and the reproduction of accident reports which, especially when they concern very minor incidents, are used primarily if not solely for insurance purposes. This task has gotten so out of hand that many police departments no longer provide such services when only minor damage is involved or the incident occurs on private property. Other nonenforcement type tasks which the police frequently perform include settling family disputes, finding lost children, aiding the sick or elderly, guiding tours through police facilities, visiting schools, and speaking before civic groups. As a result, today, many police departments find themselves so overburdened with service requests that they cannot respond to all such requests or can respond only after considerable delay. Time and manpower available solely for law enforcement work are at a premium.

In addition to forcing the police officer to realize that he is primarily a service provider rather than a crime fighter, the tremendous increase in requests for services may lead to public dissatisfaction if the police are slow in responding or fail to respond at all, although there is now some evidence that the public can be persuaded to accept diverse response strategies. Further, public perceptions of the police as crime fighters suffer, since the police often fail to fully investigate violations of law because their resources are directed elsewhere (and because, in their assessment, full investigation of certain types of offenses is seldom worthwhile).

The role of the police officer as a service provider need not involve the strong masculine identity or autonomy discussed in the opening quote in this section of the chapter. Instead, it is more likely to require skills in dealing with referrals, paperwork, bureaucratic structures, and citizens other than criminals. The idealized, television program-image of the police officer continuously involved in crime fighting clearly does not represent the reality of police work today.

It is true that one major function of police in the United States is to use force against certain types of citizens under certain circumstances. In our society, the government (federal, state, and local) monopolizes the right to use legitimate force and delegates to the police the right to employ force in the form of legal coercion. In fact, it has been suggested that the police may best be viewed as ''a mechanism for the distribution of situationally justified force.''[24] This view of the police, as Bittner (1970) aptly points out, aids in understanding both why people call the police and the expectations of the police and the citizens against whom they proceed. The gun, nightstick, mace, and handcuffs carried openly by uniformed patrol officers serve as a constant reminder that the use of force by the police is a possibility. While we seldom discuss it, one of the basic reasons for the existence of the police is the use of force. This may be one of the major reasons for distrust and hostility among citizens, especially those who would like to view themselves as ''above'' the use of force (e.g., middle-class traffic violators). The uniformed police officer, then, serves as a constant reminder that the ultimate form of power, physical coercion, can be employed against any of us under certain circumstances. While we are enthralled with movies and television programs in which the police use force on a regular basis, we would prefer not to confront this possibility in real life.

It should be noted here that although we prepare each new police officer to use weapons and force should they become necessary, the actual use of force is not involved in most police-citizen encounters. Further, although the danger of misuse of force is ever present, the actual incidence of police physical brutality is quite low.[25] Thus, most police-citizen encounters are ''carried off'' civilly if not pleasantly. Nevertheless, the realization that the use of force is a possibility when confrontation between a police officer and a citizen occurs, and the highly publicized use/abuse of police force such as that occurring in the Rodney King incident in Los Angeles, exerts both tangible and intangible influence on such encounters, as we shall see in the following sections.

As Skolnick points out, "Doctors, janitors, lawyers, and industrial workers develop distinctive ways of perceiving and responding to their environment."[26] So too, "There are distinctive recognizable tendencies in police as an occupation grouping."[27] Skolnick points out that three elements combine to create the working personality of the police officer: danger, authority, and efficiency .[28] We would add a fourth element—membership in a "blue minority." The working personality of the police officer does not generally result from selecting recruits who already possess this "personality type," although some police recruiters are very much concerned with selecting and employing officers who appear to have the physical and emotional makeup to enable them to fit the TV image. Actually, this results, instead, from the training and socialization processes which police officers encounter, as well as from pressures of the job itself. Let us examine each of the elements of the working personality individually to determine how each helps shape the nature of police community relations.

Danger is a critical element in police work, primarily because of our inability to predict when, where, and with whom it will occur. As a result, we train police officers to be alert for the possibility of attack in most types of encounters with other citizens. We teach them to approach other citizens with varying amounts of suspicion and distrust depending upon the circumstances and setting in which the encounter occurs. For example, in a routine traffic stop late at night, we ask the officer to advise the police dispatcher of her location as well as the make and license number of the vehicle stopped. In addition, we ask her to pull her car in behind the vehicle being stopped, in some cases to use the spotlight in a particular fashion, and to approach the car in a certain manner and stand in a particular position with respect to the door on the driver's side of the stopped vehicle. Since we cannot accurately predict the behavior of the driver of the car, these steps are necessary to protect the officer. Thus, the element of danger is repeatedly emphasized in police work, as the presence of the gun, nightstick, mace, and refresher courses in firearms and defensive tactics clearly indicate.

We have granted police officers the right to use legal coercion (suggestions, persuasion, and, if necessary, physical force) to enforce the law and maintain order while performing a variety of services. The badge, the uniform, and the weapons worn by the police officer are all symbols of his **authority.** These symbols, the authority we grant the police, and the training and socialization officers receive, all lead them to believe that the definition of the situation which prevails in most encounters with other citizens must be their definition. In short, the police are "in charge" and their authority must prevail. If it does not, police officers are likely to experience considerable loss of face (prestige or self-respect).

Unfortunately for some police officers, many segments of the population do not share the police perspective, nor are these groups willing to grant police officers the respect which the officers feel appropriate. Police officers, then, frequently find themselves confronted by suspicious or hostile citizens who view them as visible representatives of an establishment that, from their standpoint, leaves a great deal to be desired. The police officer is confronted by conditions which are not of her making (poor housing, poor schooling, under- or unemployment, etc.), but for which, in one way or another, she is often blamed. When the officer finds himself confronted by an unfriendly or suspicious group of citizens he feels that his authority is being threatened. Since the officer cannot obtain respect on a voluntary basis, she may resort to using her authority (sometimes inappropriately) to enforce obedience and/or respect. If citizens persist in defying the officer's authority, he may fall back on the use of physical force and/or the threat of arrest in order to gain control of the situation. If the officer does so, the level of danger is considerably escalated for both the officer and the other citizens involved, as there is the possibility of loss of face. Thus, the presence of an authority figure can have two diametrically opposed effects on citizens. It may lead to quick control of the encounter, or it may escalate the confrontation to the level of open hostility. What happens will depend upon the actions of both the police officer and the other citizens involved during and subsequent to the initial encounter.

Another element of the police officer's working personality is **efficiency.** Today, with the emphasis on maximum productivity for the tax dollar, the public demands that the police prove their efficiency. Thus, the police produce, and the public and governing bodies consume, great amounts of paperwork in the form of crime statistics, activity reports, and traffic reports. The more extensive the use of the computer and the more impressive the statistics, the more efficient we believe the police to be. As indicated in the quotation with which we opened this section, however, many police officers do not view the production of volumes of paperwork as real police work. Their frustration with the documentation of their efficiency is complicated by the requirement that they operate within the framework of due process, a demand which often takes considerable time and makes the compilation of impressive ''crimes cleared by arrest'' statistics more difficult. In addition, many officers feel that efficiency requirements place severe limitations on their discretion and sometimes hamper ''good police work.'' For example, efficiency requirements may dictate that an officer spend no more than twenty minutes handling a family dispute. The officer often feels that if she could spend an additional ten to fifteen minutes she could work out a more lasting agreement which would make future calls to the same location less likely. Ironically, while citizens often demand police efficiency, they frequently are displeased by what they consider to be impersonal, businesslike, aloof attitudes of a police officer who is trying to be efficient. The element of efficiency, then, helps determine the nature of police community relations.

Membership in a **''blue minority''** is yet another element in the police working personality. Like members of other minority groups, uniformed police officers can be readily identified and there is a tendency to divide the world into "we" and "they" groups. Like other minority group members, police officers tend to distrust members of other sectors of the population, and they tend to socialize, both on and off the job, with members of their own minority group. As a result, citizens who do not belong to the blue minority tend to be suspicious of that group because they fear the "in group" secrets and activities of its members. Even when out of uniform, members of the blue minority are frequently recognized as representatives of authority and because of this they are often excluded from activities. Thus it becomes difficult for police officers and their families to establish or maintain friendships with non-police officers who may be engaged in marginally legal (drinking too much) or illegal but often overlooked (marijuana smoking) activities. Once identification as a blue minority group member occurs, non-police citizens are likely to feel ill at ease if they are involved in such activities. As a result, police officers tend to socialize with other police officers to avoid such unpleasant interactions. It is easy, therefore, for them to view outsiders as suspicious or untrustworthy, and vice versa. The effects of such suspicion, combined with predominantly in-group activities, on police community relations are readily apparent.

Although we have discussed the elements in the police officer's working personality separately, it should be apparent that they are closely interrelated. For example, the greater the danger, the more likely the police officer is to exert his/her authority and, in certain types of cases, vice versa. Similarly, the greater the in-group activities of the police, the more suspicious the public becomes, the more suspicious police officers become, and the more dangerous police-public encounters become.

Whether it is called the "blue minority," the "fraternity," or the police subculture, there is little doubt that membership in the "in-group" of police officers has extensive influence on the way in which police officers perceive their world.[29] Along with their interpretations of the law and departmental policy, the values of the police subculture (from training throughout active duty) determine the way in which police officers approach and interact with citizens. The subculture creates categories of citizens, classifications into which the police officer believes he/she can place most of those with whom he/she interacts.[30] The officer is able, or believes he/she is able, to categorize citizens during or even prior to initial encounters. The setting, behavior, and the physical characteristics of the citizen are all clues as to the "type of character" he/she is, and to some extent these determine the course the encounter will take. For example, certain citizens may be viewed by members of the police subculture as potential troublemakers or belonging to an "outcast group," regardless of their behavior (blacks, drug addicts, prostitutes, and "hippies," are often included in these categories).[31] To the extent that police officers react negatively to such citizens even when their behavior is legal, police community relations suffer.

Finally, the police subculture requires that its members be loyal and trustworthy, even, at times, to the point of covering up illegal activities committed by its members. It is, therefore, a major force to be reckoned with in attempting to understand and improve police community relations.

The shaping of the police perspective begins with the selection and recruitment process. As Gray (1975) and Bouza (1990) point out, selection procedures, while formally directed toward fulfilling the requirements of a particular police department, are also used to select individuals who will meet the needs of the police subculture.[32] Generally speaking, those who are selected meet certain physical standards (proportionate height and weight, a certain level of agility, ability to pass a medical exam) and certain educational requirements (generally a high school diploma or G.E.D.), are morally fit and appear to have an affinity for police work.[33] Having "sorted out" all those applicants who fail to meet these requirements, examiners interview those remaining in an effort to assess the applicant's group loyalty and demeanor or general presentation of self. As Gray indicates, those who are selected frequently would have been (or actually have been) proficient in contact sports. Those selected are physically fit, often have a strong sense of "masculine identity" (including females who are selected), and are thought to be loyal and trustworthy, with a commitment to police work.[34]

Ironically, perhaps, recruiters do not always look specifically for those who understand that a major part of police work involves human relations. In some cases, interviewers still look for the "ideal" police role image described in the quote at the beginning of this section, and then expect the applicant to adapt to the "reality" of police work. Some do so with considerable success; others stay on but never fully make the transition; and still others leave when they are unable to reconcile the discrepancy. Inducted into the police ranks are those who, presumably, can fulfill the needs both of the formal police organization and the police subculture. And thus, to some extent, those entering police work are individuals whose self-image and perspective on life conform better to the ideal than to the reality. Actually, the work environment of police work is constantly changing. New laws, new departmental regulations, increasing awareness of individual and civil rights, etc., require such change.

Perhaps more difficult for many police officers to accept is the change which has occurred and is still occurring in the image of the ideal police officer. At one time, not long ago, the image was that of a physically large, strong, white male with a high school education. However, both the police department and the police subculture have been "invaded" by those previously thought to be unfit for service. Females, blacks, Hispanics, Asians, and others are among those seeking careers in law enforcement. Physical strength, while not forgotten, has become no more important than an agile mind and a knowledge of human relations. In a growing number of departments, a high school education is not sufficient to qualify for initial employment.[35] Two- and three-year college students as well as four-year college graduates are now common among applicants for police work. Promotion based on merit rather than seniority or favoritism is increasingly frequent, and lateral transfer between police agencies is possible in some areas.

Improved Image Seen by Retiring Policeman

By Norma Cunningham

Associate Editor

GALESBURG—Twenty-one years in any job is bound to produce a lot of changes, but Lt. Jim Hasselbacher thinks that may be more true in police work than most places. . . .

"There have been as many changes in law enforcement in the last 21 years as in any field," Hasselbacher said earlier this week. "A new patrolman now has an associate or bachelor's degree, and we have two who have master's," he said.

"Policemen today have much more education than they did back in the '40s, for instance. Back in those days, a policeman was a second class citizen. That image is gone."

There have been other changes, too.

Not too many years ago, a local police department was just that—local. Now there is interaction among departments and cooperation that extends effectiveness and provides better service to the public. . . .

"The modern approach to police work produces such things like 'Operation Iron Eagle' which brought together police from several cities, several counties, MEG, state and federal agencies. That wouldn't have worked 20 years ago, but now there can be that kind of cooperation. The approach is more professional, but the times dictate that's what we must do," he said.

And while law enforcement has changed in the last couple of decades, so have criminals.

"Twenty years ago, the criminals you came in contact with lived in Galesburg. That's not true of many of them now. They are more transient. They move around a lot. That's one of the things that dictates that police must cooperate and work together," Hasselbacher said.

"I felt that being a policeman would not only let me do public service, but it would be an interesting profession," he said of his decision to take the test as the first step to becoming a police officer.

He was a policeman in the late 1960s and early 1970s when there were clashes between police and protestors in many towns.

"I look back now and see that Galesburg was more fortunate than most towns. We had marches here, but they were peaceful demonstrations. The credit for that goes to an administration that granted parade demonstrations and set ground rules for the well-being of all sides. Many other towns brought on their own problems by refusing parade permits," he said. . . .

"The tensions and the emotions in domestic violence calls are way outside the norm. More policemen are injured or killed on that kind of call because they don't protect themselves and they allow themselves to become vulnerable," he said.

And what is the frustration of a veteran officer?

"It's the 13- and 14-year old who will have maybe 50 or 60 contacts with the police by the time he turns 16. That's frustrating. You get a feeling in your stomach that you're not going to be able to turn this one around."

Hasselbacher is proud of the "Neighborhood Watch" program which he shepherded along from an idea to an important part of the department's work with the community. The program is now under the leadership of another officer.

He is also pleased with his time as a court liaison officer, which required him to work with the state's attorney's office. "You learn to understand his problems and to open doors between the two agencies," he said.

Has he had any second thoughts about his decision to retire at the age of 48?

"If you'd asked me three months ago, I'd have said no. Today? Very much. But it's time to go. Most policemen will tell you that after 20 years, it's time to make a change."

"But I have no regrets. This is what I wanted to do. I'll miss it, of course. . . ."

The Register Mail, *Galesburg, Illinois.*

As we might expect, not all these changes are welcomed by the police. Nonetheless, the image of the police officer is changing and as changes occur, they have (or are expected to have) considerable impact on police community relations. More specifically, the belief is that better educated police officers will be better able to meet the legal and human relations requirements of the job by the exercise of discretion derived from reason, training, and education. Such practices, together with the presence of minority group officers and improved training, may facilitate better police community relations.

The Exercise of Discretion and Police Community Relations

Observers of police behavior are increasingly concerned about the extent and nature of **police discretion.** Skolnick, in *Justice Without Trial* (1966), notes that police are the chief interpreters of law and often test the limits of their legal authority in largely unobservable fashion.[36] Skolnick goes on to observe that: "Police discretion is hidden insofar as the policeman often makes decisions in direct interaction with the suspect. Whether it is a question of writing out a traffic citation, of arresting a spouse on a charge of assault with a deadly weapon, or of apprehending an addict informer, the policeman has enormous power: he may halt the legal process right there. Such discretionary activity is difficult to observe."[37]

Goldstein (1969) is also concerned with the difficulty of observing discretionary behavior, pointing out that police decisions not to invoke the law when they have reason to are even more difficult to observe than decisions which do invoke the law.[38]

While the assertion that discretionary behavior on behalf of the police is largely invisible is called into question by the work of Bittner,[39] Piliavin and Briar[40] and others, there is little doubt that the manner in which discretion is exercised greatly affects police community relations. If police discretion is exercised inconsistently, the public cannot know what to expect from encounters with the police. If the police exercise discretion unwisely, the public may feel that some laws are being ignored, that those who should be arrested are going free, or that some laws are being enforced too strictly.

If we define police discretion as the exercise of individual choice or judgment by police officers in the line of duty, and if we keep in mind the influences of the police subculture, police training, differing individual backgrounds, and departmental expectations, it is easy to see that the cues to which different officers respond may vary considerably. For example, a number of authors comment on the distinction between detention for harassment and arrests for prosecution. Prostitutes, alcoholics, and addicts are often detained, even though the police officer does not plan to file formal charges. This implies, of course, that the police officer has exercised his/her discretion concerning invocation of law. While it is true that there are certain limits which determine to a great extent the alternatives open to the police officer in a given situation, it is equally true that he makes personal decisions within these limits.

At the present time there appears to be considerable consensus among social scientists, police administrators, and legal scholars that police discretion is an area which warrants far more attention than it has previously received.

Examining police behavior only in terms of the law is clearly an inadequate way of understanding that behavior. Wilson, for example, points out that: "Though the substantive criminal law seems to imply a mandate, based on duty or morality, that the law be applied wherever and whenever its injunctions have been violated, in fact for most officers there are considerations of utility that equal or exceed in importance those of duty or morality, especially for the more common and less serious laws."[41]

Since these "more common and less serious" law violations constitute the majority of police work and account for most police-public encounters, the manner in which the police exercise discretion is of considerable importance to police community relations.

Finally, in any discussion of police discretion, at least three forms of discretion should be recognized. One, with which we have been most concerned in the previous discussion, involves the decision whether or not to invoke the law and make an arrest. Another form of discretion includes the selection of strategies and tactics to employ if some means other than invoking the law is chosen to deal with a problematic situation that requires some police response. The third form of discretion is often as consequential, but less often discussed than these two forms. It concerns decisions about how to enforce the law once the decision to enforce the law has been made. That is, discretion is also used in selecting the strategy and tactics to be employed in making an arrest, including decisions about time and place as well as the mode of police behavior to be engaged. The quality of decisions made in any of these three discretionary contexts may make the difference between a successful arrest with the acceptance of those directly involved and a situation that mushrooms into a large-scale social disturbance dangerous for the officers and others as well.

Of course, discretion is exercised by actors other than the police in the criminal justice system. As More puts it, ". . . discretion exists at the inception of a criminal matter and persists to the end."[42] If this is true of criminal matters, it is even more characteristic of noncriminal situations involving the police and the public. Members of the public exercise their discretion in deciding whether to report a suspicious person or a crime, whether to serve as witnesses, and whether to come to the aid of a police officer or victim of a crime. The prosecutor exercises his or her discretion in deciding whether to prosecute and what charges are to be filed. Judicial discretion is exercised when deciding what testimony or evidence is to be allowed in court and in determining sentence for a guilty party. The exercise of discretion by each of these parties affects all others, as does the other's impression of the party exercising discretion. If, for example, citizens in a certain area refuse to cooperate with the police, individual police officers may come to view these citizens as belonging to a group of outsiders, as discussed previously. Consequently, they may provide fewer services to these citizens, or harass them frequently.

The exercise of discretion by all participants in the justice network virtually assures that police-public encounters will not be trouble-free. The less agreement there is concerning the proper behavior of police officers and other citizens during encounters, the greater the police community relations problems.

In recognition of the difficulties arising from too much separation of the police from other members of the communities in which they serve, many police departments in the past five years have implemented community-oriented policing programs. Implicit in these reforms is an increase in discretionary authority for the police. In many ways, these initiatives reflect the growing popularity of service-based, consumer-oriented philosophies and policies appearing in many segments of our economy and in other social/political realms as well. In a sense, these reformers advocate a return to the core principles on which Sir Robert Peel relied in forming the New Police in London more than 150 years ago, but which seem to have been ignored all too often in American policing. While skeptical that community policing is the whole answer to the problems that plague contemporary police community relations in Great Britain or anywhere else, Reiner (1992) nevertheless asserts: "There are many welcome aspects of the emerging consensus around a service-based, consumerist approach to policing. Certainly it is infinitely preferable to the tough 'law and order' promises and practices of the late 1980s which constituted much of the initial police reaction to spiraling crime and disorder."[43]

The community policing initiative both abroad and here in the United States emphasizes the importance of the police-public partnership, positive human relations, and the obligations of citizens other than the police with respect to order maintenance and law enforcement.

Summary

It is evident that many of the problems in police community relations have deep historical roots. It is also apparent that these problems are not created solely by the police or the public, but result from inconsistencies, misperceptions, and misbehavior on both sides. In addition, it appears likely that in a society like ours some degree of conflict and dissatisfaction is built into police-public encounters.

There are a number of differences between "real" and "ideal" police work. The basic function of the police is the provision of services, not crime fighting. Because of the position they occupy in our criminal justice network the police serve to some extent as mediators between citizens and the rest of the network. As a result, the public often holds the police responsible for failures of other criminal justice practitioners.

Among other factors affecting police community relations are the potential for the use of force implied by police presence and the development of the police "working personality." Emphasis on danger, authority, efficiency, and the perception that they are part of a minority group help shape the perspective of police officers as they approach encounters with the public. The working personality is nurtured by a police subculture which often stresses the ideal police image rather than the reality of police work. This discrepancy is partially perpetuated by selection procedures based more on requirements for mythical or ideal police roles than the actual requirements of the job. However, due to increasing numbers of minority group members, changing educational standards, and, hopefully, a better understanding of the human relations aspect of police work, the police subculture may be undergoing changes which could have positive effects on both police performance and police community relations.

The exercise of discretion by all participants in the justice network is another important determinant of police community relations. Inconsistent and unfair discretionary practices make police public encounters problematic and thus undermine good police community relations.

Finally, it should be stressed that both the human relations and public relations aspects of police community relations have played, and continue to play, important roles. Encounters between individual police officers and individual members of the community have led to many of the misperceptions held by both sides; perhaps future such encounters, based upon improved mutual understanding, can improve the quality of these encounters. Similarly, the public image of the police, in many instances mistakenly projected by both the police and the media, may have to change considerably if police community relations are to improve. Attempts to improve both human and public relations are currently underway in many police departments. However, such efforts are likely to prove unsuccessful unless the various groups which comprise the community in which and for which the police operate take similar steps.

Discussion Questions

1. A number of problems characterized the watch-and-ward system as developed in England and colonial America. What were some of these problems and how are they related to problems in police community relations in the United States currently?
2. Discuss the consequences of lack of public consensus concerning the proper role of the police in terms of professionalizing the police and with respect to the exercise of discretion by police officers.
3. Discuss the following problems confronting the American police and the impact of each problem on police community relations:
   a. an emerging heterogeneous society
   b. public apathy
   c. police autonomy
   d. the "means over ends" syndrome
   e. diminishing resources.
4. Discuss some of the major forces which help mold the self-image and public image of police officers. Why is each of these forces important?

Endnotes

1. Donald H. Bouma. 1969. *Kids and Cops: A Study in Mutual Hostility.* Grand Rapids, MI: William B. Erdmans Publishing Co.: 21.
2. Peter K. Manning. 1979. *Police Work: The Social Organization of Policing.* Cambridge, MA: MIT Press: 40–41.
3. John T. O'Brien. "Public Attitudes." 307.

4. *Law Enforcement News.* 1992. ''Police Efforts to Prevent & Solve Crime Win the Approval of Majority in Survey.'' 18(368): 1, 7.

5. Jonathan Rubinstein. 1973. *City Police.* New York: Farrar, Strauss and Giroux: 11–14.

6. Ibid.: 5.

7. *Criminal Victimization in the United States, 1991.* U.S. Department of Justice. Washington, D.C.: U.S. Government Printing Office: 110–111.

8. Ibid.: 102 and Anne Groer. 1994. ''Neighbors Hire Their Own Police.'' *Journal Star.* Peoria. (January 9): A10.

9. James F. Richardson. 1975. ''The Early Years of the New York Police Department'' in Jerome H. Skolnick and Thomas C. Gray, eds. *Police in America.* Boston: Little, Brown and Company: 19–20.

10. Rubinstein. *City Police.* 7.

11. Bruce Frankel. 1993. ''Ex-NYC Officer Tells Stark Tale of Cops Gone Bad.'' *USA Today.* (September 28): 3A.

12. Albert J. Reiss, Jr. 1971. *The Police and the Public.* New Haven: Yale University Press: 2.

13. Rubinstein. *City Police.* 20.

14. Aleksandr I. Solzhenitsyn. 1973. *The Gulag Archipelago.* New York: Harper and Row: 16.

15. National Advisory Commission on Civil Disorders. 1968. Washington, D.C.: U.S. Government Printing Office.

16. Rubinstein. *City Police.* 267–274.

17. See, for example, Ed Cray. 1972. *The Enemy in the Streets: Police Malpractice in America.* Garden City: Anchor Books; or Paul Chevigny. 1969. *Police Power—Police Abuses in New York City.* New York: Vintage Books; or D. Rudovsky. 1992. ''Police Abuse: Can the Violence be Contained?'' *Harvard Civil Rights-Civil Liberties Law Review* 27(2): 467–501.

18. Sir Robert Mark. 1977. *Policing a Perplexed Society.* London: George Allen and Unwin Ltd.: 35.

19. Ibid.: 37.

20. Rudovsky. ''Police Abuse.''

21. Nicholas Alex. 1976. *New York City Cops Talk Back: A Study of a Beleaguered Minority.* New York: John Wiley and Sons: 54.

22. Anthony V. Bouza. 1990. *The Police Mystique: An Insider's Look at Cops, Crime, and the Criminal Justice System.* New York: Plenum: 67.

23. See, for example, Larry Gaines, Victor E. Kappeler, and Joseph B. Vaughn. 1994. *Policing in America.* Cincinnati: Anderson: 8–10; Thomas Barker, Ronald D. Hunter, and Jeffery P. Rush. 1994. *Police Systems & Practices.* Englewood Cliffs, NJ: Prentice-Hall: 95–112.

24. Egon Bittner. 1970. *The Functions of the Police in Modern Society.* Rockville, MD: National Institute of Mental Health: 36–44.

25. Albert J. Reiss, Jr. 1968. ''Police Brutality—Answers to Key Questions.'' *Trans-action.* 5 (July–August): 15–16.

26. We are indebted to Jerome H. Skolnick for the term ''working personality'' and for much of the following discussion. See Jerome H. Skolnick. ''Why Police Behave the Way They Do'' in Skolnick and Gray, eds. *Police in America.*: 31–37.

27. Ibid.: 31.

28. Ibid.

29. See, for example, Arthur Niederhoffer. 1967. *Behind the Shield: The Police in Urban Society.* Garden City: Doubleday and Company; Ellwyn R. Stoddard. 1968. ''The Informal 'Code' of Police Deviance: A Group Approach to 'Blue-Coat Crime'.'' *Journal of Criminal Law Criminology, and Police Science* 59(2):201–213; Joseph Wambaugh. 1975. *The Choirboys.* New York: Dell Publishing Company; Bruce Frankel. 1993. ''For NYC Cops, License for Crime.'' *USA Today* (October 7): 3A; or Richard Lacayo. 1993. ''Cops and Robbers.'' *Time* (October 11): 43.

30. See John Van Maanen. 1978. ''The Asshole'' in Peter K. Manning and John Van Maanen, eds. *Policing: A View from the Street.* Santa Monica, CA: Goodyear Publishing Company: 221–237.

31. Chevigny. *Police Power.*; Lacayo. "Cops and Robbers."
32. Thomas C. Gray. "Selecting for a Police Subculture," in Skolnick and Gray. eds. *Police in America.*: 46–54; Bouza. *The Police Mystique.*: 70–77.
33. Gray. "Selecting for a Police Subculture.": 46–47.
34. Ibid.: 52.
35. Robert E. Worden. 1990. "A Badge and a Baccalaureate: Policies, Hypotheses, and Further Evidence." *Justice Quarterly* 7(3): 565–592.
36. Jerome H. Skolnick. 1966. *Justice Without Trial: Law Enforcement in a Democratic Society.* New York: John Wiley and Sons: p. 4.
37. Ibid.: 233–234.
38. Joseph Goldstein. 1969. "Police Discretion Not to Invoke the Criminal Process: Low-Visibility Decisions in the Administration of Justice" in Donald R. Cressey and David A. Ward, eds. *Delinquency, Crime, and Social Process.* Englewood Cliffs, N.J.: Prentice-Hall: 166–167.
39. Egon Bittner. 1967. "Police Discretion in Emergency Apprehension of Mentally Ill Persons." *Social Problems* 14: 278–292; and Egon Bittner. 1967. "The Police on Skid-Row: A Study of Peace Keeping." *American Sociological Review* 32(October): 699–715.
40. Irving Piliavin and Scott Briar. 1964. "Police Encounters with Juveniles." *American Journal of Sociology* 70(September): 206–214.
41. James Q. Wilson. 1968. *Varieties of Police Behavior.* Cambridge: Harvard University Press: especially 83–90.
42. Harry W. More, Jr. 1972. *Critical Issues in Law Enforcement.* Cincinnati: Anderson: 151.
43. Robert Reiner. 1992. "Fin De Siecle Blues: The Police Face The Millennium." *The Political Quarterly* 63(1): 47.

Suggested Readings

Bordua, David J. and Albert J. Reiss, Jr., eds. 1967. *The Police: Six Sociological Essays.* New York: John Wiley.

Bouza, Anthony V. 1990. *The Police Mystique: An Insider's Look at Cops, Crime, and the Criminal Justice System.* New York: Plenum.

Carter, Gerald. 1980. "Police Discretion: Desirable or Undesirable?" *The Police Chief* (November): 34–35.

Meehan, Albert J. 1992. "I Don't Prevent Crime, I Prevent Calls: Policing as a Negotiated Order." *Symbolic Interaction* 15(4): 455–480.

Richardson, James F. 1970. *The New York Police: Colonial Times to 1901.* New York: Oxford University Press.

———. 1974. *Urban Police in the United States.* Port Washington, New York: Kennikat Press Corporation.

Skolnick, Jerome H. 1969. *The Politics of Protest: A Task Force Report Submitted To The National Commission On The Causes And Prevention Of Violence.* New York: Simon and Schuster.

Skolnick, Jerome H. and David H. Bayley. 1986. *The New Blue Line: Police Innovation in Six American Cities.* New York: Free Press.

Chapter 3

Human Relations and the Police

I n the preceding chapter we considered some aspects of the history of policing and of the police role that are important in understanding contemporary American police community relations. This chapter will focus on the human relations dimension of police community relations.

Human relations, as we noted in Chapter One, is a concept that refers to the ''nitty-gritty'' of police community relations: person-to-person contacts between police officers and other citizens. At one level, these interactions are organized according to the different roles being played. But, underlying this are more fundamental relationships based on what participants have in common: their citizenship and humanity. Emphasizing the human relations dimension of police-citizen interaction, then, invites consideration of the civil and human rights of all participants as they are manifested in these contacts.[1]

While there is relatively little conflict during most encounters between the demands of specific roles being enacted and this underlying set of expectations and obligations, serious difficulties arise in some cases. Those involving police officers in a heterogeneous democratic society offer prime examples.

Police contacts with other citizens can occur in writing or by phone. But compared to these types of interaction, there is a great deal more to gain or lose for the individual participants and for police human relations during face-to-face meetings. Such in-person contacts are more intimate and offer the greatest opportunity for effective communication. Immediate feedback is available and messages can be clarified if necessary on the spot. Nonverbal (e.g., dress, facial expressions, gestures, and sometimes smells) as well as spoken exchanges occur, and participants can compare these various channels of information with each other for consistency. In short, there is ample opportunity for getting a real sense of the person(s) with whom one is dealing. At the same time, however, because they are intimate and participants are physically accessible to each other, emotions may be easily aroused, self-control is sometimes difficult to maintain, and embarrassments, insults, and even physical injury are ever-present possibilities. Hence, in-person interactions are the most appropriate context for observing, analyzing, and evaluating the quality of police human relations practices.

Depending on the size of the community and its police force, there may be hundreds—even thousands—of police interactions with other citizens every day. As we noted in Chapter Two, most police-citizen interactions are initiated by citizens seeking general (i.e., not directly crime-related) services; most are also at least civil in tone and many reflect positively on police community relations.

Unfortunately, however, the majority of relatively positive encounters does not necessarily determine the prevailing tone of police human relations. Unpleasant experiences seem to be remembered longer and their impact often extends well beyond those directly involved. Participants may share their versions of what transpired with family members, friends, and coworkers. The media often spread details of such interactions to a much larger audience. Rumors may circulate quickly and broadly throughout a neighborhood, even without media involvement. A few unpleasant interactions, especially those which attract media attention, can sour police community relations way out of proportion to their actual frequency of occurrence. Thus, improvements in human relations practices which reduce this already relatively small number of unpleasant encounters can produce substantial benefits for police community relations. Let us now turn our attention to some of the more salient aspects of police interaction with other citizens.

Routine Police-Citizen Encounters

An encounter begins when two or more people recognize each other's presence.[2] During an encounter, participants present themselves to each other as individuals and as players of (typically complementary) roles (e.g., teacher–student, police officer–suspect, parent–child). They claim identities (self-definitions or self-concepts) corresponding to the roles being enacted. They try to achieve a consensual definition of the situation (answers to questions like: What is going on here? What kind of social scene is this? A party? A fight? A burglary?). Communication with each other is attempted. Throughout the encounter each party forms some impressions of the other party.[3] But what kinds of impressions do the participants bring with them to such encounters? Where do such impressions come from? And, what are the basic concerns of the participants during the encounter?

Characteristics and Experiences That Affect Police Encounters with Other Citizens

What happens during an encounter in terms of human relations depends, in part, on what the participants bring to it. In addition to their roles, they bring their primary culture and one or more subcultures, their gender and personality, a history of previous interactional experiences with the same (or similar) others, and their (typically clothed) bodies.

Most encounters take place between people who share what may be called a primary culture. In fact, having a culture in common is a virtual necessity for meaningful interaction because the culture provides the general framework within which participants make sense of themselves, each other, their roles, and the social situation. A culture is learned through the process of socialization and has both material and nonmaterial (symbolic) aspects. Among the nonmaterial cultural components are a language, basic values (goals or principles that are regarded as ultimately important), norms (rules that define acceptable and unacceptable behavior), and beliefs (ideas about what is real and theories about how the social and physical worlds operate). Material components of culture include tools and other forms of equipment (e.g., automobiles, computers), physical markers of roles and identities (e.g., licenses, I.D. cards, or badges), works of art, food preferences, clothing, etc. Some core cultural elements are shared by the majority of Americans (the English language and at least some of the values enunciated in the constitution and Bill of Rights, for example). To the extent that those involved in an encounter share a culture, interaction is facilitated.

Even though most Americans share many cultural elements, the cultural homogenization implied by the ''melting pot'' metaphor is largely a myth. Our society is quite diversified and fragmented and, in addition to being socialized into the ''American'' culture, each of us becomes a member of one or more subcultures. Material and nonmaterial concerns of a particular subculture may vary considerably from those of the primary culture and other subcultures. These differences may significantly complicate an encounter for all participants by increasing the likelihood that misinterpretations of verbal and nonverbal messages will occur.

Subcultures tend to form within specific age and ethnic groups, as well as within social classes, occupations, and life-styles. Thus we hear references to youth or delinquent subcultures; Black, Hispanic, and Asian subcultures; the subcultures of computer buffs, or physicians, or the police; and homosexual, criminal, and drug subcultures, for example. In many cases, of course, these subcultures overlap and a particular individual may participate in several of them.

The police must interact with a number of different subcultures. The youth subculture (about which we will have more to say in Chapter Five) is of special significance to the police. For a variety of reasons (lack of employment opportunities, the turmoil of adolescence, the ''generation gap''), members of the youth subculture, especially minority group members, are in frequent contact with, and present special problems for, the police.[4] Similarly, the elderly, who comprise the fastest growing age group in our population, wield increasing political power, and fear crime more than those in other age groups, represent a subculture increasingly important to the police.[5]

Periodic waves of immigration from many regions of the world have led to the proliferation of ethnic groups in our society. It is projected that people of color (nonwhites) will constitute the majority of U.S. citizens by the year 2080. These groups, too, are growing in political influence, especially in urban areas. While ethnic subcultures add healthy and colorful variety to the social and cultural life of our society, racist stereotyping, employment discrimination, and intergroup conflict continue to plague us and to create serious problems in police community relations.[6] While some progress has been made in police minority relations in recent years (Chapter Eight),[7] tensions at times still run high.

Working effectively with people from a number of different age, ethnic, class, and life-style subcultures, as the police must if they are to succeed in their missions, requires knowledge of and sensitivity to the human differences represented in these various groups. Separating personal beliefs and values from the execution of duty is difficult but vital. The occupational subculture to which the police belong, the training they receive, and personal experiences with members of different subcultures all affect the ability of police officers to cope with their personal beliefs and values in the performance of their duties.

As noted earlier in this chapter, people are socialized into subcultures and the police are no exception. Most recruits are required to participate in formal training academies that focus on the law, investigative techniques, use of fire-arms, self-defense tactics, etc., and, to a lesser extent, police community relations.[8] This formal academy training is typically followed by a period of street apprenticeship (the probationary period) under the supervision of more experienced officers. Often there are serious differences between what the recruit learned in the academy and the ''street rules'' to which the new officer is introduced during the apprenticeship; almost always the latter has greater influence on the new officer's philosophy and behavior.[9]

The values comprising the police subculture have been characterized in several different ways,[10] but there are some consistencies. Among the values and norms most frequently cited are strong in-group loyalty (the ''blue fraternity''), political and moral conservatism, an emphasis on physical strength and machismo, rugged individualism, autonomy, and a sense of alienation and isolation that arises, in part, from the inevitable tensions between the police and other citizens in a democratic society. Insofar as this is an accurate portrayal of the police subculture, human relations, especially with those perceived as ''outsiders,'' are likely to be problematic. And, of course, the definition of outsiders changes over time. For example, the changing role of women in our society has heightened tensions between the police and women in some cases. Policing has been, and remains, a male-dominated occupation, and some male officers are viewed by some women as being unresponsive to their requests for services or too quick to find fault with their reports of victimization, especially with respect to domestic and sexual assault.[11] Some elements of the police subculture, conservatism and machoism, for example, would lead us to expect these conflicts. Resolving them remains an important human relations challenge.[12]

People also bring their personalities to an encounter. A personality is a mode of response or personal style that the individual typically employs in relating to others. For example, one person may be an extrovert (very outgoing

and sociable) while another is an introvert (shy and retiring); one may be authoritarian, another unconventional; one may be inner-directed while another is other-directed. Sometimes people are drawn to a particular career because they believe their personalities and self-conceptions fit well with its occupational subculture and roles. As we noted in Chapter Two, Skolnick saw the ''working personality'' of the police officer as shaped by danger, authority, efficiency, and membership in the ''blue minority.''[13] Others have characterized the police personality as inner-directed (self-motivated), task-oriented (get the job done even if the law and civil or human rights must occasionally be compromised), action-oriented (excited by danger, the thrill of pursuit), loyal to the ''blue brotherhood,'' distrustful and suspicious of the public, aggressive, macho, cynical, patronizing, authoritarian (both submissive to those with greater authority and demanding obedience from those with less authority), defensive, and overly concerned with controlling both situations and people.[14] ''Stressed'' is also a frequently cited description of the police personality.[15] Stress is produced by departmental demands for efficiency and productivity, the resentment of the public, the uncertainties associated with many aspects of officers' dealings with superiors and the public, danger,[16] and other conflicting and contradictory pressures inherent in the police role. These factors, combined with the heavy burden of paperwork (perceived as not ''real'' police work) and the frustrations arising from the fact that so few crimes are solved and so few criminals caught, often result in depressed morale.[17] Low morale is, in major part, a function of the perception that key objectives have not been achieved. Low morale, frustration, and stress as major influences on the police may create serious difficulties in building positive relationships with others.

People bring personal histories of previous encounters with the same individuals or persons who are perceived as being of the same "type" to encounters as well. Typing people and situations is inevitable; it is simply not possible for the police or anyone else to treat every person and every situation as completely unique. But focusing on human relations emphasizes the importance of police officers knowing as many other citizens as possible individually and personally—and vice versa. When typing is involved, the nature of the categories employed is crucial. Those that reflect racist or sexist stereotypes, for example, are a major barrier to positive human relations.

And, people bring their bodies to encounters, typically clothed in a way which provides others with some cues about the identities and roles being claimed and an appropriate definition of the situation, together with whatever tools or equipment they may carry on their persons. Uniforms are a common example and they sometimes present difficulties in human interactions as we shall see shortly.

Focal Concerns in Police Encounters with Other Citizens

The focal concerns of participants are the second general feature of encounters. Here we shall consider three with special significance for police human relations: saving face, effective communications, and the distribution of power and authority among participants.

Perhaps the most general and most important concern in encounters is with protecting or saving "face."[18] Face may be defined as the reputation of an actor as a person in good social standing—as a person with honor, dignity, and moral integrity, worthy of the respect of others. The face of each participant is always at stake during an interaction. Usually, the concern for protecting face remains in the background, but its significance is immediately clear when one of the interactants interprets another's actions as face-threatening. Any physical gesture or verbalization that impugns one's honor, diminishes one's dignity, or attacks one's integrity does damage to one's social face. When such insults or embarrassments occur during the course of an interaction, the usual response is defensiveness and/or hostility. The focus of the encounter immediately shifts either to restoring the lost face or to a "face contest" in which escalating insults are exchanged. The former, if successful, permits a return to other matters that were being considered before the offense was committed; the latter may lead to physical violence. If a threat to face emerges during a routine interaction, it is vital to alleviate it as quickly as possible. Apologies are seldom easy, especially for the person with the greater authority (or power) in a particular encounter (the usual circumstance in which police officers find themselves), but they are the simplest and surest way of accomplishing this goal. Protecting one's own face and showing appropriate respect for another's are powerful norms in human encounters. As we shall see shortly, several aspects of the police role make abiding by these norms difficult.

Using appropriate social manners is one of the more important means of protecting one's own face while demonstrating proper respect for others in any human relationship, including those between police officers and other citizens. Doing so signals one's own respectability and readiness to conform to the rules of polite social discourse. At the same time, the other is acknowledged as a person of honor and dignity, likewise worthy of respect.[19] Forgetting basic social manners is easy in the press and stress of routine duties and personal problems, but applying them has a remarkable salutary affect on first and lasting impressions formed during an encounter.[20]

Another focal concern is effective communication.[21] Symbolic communication is inherently difficult. Words have multiple meanings that change from one social context to another. As a result, the potential for misunderstanding is enormous. Especially when some "business" is being transacted during an encounter, careful attention to what one says (as well as how one says it) is vital. Those employed in particular professions communicate with colleagues through a shorthand of technical codes and specialized vocabulary. Because their use comes so naturally, it is easy to forget that few outside the profession understand them. A prerequisite of clear and effective communication is tailoring the message to the audience. In communicating with the public, for example, police jargon and codes can cause confusion, apprehension, and misunderstanding.

Keeping people informed regularly about matters that are of interest to them is another feature of good communication practices. Here, perhaps, victim relations are the clearest example. In recent years, much has been said (and in some cases done) about improving communications with victims, one of the principle types of criminal justice clients. In some jurisdictions, for instance, victims have been given a voice in sentencing and parole hearings. A few police departments and prosecutors' offices have made a point of keeping victims better apprised of the progress of investigations.[22] The human relations implications of informative contact (or lack thereof) with crime victims, not just for the police but for prosecutors and other criminal justice practitioners are substantial.

Good listening is also important in effective interpersonal communication. This involves a number of aspects.[23] Both the speaker and the message must be taken seriously (deliberately suspending disbelief), at least at the beginning of the interaction. For police officers, whose job often entails being suspicious of the claims of other citizens, this may take a special effort. Various aspects of nonverbal communication (posture, gestures, etc.) are at least as important as what people say to each other. Good eye contact should be established initially and reestablished periodically throughout the exchange. Paying close attention to messages being sent, repeating the message in one's own words for confirmation, and asking clarifying questions are also important. Avoiding a superior air and a "know-it-all" attitude is also crucial to being a good listener.

Employing good verbal and nonverbal interpersonal communication practices creates a positive impression with the public and maximizes the likelihood of effective police response to requests for service from other citizens.

The last focal concern to be considered is the distribution of power and authority among the participants in an encounter. The power of an actor is his/her ability to coerce (through physical force, if necessary) another to obey. That is, some actors, by virtue of their position or role, are permitted (sometimes legally or morally obliged) to exercise power over others. Usurped or illegitimate power is force or the threat of force used by someone who is not authorized to coerce others to comply with their wishes. Participants in an encounter may be of equal power but unequal authority, equal authority but unequal power, or equal in both power and authority. One of the significant sources of trouble in police human relations is disagreement between officers and other citizens over whether an officer's compliance demands are a legitimate or illegitimate use of power.[24] In general, as we noted above, the fact that a police officer has, at least implicitly, the greater authority in virtually all of the interactions in which he or she is involved creates some special human relations problems.

Special Characteristics of Police Interaction with Other Citizens

The police officer's role may be defined in general terms as consisting of two elements: law enforcement and order maintenance. Both involve the exercise of coercive authority[25] and the line between the two is often blurred. At the very least, because there is almost always some ordinance or statute that could be cited, it is not unusual for an encounter that begins as an order maintenance activity to culminate with an arrest. In fact, as we noted in Chapter Two, discretion concerning when and when not to formally invoke the law is a primary component of the police officer's role. However ambiguous the distinction between the two police functions may be, both present significant human relations problems. Almost always, whatever the officer decides to do, someone is displeased.

Consider the uniformed officer. Wherever the officer goes and whomever he or she encounters, the uniform, complete with badge and gun, nightstick and handcuffs, announces to others this person's official role as an officer of the law. Included in this announcement is the message that the officer has authority and that he or she can, if necessary, use force—even deadly force—in gaining compliance with his or her instructions. While these aspects of the officer's role and equipment do not automatically resolve either the power or authority issue in an encounter (if they did, no officer would ever be resisted or assaulted), they do confer significant advantage in controlling most people and situations.[26] It would be absurd to suggest that things should be otherwise.

Along with this necessary and appropriate advantage accorded the police, however, inevitably comes a number of serious human relations problems. First,

Police Respond to Special Populations

Critical Issue

Handling the Mentally Ill, Public Inebriate, and the Homeless

By Peter E. Finn and
Monique Sullivan

- *Two police officers are dispatched to a housing project to handle a disturbance call. The officers find a terrified man hurling rocks at neighbors he says are trying to kill him with ray guns. A check by the officers fails to find any nearby family members or close friends.*
- *A deputy sheriff cruising a suburban shopping mall is stopped by a store manager and asked to get rid of two public inebriates sitting next to a dumpster behind the store. The merchant says the two have been accosting passers-by for "spare change."*
- *A bus terminal manager calls the police to have several homeless people evicted from the waiting area where they have piled up their belongings on the seats.*

The public repeatedly calls on law enforcement officers for assistance with people who are mentally ill, drunk in public, and homeless. They do so because peace officers are unique in providing free, around-the-clock service, mobility, a legal obligation to respond, and legal authority to detain.

In recent years, these requests have increased. Laws making it more difficult to commit the mentally ill have left many disturbed people on the streets, while the deinstitutionalization policies of the 1960s and 1970s have led to the release of thousands of mentally ill individuals from mental hospitals.

Jail crowding and the decriminalization of public intoxication have left more inebriates in public view. Various changes in employment patterns and public assistance programs and decreased availability of low-income housing have increased the number of homeless. At the same time, the number of facilities to assist these groups has either declined or not kept pace with the increasing need.

To help lessen the burden on police officers and deputy sheriffs who must handle special populations, some jurisdictions have created formal networks between law enforcement and social service agencies. . . .

Challenge to Law Enforcement

The mentally ill. Handling the mentally ill is perhaps the single most difficult type of call for law enforcement officers.[1] Today, these encounters are becoming more frequent. In one urban police department, 8 percent of more than 1,000 police-citizen encounters involved dealing with mentally ill persons, according to a study funded by the National Institute of Justice and the National Institute of Mental Health.[2]

In most of these situations—nearly 72 percent—police used informal dispositions, such as calming the person down or taking the person home. Less than 12 percent of the mentally ill were hospitalized. Nearly 17 percent were arrested.

Regardless of disposition, police officers usually found themselves saddled with sole responsibility for suspected mentally ill persons whose public behavior warranted some form of social intervention.

The public inebriate. Police officers also have to cope largely on their own with people found drunk in public. A recent National Institute of Justice study[3] found that limited bed space and

Continued

1. Hanewicz, W. B. 1982. "Improving the Linkages Between Community Mental Health and the Police." *Journal of Police Science and Administration* 10: 218–223.
2. Teplin, L. A. 1986. *Keeping the Peace: The Parameters of Police Discretion in Relation to the Mentally Disordered.* Washington, D.C.: National Institute of Justice.
3. Finn, P. 1985. "The Health Care System's Response to the Decriminalization of Public Drunkenness." *Journal of Alcohol Studies* 46: 7–23.

selective admission practices at detoxi-fication and other alcoholism facilities have curtailed the ability of the police to transport public inebriates to health care facilities.

Jail crowding and the perception that the stationhouse lockup is an inappropriate place to take the public drunk increasingly limit other police alternatives.

The homeless. Police are often called on to remove the homeless from streets and parks. The homeless have a dampening effect on business, and they invite crime by creating an appearance of community neglect. The homeless are often a danger to themselves, particularly in subfreezing weather. Law enforce-ment officers dealing with the homeless on the street have few options: Not only is shelter space limited, but most shelters refuse to admit the large percentage of homeless who are also mentally ill or alcoholic.

Networks with Social Service Agencies

One way of expanding the options for handling these populations is to share re-sponsibility for them with the social ser-vice system. Networks between law enforcement agencies and human ser-vices agencies can yield substantial ben-efits not only for the agencies involved, but for individuals who need help. . . .

U.S. Department of Justice, National Institute of Justice Reports, May/June 1988.

---

while citizens generally concede, in the abstract, that there are others who have more power and authority, they dislike being reminded of the fact in concrete situations. When they become aware of an officer's presence, most people go ''on guard,'' taking special care to comport themselves appropriately. Whether or not the officer intends it, his or her uniformed presence is easily interpreted by other citizens as a compliance demand. To encounter a uniformed officer, then, is to be placed, at least implicitly, in a subordinate position. Demands made by superiors of free citizens in a free society invite resistance.

Second, when citizens enter into an encounter with another who is more powerful and carries more authority like the police, the less powerful are likely to be anxious and tense. Of course, police officers are aware, and sometimes try to take advantage of, the vulnerability of citizens; citizens often try to hide their nervousness from the officers. But the anxiety, tension, defensiveness and sometimes near panic of citizens, whether well concealed or not, can easily lead to serious interactional problems. It is difficult to view the current circumstance in a larger and more balanced perspective. Attention tends to focus on the im-mediate situation and to become more rigid. Responses tend to be more exag-gerated and dramatic. What happens during the encounter is seen as more important or consequential than it may in fact be.

Third, as a result of power differentials just discussed and other factors as well, such as cultural differences, effective communication is difficult to achieve. An interesting illustration of this is provided by Vrij's (1993) study of interaction between Amsterdam police and Surinamer citizens. In this case, Vrij reports that cultural differences in nonverbal gestures (e.g., gaze aversion, smiling) as well as norms concerning answering questions (Surinamer cultural norms encourage indirect answers to potentially troublesome questions) were more important than skin color in creating difficult human relations. He also found that black skin color was an advantage in some circumstances, namely those where the demeanor and deportment of the Surinamer otherwise complied with ''white'' Dutch middle-class cultural norms (e.g., cleanliness, neat dress, etc.).[27] Whether the same results would be found in the U.S. is an empirical question, but it would not be surprising.

Fourth, persons who are used to being in authority, such as police officers, are likely to expect—and in some cases demand—that others whom they encounter accept and respect their superiority on both legal and moral grounds. Officers are likely to take challenges to their authority as serious breaches of citizens' legal and moral obligations, and as threats to their control of the situation. An escalating spiral of subordination demands and resistance may ensue, with increasingly severe face damage and possible physical injury resulting.

Fifth, because officers often see themselves as loyal members of a tightly knit fraternity that maintains a ''thin blue line'' between social order and chaos, challenges to a particular officer's authority may be seen as a threat to other members of the fraternity and to the very foundations of society. As a result, officers may feel compelled to respond more quickly and with greater force than may be required by the situation to preserve not only their own individual authority, but that of the whole blue fraternity.

Things can get especially dicey if the encounter occurs in front of other officers or citizens. Both officers and other citizens may play their roles as much to the audience as to those directly involved in the interaction. Furthermore, an audience tends to specify each participant's concerns about saving face vis-à-vis each other, and the audience as well. A further complicating factor is that officers may quickly find themselves substantially outnumbered, particularly in ethnic minority neighborhoods where the police are seen as agents of a repressive political establishment. Such circumstances increase the likelihood of disastrous human relations consequences and may produce serious public relations problems as well.

Informal reprimands and arrest are perhaps the most frequent overt expressions of the police officer's authority. Whenever possible, informal reprimands and official arrests should be made outside the purview of others. Doing so is one way of overtly demonstrating the officer's concern for saving as much of the citizen's face as possible and indicating her or his sensitivity to the feelings of others as human beings. While it is tempting to believe that the extra humiliation which comes with subordination in front of others is a more effective deterrent, it seems more likely to increase resistance and produce deeper resentment of the police and the system than contribute to the reformation of a person's behavior.

Arrest is, of course, sometimes required in the interests of public safety and security. A ''good pinch'' is also often personally satisfying to the arresting officer. But what Seabrook (1987) says of the British police officer is probably true of the American officer as well.

. . . few policemen harbor any personal hostility towards persons they arrest or otherwise deal with as offenders simply because the persons are in breach of the law. They are always ready to take up a hostile stance, simply because they are realistic enough to know that nobody actually likes being policed by being arrested or reported for offences or being told off or being caught in any act of wrongdoing.[28]

Because arrest involves taking people into legal and physical custody against their will, it is extremely face denigrating. Furthermore, once a decision to arrest has been announced, the encounter shifts to a new level of intensity for all participants. Neither the officer nor the other party involved is free to withdraw from the encounter without suffering serious consequences.[29] Nevertheless, even people under arrest and in custody are likely to feel they are still citizens and humans (which, of course, they are) and deserve to be treated as such (which, of course, they do). When an arrest or reprimand is accompanied by personal insults, racial epithets, or excessive force, especially in the presence of others, unnecessary and possibly dangerous complications may arise.

The use of physical—sometimes deadly—force (physical abductions and shootings) starkly reveals the coercive nature of the power and authority inherent in the police role.[30] For that reason, among others, such actions are potentially the most controversial actions an officer takes. Strict guidelines governing weapons discharge by officers have been established in most departments and almost all departments have mandatory review procedures following a shooting incident.[31] The Supreme Court has permitted civil damage suits against the police and forbidden shooting at suspected property felons.[32] In fact, officers rarely wrestle with suspects or fire their weapons, and are apparently doing so less often now than in the past.[33] When they do, however, the most serious human relations problems may be created: physical injury, and possibly deprivation of life. Severe public relations problems may emerge as well, as we shall see in the next chapter.

Other aspects of the police officer's role are also problematic for human relations. Even though most police activity is a result of citizens' requests for services, the persons whom the officer encounters in responding to these requests are often not the same as those who initially requested the services. This would be the case, for example, in investigations of noisy parties or domestic disputes that have aroused the concern of neighbors. Those who are the object of the investigation often regard the officer as an unwelcome intruder—a circumstance bound to create tensions. Then too, many of these encounters involve officers and other citizens who are strangers to each other and take place in settings about which the officer has little knowledge and over which he or she has little control. None of the participants know what to expect from the others with whom they are involved. Danger is, therefore, a recurrent theme in police work—both for the police and for other citizens. As might be expected, these circumstances often put all participants "on edge," lending an extra emotional charge to the encounter.

Third Shift Presents Different Challenge

Critical Issue

By Paul Swiech

Staff Writer

GALESBURG—"I think most people have respect for police. I had a college professor who said most people have this underlying fear of police, like of their father or teacher. Somebody that makes 'em check their Ps and Qs even if they're doing nothing wrong. . . . The way I like to get through that is to wave at 'em and show 'em a friendly face. Any way you look at it, the majority of people are law abiding and decent citizens. That's the people we are trying to work for."

The police officer was patrolling Henderson Street and talking about what he does. It was early morning on a Saturday and the car he was driving was one of about six on the streets of Galesburg to protect the people from any third shift problems. He and the emergency police officer beside him have been busier than usual tonight.

One of the younger members of the police department, the officer described how to handle matters "by the book." Yet he said "there is no substitute for experience," an important quality for an officer is "the gift of gab" and spoke highly of the street smarts of the older officers.

HE SPOKE FORMALLY, using words such as "allegedly," "thereof," "advised," and "perimeter," yet fell easily into informal street talk when questioning four youths.

He appeared to be several things at the same time, probably because like any good police officer he is part teacher, part big brother, part sociologist. All showed themselves this night. . . . Working the third shift presents slightly different challenges from those of other shifts, he said.

A major difference is the number of calls related to intoxicated persons, he said. During the third shift, the numbers of persons arrested for driving under the influence of alcohol and the numbers of calls officers receive in which one or more of the persons is drunk drastically increase, the officer said. Most of these are the so-called domestic disputes—arguments between family members. Domestic disputes spurred by drunkenness increase about 75 percent during third shift, he estimated. . . .

Because of the increased number of people who are intoxicated, police officers are physically threatened more during the third shift, the officer said. He said in 2½ years he has been threatened several times—including once by a person with a hammer, and has been in several scuffles with persons resisting arrest in which he has caught several elbows and his shirt has been ripped. But he said he has not yet been punched or threatened with a gun. He said he has yet to pull his gun completely out of the holster.

When a person begins wrestling with a police officer or officers who are arresting him, the officers can only use "force necessary to effect that arrest," and generally force the person to the ground and handcuff him, the officer said. He said scuffles between persons arrested and police officers seldom go beyond this.

"You're not intoxicated, you're alert; they are usually intoxicated, so that gives you a clear-cut advantage right there," the officer said. . . .

The Register Mail, *Galesburg, Illinois.*

Part of the officer's role is to be on the lookout for possible crimes in progress and/or suspects in previous offenses. Especially during crime investigations, the officer seeks information which, if discovered, threatens the face and freedom of others. During such encounters, officers are routinely skeptical of other citizens' accounts of their activities. Police expect to be lied to in some circumstances; frequent experiences of this nature contribute to the cynicism of some officers. All participants in such encounters are gleaning all the information they can about how much each of the others knows, what their intentions are, and so on. Thus, the mutual distrust which suspicion engenders may contribute to difficulty in police encounters with other citizens.

Many of the dilemmas and tensions we have discussed are to some extent inherent in the role of the police in a democratic society and will, therefore, never be entirely resolved. But improving human relations practices can lessen their negative impact on police community relations.

Human Relations Programs and Policy

Training in human relations has been a part of some police academy and in-service training curricula since the racial unrest of the 1960s. In some states it is required by law, but the amount of time actually spent in human relations training is very short in most cases.[34] The theory underlying one version of these programs (variously referred to as "T groups," "sensitivity training," and "encounter groups") is well summarized by Cooper and Mangham (1971):

> The training or T-group is an approach to human relations training which, broadly speaking, provides participants with an opportunity to learn more about themselves and their impact on others and, in particular, to learn how to function more effectively in face-to-face situations. It attempts to facilitate this learning by bringing together a small group of people for the express purpose of studying their own behavior as it occurs when they interact within a small group.[35]

Most of the earlier training programs of this sort focused on problems of racism and stereotyping in police-minority encounters. The idea was that destructive stereotyping could best be broken through—and mutual understanding could best be developed in—intimate, face-to-face meetings where people could get to know each other, not just as representatives of categories or players of particular roles, but also as individuals, with human feelings and thoughts.

The typical encounter group session included role-playing exercises which involved participants "taking the role of the other"—that is, police officers pretended to be minority citizens and minority citizens pretended to be police officers. Scenes would be set by the instructors and participants would play out the interaction, making up the script as they went along. Discussions of the events that occurred and the emotions aroused would then take place. Research evaluating these efforts indicates some short-term positive change in the participants' attitudes, but long-term benefits were more difficult to substantiate.[36]

More recent programs, whether in the encounter group or the more traditional classroom format, have focused on human relations involving youth, women, and the elderly, in addition to racial and ethnic minorities. Films, lectures, discussion sessions, and analysis of written case studies are frequently employed in these courses and training sessions. The advent of relatively inexpensive videotaping equipment presents an additional and potentially useful tool for such training efforts. Actually seeing oneself in action through the cold, hard eye of the camera may have more lasting effects than simply hearing others' impressions of how one behaved. At the very least, videotaping may be a valuable adjunct to role-playing/discussion exercises.

It is worth noting that many previous reforms of the strategy and tactics of policing have substantially decreased both the frequency and the intimacy of routine police encounters with other citizens. The replacement of foot with motorized patrol is perhaps the most dramatic example. As Brown suggests: "Modern patrolmen do not so much involve themselves with people as they observe them from a distance."[37] If, as we believe, frequent face-to-face interaction is a necessary prerequisite of building community cooperation and support, the motorized patrol strategy may actually diminish the likelihood of positive police community relations. For example, a "20/20" television show (January 26, 1990) dealt with traffic stops made by the police in a Florida county in an attempt to control drug traffic. These stops are based on profiles of drug runners and many argue they discriminate against minority group members. While a sizable proportion of these stops, made in many instances for minor traffic violations, result in confiscation of drugs or cash, many do not and those innocent citizens who are stopped resent the intrusion into their privacy without probable cause. Such actions almost certainly exacerbate the sense of exploitation and victimization of the ethnic groups who are the targets of such profile policing. Likewise, the strong criticism of these police tactics mounted by civil rights and civil libertarian groups enhances the sense of alienation and isolation among the police, intensifying their immersion in and reliance on the police subculture.

The community policing initiative recognizes and attempts to alleviate some of the human relations problems that have been identified. Many of the particular programs promoted under this philosophical umbrella address the issue of police-citizen estrangement, attempting to humanize law enforcement and to enter into partnerships with community citizens to deal with crime and related problems. In some cities, for example, mini-police stations have been established in selected neighborhoods in order to make individual police officers more familiar and police services more accessible. In commercial districts, patrol officers are getting out of their patrol cars and away from the emergency response mode of policing. Instead, they are walking a beat, attempting to establish ongoing informal relationships with business owners and employees. Such efforts reflect a growing appreciation among police officials for the benefits of person-to-person contacts in police community relations.

Whether they are cast in the community policing frame or in some other language, a clearly articulated departmental policy is crucial to the successful implementation of good human relations practices. The higher-ranking officers must, of course, both practice and preach the message. But to achieve maximum benefit, the policy must be reflected in the conduct of lower-ranking personnel. It is they, after all, who have the vast majority of person-to-person contacts with other citizens and it is in such contacts that the real effects of good (or bad) human relations practices are felt. Since human relations are a two-way street, the practices of other citizens with whom the police interact are equally important.[38]

Summary

Human relations are one of the key components in police community relations. Improving the quality of human relations depends on paying attention to what happens during the many daily person-to-person encounters between police officers and other citizens. Of particular relevance are those aspects of interaction that reflect the shared citizenship and common humanity of the participants. Interactions that involve faulty human relations practices can influence disproportionately the substance and tone of community relations.

What transpires during an encounter between police officers and other citizens is influenced by what the participants bring to the encounter and the focal concerns of participants during the encounter. The cultures, subcultures, genders, personalities, previous interactions, and clothed bodies of participants affect the quality of human relations that emerge during the encounter. So does the manner in which the participants deal with their focal concerns: saving face, communicating effectively, and distributing power and authority.

Many of the human relations problems that are more or less unique to police encounters with other citizens are related to the officer's visible authority and the dilemmas posed by the exercise of coercive force in a free, open, and democratic society. Aspects of the police subculture sometimes exacerbate human relations problems.

Police officers often find themselves dealing with people who are different from themselves in culture, gender, race, age, and life-style. Human relations training programs are intended to increase participants' sensitivity to these human differences. And there is much to be gained from the effort: "For if it is what people do rather than what people are that causes problems, then some misery is optional and can indeed be prevented."[39]

Human relations policy leadership must come from the top, but it is the practices of both police officers on the front line and the other citizens with whom they interact that determines the quality of human relations in the community. Good human relations practices must be rewarded in clearly recognizable ways if policies are to succeed and practices are to be implemented.

Discussion Questions

1. What are police human relations? What do civil and human rights have to do with them?
2. Describe in detail an encounter in which you recently participated. What roles were you and others playing? What part did social manners play in the encounter? What were their significance in the context of human relations?
3. When we meet someone we don't know personally, what produces positive impressions of the person? What produces negative impressions?
4. Why are police relations with youth and members of racial and ethnic minorities often negative? Do aspects of the police subculture have anything to do with these relationships?

5. What impact do you think the increasing numbers of minority and women police officers will have on the police subculture?
6. What is it about the police role in American society that creates human relations dilemmas?
7. How might police human relations practices be improved?

Endnotes

1. For an interesting discussion of human rights in the international context, see J. Alderson. 1984. *Human Rights and the Police.* Strassbourg: Council of Europe, Directorate of Human Rights. Also see R. Reiner. ed. 1985. *Police, the Constitution, and the Community.* Abingdon: Professional Books; Donald O. Schultz. 1984. *The Police as Defendant.* Springfield, IL: Charles C Thomas; Charles E. Friend. 1979. *Police Rights: Civil Remedies for Law Enforcement Officers.* Charlottesville: The Michie Co.; and Lee W. Potts. 1983. *Responsible Police Administration: Issues and Approaches.* Tuscaloosa: University of Alabama Press.
2. For a discussion of the various aspects of encounters, see Erving Goffman. 1961. *Encounters.* New York: Bobbs-Merrill and Erving Goffman. 1959. *Presentation of Self in Everyday Life.* Garden City: Doubleday and Co.
3. Richard E. Sykes and Edward E. Brent. 1983. *Policing: A Social Behaviorist Perspective.* New Brunswick, NJ: Rutgers University Press.
4. Troy Duster. 1987. "Crime, Youth Unemployment and the Black Urban Underclass." *Crime and Delinquency* 33(April): 300–316; Peggy Sullivan, Roger Dunham, and Geoffery Alpert. 1987. "Attitude Structures of Different Ethnic and Age Groups Concerning the Police and Police Procedures." *Journal of Criminal Law and Criminology* 78: 177–196.
5. See Lou Harris. 1987. *Inside America.* New York: Vintage Books: 185; Mark Moore and Robert C. Trojanowicz. 1988. "Policing and the Fear of Crime." *Perspectives on Policing.* 3. National Institute of Justice and Harvard University(June); and Sullivan et al. "Attitude Structures."
6. Sullivan et al. "Attitude Structures."; John L. Cooper. 1980. *The Police and the Ghetto.* Port Washington, NY: Kennikat Press; Louis Harris. 1981. 1982. *The Harris Survey.*(February 26 and May 24 respectively); Paul Kim. 1994. "Specialized Unit Helps Overcome Cultural Barriers." *The Police Chief* 61(2): 50–51.
7. Larry E. Moss. 1977. *Black Political Ascendancy in Urban Centers and Black Control of the Local Police Function: An Exploratory Analysis.* San Francisco: R & E Research Associates. For an interesting exchange reflecting different cultural perspectives on rap music, see Dennis R. Martin. 1993. "The Music of Murder." *ACJS Today* 12(3); and Mark S. Hamm and Jeff Ferrell. 1994. "Rap, Cops, And Crime." *ACJS Today* 13(1).
8. N. G. Fielding. 1987. *Joining Forces: Police Training, Socialization and Occupational Competence.* London: Tavistock; K. Harris. 1973. *The Police Academy: An Inside View.* New York: Wiley.
9. Jerome H. Skolnick. 1966. *Justice Without Trial.* New York: John Wiley and Sons.
10. Orlando Wilson. 1983. *On This We Stand.* Chicago: Chicago Police Department; Robert Wasserman and Mark H. Moore. 1988. "Values in Policing." *Perspectives on Policing.* 8(November); Peter K. Manning. 1979. *Police Work.* Cambridge: MIT Press; William Westley. 1970. *Violence and the Police.* Cambridge: MIT Press; Michael K. Brown. 1988. *Working the Street.* New York: Russell Sage Foundation: 76–87 and chapter 6; Douglas S. Drummond. 1976. *Police Subculture.* Beverly Hills: Sage; Arthur Neiderhoffer and Abraham S. Blumberg. 1973. *The Ambivalent Force: Perspectives on the Police.* San Francisco: Rinehart Press: especially Part 6; A. Conser. 1980. "A Literary Review of the Police Subculture: Its Characteristics, Impact and Policy Implications." *Police Studies* 2(4): 46–54; and Elizabeth Reuss-Ianni. 1983. *The Two Cultures of Policing: Street Cops and Management Cops.* New Brunswick, NJ: Transaction Books.

11. Amy Eppler. 1986. "Battered Women and the Equal Protection Clause: Will the Constitution Help When the Police Won't?". *Yale Law Journal* 95: 793; Daniel G. Saunders and Patricia B. Size. 1986. "Attitudes About Woman Abuse Among Police Officers, Victims, and Victim Advocates." *Journal of Interpersonal Violence* 1(1): 25–42; D. M. Moore. ed. 1979. *Battered Women.* Beverly Hills: Sage; D. V. Stephens. 1977. "Domestic Assault: The Police Response" in M. Roy, ed. *Battered Women: A Psychological Study of Domestic Violence.* New York: Van Nostrand-Reinhold: 164–172.

12. Harris. *Inside America.*, Moore and Trojanowicz. "Policing."

13. Skolnick. *Justice Without Trial.*

14. Robert W. Bolch. 1972. "The Police Personality: Fact or Fiction?". *Journal of Criminology, Criminal Law, and Police Science* (March): 106–119; Gordon Pitter. 1994. "Police Cynicism in the 1990s." *The Police Chief.* 61(5): 57–59.

15. William H. Kroes. 1988. *Broken Cops: The Other Side of Policing.* Springfield, IL: Charles C Thomas; Daphne Dodson-Chaneske. 1988. "Mental Health Consultation to a Police Department." *Journal of Human Behavior and Learning* 5(1): 35–38.

16. See Joel Garner and Elizabeth Clemmer. 1986. "Danger to Police in Domestic Disturbances—A New Look." *Research in Brief.* National Institute of Justice. Washington, D.C.: U.S. Government Printing Office for a summary of recent data on circumstances associated with harm to police.

17. Westley. *Violence and the Police.* John Van Maanen. 1972. "Pledging the Police" and Jesse Rubin. 1972. "Police Identity and Police Role" both in Robert Steadman, ed. *The Police and the Community.* Baltimore: The Johns Hopkins University Press; Manning, *Police Work.*

18. For an insightful analysis of "face work" see Erving Goffman. 1967. *Interaction Ritual.* Garden City, NY: Doubleday and Co.: 5–45.

19. Ibid.

20. Robert C. Wadman and Stephen M. Ziman. 1993. "Courtesy and Police Authority." *FBI Law Enforcement Bulletin* 62(2): 23–26.

21. George I. Thompson. 1983. *Verbal Judo: Words for Street Survival.* Springfield, IL: Charles C Thomas.

22. For a review of the criminal justice system's relationships with victims, see Andrew Karmen. 1990. *Crime Victims.* 2ed. Pacific Grove, CA: Brooks/Cole Publishing Co.

23. Thompson. *Verbal Judo.*

24. See James R. Hudson. 1970. "Police-Citizen Encounters that Lead to Citizen Complaints." *Social Problems* 18(2): 179–193.

25. Westley. *Violence and the Police.*; Terry R. Armstrong and Kenneth M. Cinnamon. eds. 1976. *Power and Authority in Law Enforcement.* Springfield, IL: Charles C Thomas; Roberg and Kuykendall. *Police and Society.* especially 199–237.

26. Peter Southgate. 1986. *Police-Public Encounters.* London: HMSO Books; Mary Glenn Wiley and Terry L. Hudik. 1980. "Police Citizen Encounters: A Field Test of Exchange Theory" and Richard E. Sykes and John P. Clark. 1980. "Deference Exchange in Police Civilian Encounters" both in Richard J. Lundman. *Police Behavior: A Sociological Perspective.* New York: Oxford University Press.

27. Aldert Vrij. 1993. "An Impression Formation Framework on Police Prejudice: An Overview of Experiments on Police Bias in Police-Citizen Interaction." *Police Studies* 16: 28–32. See also Aldert Vrij and Frans Willem Winkel. 1992. "Cross-cultural Police-Citizen Interactions: The Influence of Race, Beliefs, and Nonverbal Communication on Impression Formation." *Journal of Applied Social Psychology* 22: 1546–59.

28. Dolfe Seabrook. 1987. *Coppers: An Inside View of the British Police.* London: HARRAP Ltd.: 31.

29. Hudson. "Police-Citizen Encounters."

30. Donald O. Schultz and J. Gregory Service. 1981. *The Police Use of Force.* Springfield, IL: Charles C Thomas; Bill Clede. 1987. *Police Non-lethal Force Manual.* Harrisburg, PA: Stackpole Books.

31. Ibid. appendix.
32. Ibid.; Potts. *Responsible Police Administration.*: ch. 3.
33. Brown. *Working the Street.*
34. For an excellent review of the early history of the human relations training movement in a variety of different contexts, see Kurt W. Back. 1972. *Beyond Words: The Story of Sensitivity Training and the Encounter Movement.* New York: Sage; for applications in the police context, see Priss Dufford. 1986. *Police Personal Behavior and Human Relations.* Springfield, IL: Charles C Thomas; D. K. Das. 1985. ''A Review of Progress Toward State Mandated Human Relations Training.'' *The Police Journal* 58(2): 147–162; Donald Bimstein. 1975. ''Sensitivity Training and the Police'' in Michael E. O'Neill and Kair Martensen, eds. *Criminal Justice Group Training.* La Jolla, CA: University Associates, Inc.; Peter Southgate. ed. 1988. *New Directions in Police Training.* London: HMSO Books; Rod Morgan and David J. Smith. eds. 1989. *Coming to Terms with Policing.* London: Routledge; and St. George. '' 'Sensitivity' Training.''
35. C. L. Cooper and I. L. Mangham. eds. 1971. *T Groups: A Survey of Research.* New York: John Wiley and Sons; St. George. '' 'Sensitivity' Training.''; Ray Bull. 1986. ''An Evaluation of Police Recruit Training in Human Awareness'' in John C. Yuille, ed. *Police Selection and Training: The Role of Psychology.* Dordrecht, The Netherlands.
36. Joyce St. George. 1991. ''Sensitivity Training Needs Rethinking.'' *Law Enforcement News.* Nov. 30. pp. 8–9.
37. Brown. *Working the Street.*
38. Edwin Meese III. 1993. ''Community Policing and the Police Officer.'' U.S. Department of Justice. *Perspectives on Policing* (January) No. 15. See also National Institute of Justice; *Research in Brief.* August 1992. ''Community Policing in Seattle; A Model Partnership Between Citizens and Police.'' U.S. Department of Justice.
39. Alan Coffey, Edward Eldefonso, and Walter Hartinger. 1971. *Human Relations: Law Enforcement in a Changing Community.* Englewood Cliffs: Prentice-Hall.

Suggested Readings

Alpert, Geoffrey P. and Roger G. Dunham. 1988. *Policing Multi-Ethnic Neighborhoods: The Miami Study and Findings for Law Enforcement in the United States.* New York: Greenwood Press.

Bagley, David H. and James Garofalo. 1989. ''The Management of Violence By Police Patrol Officers.'' *Criminology* 27: 1–29.

Cohen, Howard S. and Michael Feldberg. 1991. *Power and Restraint: The Moral Dimensions of Police Work.* New York: Praeger.

Eppler, Amy. 1986. ''Battered Women and the Equal Protection Clause: Will the Constitution Help When the Police Won't?''. *Yale Law Journal* 95.

Goffman, Erving. 1959. *The Presentation of Self in Everyday Life.* Garden City: Doubleday and Company.

————. 1967. *Interaction Ritual.* Garden City: Doubleday and Company.

Ohlin, Lloyd E. and Frank J. Remington, eds. 1993. *Discretion in Criminal Justice; The Tension Between Individualization and Uniformity.* Albany: State University of New York Press.

Peak, Ken, Robert V. Bradshaw, and Ronald W. Glensor. 1992. ''Improving Citizen Perceptions of the Police: 'Back to the Basics' with a Community Policing Strategy.'' *Journal of Criminal Justice* 20: 25–40.

Reiss, Albert J., Jr. 1971. *The Police and the Public.* New Haven: Yale University Press.

Sykes, Richard E. and Edward E. Brent. 1980. ''The Regulation of Interaction By Police: A Systems View of Taking Charge.'' *Criminology* 18(2): 182–197.

Walker, Samuel. 1993. *Taming The System: The Control of Discretion in Criminal Justice.* New York: Oxford University Press.

Chapter 4

Police Public Relations

*I*n Chapter One, we indicated that police community relations consisted of two major elements: human relations and public relations. Having considered human relations in Chapter Three, we turn now to a discussion of public relations.

Organizations that sell products or provide services to the public typically want to establish relations as collective entities, that is, as organizations, with their public; police agencies are no exception. These relations typically involve communications of three closely related types. The first is concerned with establishing a linkage with the public—making the public aware of the agency's identity, the services available, and how to access those services—and sometimes to increase the demand for the available services (in the business world these are among the functions of advertising). A second kind of organizational communication is educational. Here, the activity is aimed at providing information or instruction that the public might use to help themselves or to solve their own problems. A third kind of communication is directed toward establishing and maintaining a good organizational image or reputation among the public. Of course, both the quality of the communications and the quality of the product or service actually delivered are crucial to establishing good organizational relations. And in an age dominated by the media as much as is ours, press relations are also vitally important. In any event, these activities and communications, sponsored and funded by the organization as an organization, are referred to as **public relations.**

To the extent that the uniform of the officer, the symbol on the squad car, and the response of the dispatcher or receptionist at police headquarters convey an impression, they are part of police public relations. Educational pamphlets prepared and distributed in the name of the department, public speaking engagements, news conferences, department sponsored youth programs, and a host of other activities also fall within the scope of police public relations. So, too, does controlling the damage arising from ''bad press'' concerning controversial or discrediting events involving the police. Although many of these activities also involve human relations, we will concentrate in this chapter on the nature of public relations. You should keep in mind, however, that in this area as well as others, the police are not an isolated, independent agency, but part of a large network of governmental and political bodies. Therefore, although police administrators may plan, develop, and implement public relations strategies, they should consult not only with their own personnel and citizen groups, but also with mayors, city managers, councilpersons, and commissioners with whom or for whom they work.

Problems in police public relations may be traced to a variety of sources and circumstances. We shall mention here only a few of the more common ones. Too little attention may be given by administrators and/or other departmental personnel to planning and implementing public relations efforts. Information about the public's view of the police and the quality of the services they provide may be incomplete or inaccurate. The public may desire other services or that existing services be delivered in a different way, for example. Ties between community political entities and the police may be perceived by the public as too close, resulting in suspicions of favoritism or unequal treatment. Police officers may be involved in activities that are illegal, corrupt, or brutal. Police unions may be the source of difficulties, too. The "blue flu" or strike actions, however justified they may be, are not often greeted by the public with sympathy or approval. They may also clash openly with departmental administrators, other public officials, or citizen groups. Then, too, bad human relations practices inevitably tarnish a department's public image. Finally, physical (especially mortal) injury to citizens is sometimes the source of serious public relations problems for the police. As with human relations, some public relations difficulties are inherent in the task of policing a free, democratic society.[1] But well-planned and executed public relations efforts can increase public support for police efforts and improve the quality of life in the community.

Public Relations—Policy and Practice

Public relations may be viewed as an activity consisting of two major elements—policy and practice.[2] **Policy** consists of decisions, statements, and plans made by management in an attempt to connect with, educate, and/or create a positive public opinion about the agency in question.[3] In most police agencies, public relations policy is made by the police chief in consultation with a public relations officer or unit and with other appropriate staff members, and political or governmental authorities who may be involved; sometimes these include public relations specialists or leaders of concerned citizen groups. **Practice** is the process of putting these policies into action. Public relations, then, consists of all the measures a police department initiates in order to inform and establish connections with its public and to encourage a favorable public opinion about the department. Policies not formulated when needed, problems not dealt with on a timely basis, and programs planned but not implemented, may well influence public opinion, but not always in a positive direction.

Officer Spends 20 Minutes Ticketing Woman in Labor

KANSAS CITY, Kan. (AP)—A woman in labor had to wait for 20 minutes while a police officer wrote a parking ticket on the car her husband had borrowed to take her to the hospital, the husband complained.

Jim Sanchez said the officer ignored his pleas to allow him to get his wife, Viola, to a hospital, where she gave birth to twins about two hours later. The babies were listed in good condition Monday.

"I ran out to tell him that my wife's labor pains were four minutes apart and that I needed to get her to the hospital," Sanchez said. "He called me an idiot and told me to shut up."

Police Chief Allan Meyers said Monday he was initiating an investigation.

The officer who wrote the ticket has not been identified. His name is not legible on the ticket.

Sanchez said he had borrowed a friend's car Friday afternoon, parked it just past his house and went in to get his wife.

When they left the house the officer was writing the ticket, explaining they could not park in that spot between 4 and 6 P.M., Sanchez said.

Sanchez said his wife stood in front of the house waiting while the officer filled out the ticket.

"I explained it to him three times," Sanchez said. "We have four kids and we know how pregnancies go."

Associated Press, 1988. Used with permission.

Figure 4.1 The relationship between policy and practice.

From Fundamentals of Public Relations, Second Edition *by Lawrence W. Nolte, copyright 1979 by Pergamon Press, Inc. Reprinted by permission.*

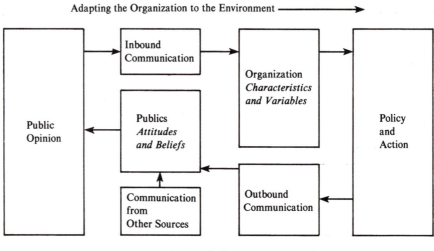

The diagram in Figure 4.1 indicates the relationship between policy and practice and provides guidelines for establishing a public relations program. We may begin with action which is publicized in the form of outbound communication.[4] These communications reach the various publics in the community (e.g., youth, the elderly, blacks). Members of these public groups form opinions that help determine the success or failure of the organization (in this case, police department) in attaining its goals. In order to succeed, organizational personnel must receive, analyze, and evaluate communications from the various public sectors. Once this is accomplished, public relations programs may be developed and put into action which is, in turn, made known to the public sectors by outbound communication (as well as communication from other sources). The cycle is then repeated over and over, since public relations is a continuous process.[5]

It should be clear from our discussion of the diagram, that good public relations policies alone are insufficient to create a favorable public image of the police or of any other organization. As Nolte points out: "what the organization really **does** is just as important as policy. It is imperative that an organization live up to what it says about itself."[6] In other words, public relations programs can only project a favorable public image if they accurately reflect practices which are, or can be, accepted by the publics concerned. For example, the police may spend a great deal of money publicizing the fact that officers are courteous, fair, and professional, but if police-citizen encounters do not reflect matching police behavior, sooner or later the public relations effort will fail. Honesty and coordination of policy and practice, then, appear to be indispensable to the public relations process.

> Effective public relations do not just happen. They require a lot of time and effort. Everyone in the organization should be concerned with public relations, but someone must be specifically responsible if anything is to be accomplished.[7]

Unfortunately, police departments have often tended to rely either upon a public relations officer or unit or upon each individual officer to promote public relations. In the former case, many individual officers (and police administrators) remain relatively unconcerned about public relations because these are thought to be the responsibility of a specially designated officer or unit. In the latter case, each individual officer may be told that she is responsible for public relations, but there may be no one appointed to supervise or evaluate the total public relations effort. In either case, it is easy (and tempting) for the police chief and his staff to assume that public relations (and community relations) are receiving sufficient attention. Provided no major misunderstandings arise in the community, the chief or his staff may assume that all is well. However, often all is not well in either of these two common types of public relations programs. Frequently, complaints from the community reflect the lack of unified, systematic public relations efforts. These complaints include police indifference, ignorance of problem areas, high-handedness, and unfairness in dealing with one or more of the public sectors (groups) residing in the community.[8] Not infrequently, these complaints exist even though police administrators express confidence that the public views them as concerned, intelligent, courteous, and fair. Since, in many police departments, there is no systematic effort to find out what the various public sectors actually think about police services, these two conflicting views can exist side-by-side until some crisis indicates to the police that all is not well. For example, we have heard police administrators claim that they have developed highly successful public relations in the areas of traffic control, or crime prevention, only to be told by other citizens that the police are extremely ineffective in traffic control or crime prevention. Similarly, police personnel may assert that they have a favorable image among minority group members, while members of the minority group in question may feel that the police know little or nothing about their problems or feelings and care even less. In addition, they may believe that the police are high-handed or unfair. However, since any complaints about particular officers would have to be taken to the police themselves, they may not communicate their beliefs directly to the police. Thus it may be some time before police administrators become aware of the problem.

When a police department fails to systematically collect and analyze public opinion, or to develop public relations programs based upon such collection and analysis, a great deal of unnecessary, potentially damaging misunderstanding can occur. Perhaps a specific example will help to illustrate this point. The chief of a small, midwestern police department was quite pleased to announce that he had improved his department's public image considerably by implementing a new traffic control program concerned with speeding. The new program required only one patrol car which was used both to time oncoming traffic and to pursue and stop violators. This program left most patrol officers free to pursue other activities and, in the opinion of the chief, was an important advance in efficiency over the more traditional two-car system. The program demonstrated what a progressive department, concerned with giving citizens maximum efficiency, could accomplish. Some members of the public, however, took exception to this view. A large number of citizens stopped for speeding indicated that they thought the new system was very unfair because, while the officer involved was writing citations for those drivers who had been clocked over the speed limit, many other cars which were obviously speeding passed without incident. Some of these drivers did not view themselves as guilty of violating the speed limit, but as victims of selective, unfair police practices.

As this example indicates, if the police want to be aware of citizen complaints, and if they want to do something to correct the situations that lead to these complaints, they must keep informed of the attitudes, interests, and perceived problems of these citizens. In other words, they need to analyze public opinion about themselves in systematic (not hit-and-miss) fashion.

Although there are many public relations professionals available today, most police departments use police officers to perform public relations functions. The number of officers specifically assigned to public relations functions fluctuates with concerns about budgetary cutbacks, maximum efficiency for tax dollars, and public relations crises. Although, as we have seen, public relations programs are often viewed as auxiliary services and are among the first services to be cut back during financial crises, their role is crucial to the overall functioning of any police department.

The use of police officers in public relations has both advantages and disadvantages. These officers have a great deal of information about police procedures and operations, and they understand very well the day-to-day operations of the police department. In addition, they have close contact with police officers at different levels, to whom they can turn for assistance in developing new programs. At the same time, however, there is a danger that police personnel who are designated as public relations officers will not be able to maintain their objectivity in assessing citizen complaints and will not be trusted by certain of their audiences simply because they are, after all, "cops." Thus, even when they communicate to the media or citizen groups honest and objective reports of departmental activities, these reports may be viewed as departmental propaganda or "whitewash." Nonetheless, in the foreseeable future, in the vast majority of police departments, public relations are likely to be the responsibility of police officers.

Politics may be an especially troublesome area for police public relations.[9] On the one hand, being a part of the local political structure provides legitimacy for the police and their activities and some measure of accountability to the public. A local police force completely independent of community influence and control would be a serious threat to basic democratic principles. On the other hand, when the police are tied too closely to particular political parties or factions within the community, unequal and discriminatory law enforcement and order maintenance activities may be the result. A police agency unable to demonstrate in policy and practice that it serves the whole community is a police agency with serious public relations problems.

The political structures within which the police are located as well as the way they are tied to them vary from one locality and police agency to another. Typically, county sheriffs are elected directly by the public while police chiefs are not. In this sense, sheriffs are more directly accountable to the public than are police chiefs, but their entanglement in political patronage pressures and party or factional politics is an almost inevitable consequence. Perhaps for this reason more than any other, sheriffs seem more prone to charges of political corruption than their municipal police counterparts.

In some cities, police chiefs are appointed directly by city managers or mayors, typically with the approval of city councils. In others, they are appointed by a board of police commissioners who may themselves be appointed by elected officials or elected directly by the public. These arrangements provide varying amounts of insulation from particular political forces within the community, but also render them somewhat less directly accountable to the public for their policies and procedures. Perhaps as a result, police departments seem more prone to charges of graft and nepotism.

How other departmental personnel are hired, promoted, and fired, can also influence the reputation of a department. Again, arrangements vary from one locality to another. In some cases, hiring, promoting, disciplining, and firing decisions are made solely by the department administrator; in others city government officials or boards of police commissioners make these decisions. In still others, civil service commissions have these responsibilities. Here, too, there are public relations implications attached to whatever the particular arrangements are in a particular community.

Perhaps the clearest indicator of the persistent tensions between local accountability and independence was the emergence of citizen review boards, another product of the civil rights movement of the 1960s.[10] Many citizen groups, especially minority groups, were dissatisfied with police services, critical of their treatment by the police, and distrustful of internal departmental review and disciplinary procedures. The purpose of citizen review boards was to make police less dependent on white-dominated political machines and more accountable to the citizens of local ethnic communities and neighborhoods. While they were not established in all major cities and they have fallen somewhat out of favor in recent years, they reflect the severe public relations (and often human relations) problems that can result when police agencies are not perceived as acting in the interests of the whole community.

In the end, as many observers have noted, the quality of police services tends to match the political health of the communities they serve. Skolnick summarizes this connection quite well: "As an institution dependent on rewards from the civic community, police can hardly be expected to be much better or worse than the political context in which they operate."[11]

Techniques and Strategies for Police Public Relations

The diagram presented earlier in this chapter may serve as a useful starting point for outlining a good police public relations program. The diagram indicates that a necessary step is the systematic collection of information concerning public attitudes, perceptions, complaints, needs, and desires (inbound communication). Such information may be collected on a day-to-day basis by patrol officers during their encounters with citizens, and by police administrative personnel in their contacts with leaders of civic organizations, other public service agencies, and political groups. Such information may also be collected at regular intervals by means of questionnaires distributed to a representative sample of the public served. This latter task may be assigned to trained departmental personnel who have knowledge of appropriate sampling and survey techniques or it may be farmed out. We know, for example, of several communities in which police officials have worked out arrangements with nearby universities to conduct, and/or to analyze the results of, public opinion polls. Police agencies wishing to be accredited and those participating in certified city programs are required to conduct such surveys.

The information collected through these methods may be analyzed on a continuing basis, helping police chiefs and other top-level administrators make decisions concerning appropriate courses of action. One advantage of regular surveying is that these surveys provide a comparison standard against which the effectiveness of new public relations initiatives can be measured. Data collection and analysis processes should be continuous if this benefit is to be maximized. Let us now turn our attention to some of the resources available to police departments for putting public relations policies into effect.

Among the most important public relations resources available to any organization are its employees. The public image of any police department depends to a great extent upon the dress, bearing, and actions of police officers involved in street encounters, public speaking, traffic direction, and other interactions with the public. Most of us have seen police officers who were overweight, sloppily dressed, inefficient, and abusive. These officers create a far different impression than those who are properly dressed, in good physical condition, efficient, and courteous. Equally important may be the officer's uniform and arm patch, the insignia he wears, the decal on the patrol car, and the physical appearance of the police station. We recall a police department which was housed in an old, deteriorating building accessible only by walking or driving through an alley in front of which hung a neon sign saying "Police" with an arrow pointing into the alley. Numerous critical comments were made by visitors to the community, residents, and police officers themselves concerning the facility and what it signified. One visitor remarked, "more like visiting a whorehouse than a police station." Others said it gave them "the creeps." The move to a new, spacious, visible facility was hailed by police and public alike as a major improvement for the department. This move made possible a variety of public relations activities (tours, open houses, displays, meetings and conferences, etc.), that before had been rarely offered. Employees, facilities, and equipment (e.g., the use and display of modern communications and computer equipment), all affect public relations.

Another public relations tool available to police officials is the written report. Accurate and timely reports indicating improvement in the qualifications of officers, increased frequency of crimes cleared by arrest, a greater number of service requests received and responded to, or new programs sponsored, may help improve the image of the police.

The police can also utilize public meetings, open houses, guided tours, exhibits and displays, and ride-along programs to inform the public about police activities and procedures and help create and/or maintain a favorable public image. Public meetings in which members of the public are invited to discuss their grievances with police personnel in open, frank fashion can be of value, particularly where mutually agreeable solutions can be found. These meetings may also be of considerable value to police administrators in collecting information about citizen attitudes and needs as indicated above. When using such meetings for this purpose, however, police administrators should keep in mind the fact that people who attend these gatherings may not be representative of the groups which they appear or claim to represent. Therefore, efforts to discover the attitudes and problems of a racial minority, for example, cannot with assurance be limited to such meetings. Open houses, tours of police facilities, and ride-along programs are often used to help convince the public that the police have nothing to hide and are indeed public servants. The use of police facilities to exhibit new equipment or to explain new procedures may also produce positive effects. Audiovisual presentations which help explain how police speed-checking equipment operates, demonstrate how fingerprints are taken, or describe and illustrate first aid procedures, are examples of programs of this type. Information concerning these efforts may be published in weekly columns in local newspapers or in the form of pamphlets prepared and distributed by police personnel.

Police facilities—old. . . .
. . . And new.

Photos courtesy of Galesburg
Police Department, Galesburg,
Illinois.

Community programs sponsored by the police may also have considerable public relations value. Seminars or TV programs featuring police experts talking about self-defense, child safety, drug abuse resistance, gang activity, property marking or other burglary prevention strategies that can be employed by business or home owners are appropriate. So also are Police Cadet programs, police baseball and football leagues, and junior police programs. In the author's community, for example, the police have sponsored an Explorers Post for the Boy Scouts, as well as Silver and Golden Gloves boxing events. They also present programs for the elderly dealing with how to protect persons and property. In addition, they conduct seminars for local businesspersons dealing with the prevention of theft by customers and employees. All these projects can be effective in showing citizens that the police are concerned about them. And, of course, community-oriented policing is an attempt to involve the entire police department and the community which it serves in joint programs. Publicity concerning community policing is aimed at improving the police image or changing it to that of problem-solver and partner in improving the quality of life within the community.

Police Public Relations and the Media

Of major concern to any police agency interested in good public relations are the media. The use or misuse of the press, radio, and television can do a great deal to shape public opinion concerning the police. These media reach large

Cops Or Gestapo?

FBI Accused Of Faking Evidence Against Minorities

Woman, 60, Bites Trooper, Won't Let Go

Police Officer Accused Of Kidnapping

2 cops indicted in cocaine deals

Former Police Officer Gets 60 More Years; Other Charges Pending

Police Officers Plead Innocent To Drug, Extortion Charges

Man, 36, Dies; Shot By Sheriff's Deputy In Dispute

Police Procedures To Undergo Scrutiny Following Jail Death

10 Policemen Indicted

numbers of people on a regular, frequent, and continuing basis, and no police department can long maintain a favorable image without their support as can be seen from the headlines above.

Relations between media and police personnel should be based upon openness, honesty, and availability. As Davis pointed out some time ago: "It is very important that a police agency have an open media policy. A media policy should permit anyone in the department who has adequate knowledge of relevant information, from the lowest to the highest ranking person, to talk to the press.''[12] He goes on to state that the media should be provided with all the information they can legally be given without jeopardizing the rights of concerned parties or compromising ongoing investigations.[13]

In discussing his views of the relationship between the police and the press, Sir Robert Mark, Commissioner of the London Police Department says:

> We had always adhered to the principle "Tell them only what you must." After consultation with most of the principal editors in London, we reversed this to "Withhold only what you must" and we delegated to station level the authority to disclose matters of fact not subject to judicial privacy or policies within the sphere of the Home Office.[14]

Mark also states:

> There are two main ways in which public backing can be obtained or strengthened. The first is obviously by the adoption of a courteous and helpful attitude at all possible times by every member of the force. The second, equally important, is by means of publicity given to the activities of the force in the press and on television and radio. Most members of the public come into direct contact with policemen infrequently and it follows that their image of and attitude towards the force, when not dictated by hearsay, is largely governed by the approach adopted by the news media.[15]

He concludes by pointing out that good police media relations are often difficult to obtain as a result of the fact that the police often withhold information that could safely be made public.[16] Although not all police administrators agree with the policy that any officer ought to be accessible to the media at any time, many seem to have adopted policies similar to those outlined by Davis and Mark. In 1988, for example, police information officers from several police agencies in the state of New York and representatives of the print and electronic media formed the Capital District Law Enforcement/Media Group. The purpose of the group is to improve mutual understanding between the police and media personnel and the results to date appear to have been quite positive.[17]

Further, recognizing the need for solid long-term relationships between the police and the media, the National Highway Traffic Safety Administration has developed and offered Law Enforcement Public Information Workshops to introduce model policies, procedures, and techniques for establishing effective public information programs.[18]

Weinblatt confirms the importance of good media relations: "A working, proactive relationship with the press is an essential component in the success or failure of an agency in its service to the community."[19]

There may, of course, be times when information must be denied to representatives of the media. At such times a courteous, accurate statement of the reasons for such denial should be made. Deception and falsehoods have no place in police media relations. For an example of a news media relations policy, see Appendix A.

Perhaps the most difficult situations with which police agencies must deal from a public relations standpoint are those involving charges of police misconduct that attract media attention. Among these may be included accusations of police brutality, corruption (graft, bribes, shakedowns), drug dealing, prejudicial law enforcement, and discrimination in personnel matters. Shootings are also almost always problematic. One difficulty that runs through police agencies' efforts to deal with these sorts of events is the credibility of department officials. The public is often skeptical of statements made by police spokespersons (or representatives of any other agency) when the organization is under siege for its conduct. Official statements are often perceived by the public as nothing more than public relations cover-ups or whitewashes. As we saw in Chapter Three, certain elements of the police subculture (e.g., in-group loyalty, the perception of public hostility) may reinforce this public skepticism.

Nothing the police do can completely eliminate this public distrust of departmental self-defense, but some steps can be taken to minimize the damage to the agency's image. Providing the public with as much accurate and legally permissible information as possible is important. Playing things too close to the vest only exacerbates the images of secrecy and self-protection. Informing the public about the procedures (content is typically legally protected) of internal review as well as the rights and obligations of accusers and accused is also useful. Perhaps most important of all is establishing a record of honesty and integrity in communicating with the local media and community leaders. Vigorous but courteous defense of good police practice is certainly appropriate; so also is candid admission of mistakes and willful misconduct, along with apologies for violating public trust.

No discussion of the effects of media coverage on police public relations would be complete without mentioning the numerous television shows and movies which deal with the police. In many cases, of course, the police have no control whatever over these shows. In other cases, they are called upon to serve as technical advisors, and on other occasions, active or former police officers write, produce, or direct the shows. In any case, these productions often are misleading, in that they stress the violent, dramatic aspects of police work which actually occur quite rarely. Millions of people who see these shows (among them some future police officers) are led to believe that a police officer goes from one gun battle to another, is constantly involved in investigating a never-ending stream of violent crimes, possesses superhuman powers as a lover, seldom has a satisfactory family life, and never, **never** gets bored with police work.

To be sure, most viewers are fully aware that they are being entertained and that what appears on the screen doesn't coincide one-to-one with reality. But since many have no real firsthand knowledge of the police, it is sometimes difficult to separate fact from fiction. To the extent that such shows are technically accurate, reasonable portrayals of police work, the public has access to a valuable source of information. To the extent that they portray the police as concerned public servants, police officers probably benefit from these shows. Yet when they portray all police as cruel, violent, sadistic, not very intelligent tyrants, the police image is distorted. Since the truth usually lies somewhere between these two extremes, it is difficult to accurately assess the impact of television and movies on police public relations.

Honesty and Accessibility: Public Servants on Display

Public relations are, of course, crucial for all public service agencies. By creating and maintaining a positive public image the police can expect to benefit in terms of citizen cooperation in pursuing the goals of order maintenance and law enforcement; they may also gain in terms of salaries and equipment. The extent to which the police are viewed as an important, integral part of the community depends in part upon public relations. Successful public relations require that the police make a determined effort to be accessible to the public and to provide the public with accurate information. In addition, successful public relations require that the police practice what they preach. Projecting a positive image of the police will have no long-term positive effects unless the image reflects reality. As public servants, the police are, and must realize that they are, constantly on display. The widespread private ownership of portable video cameras gives a special, concrete edge to this sweeping generalization, as those officers involved in the arrest of Rodney King can testify. Piecemeal, inconsistent attempts to foster a positive organizational image are doomed to failure. Only continuous, day-to-day efforts on behalf of all officers will produce the desired effects. And even these efforts will fail if the department has not demonstrated a commitment to serving the community with sensitivity and integrity.

The community policing movement has encouraged police agencies to take the improvement of public relations seriously. Department sponsored community based crime prevention programs, such as Neighborhood Watch, child finger printing, property marking, antiburglary and antitheft brochures and workshops are part of the community policing effort. So also are decentralized command structures that disperse some decision making to the particular neighborhoods where problems occur and that are designed to make the police agency more responsive to community needs and interests as defined by the community, through departmental liaison with neighborhood councils.

By providing accessibility, education, quality service for the community, and engaging in other activities that foster a positive agency image, the police can expect to benefit in terms of increased citizen cooperation in law enforcement and order maintenance; perhaps increased financial resources will be available as well.

Summary

Police public relations are an important component of police community relations. Public relations include all of the activities engaged in by the police in an attempt to connect with and educate the public as well as to develop and/or maintain a favorable public image.

Any successful public relations programs must include both **policy** and **practice,** or **planning** and **action.** Public relations are based upon public opinion as influenced by the media. Organizations concerned with public relations sample public opinion, analyze the data collected, make decisions concerning proper courses of action, and translate these decisions into action.

Public relations campaigns will be successful only when they accurately reflect behavior. In order for this to occur, someone in the organization must be responsible for public relations. Too often police departments have tried to make everyone responsible for public relations, but have placed no one in charge of this task. On the other hand, one officer or one section may be made responsible for public relations and all other officers tend to forget it.

A number of strategies and techniques for improving public relations are available to police personnel. The appearance and bearing of the police officer, the equipment he uses, the speeches she gives, etc., are all important to public relations. Departmental reports, community education, open houses, and public meetings may be used to inform the public and improve the police image.

Relations with the media are a crucial concern in improving police public relations. Contacts with the media are most successful when they reflect the honesty and accessibility of police personnel. When police officers consider themselves public servants, realize that they are constantly on public display, and attempt to act in such a way that the public recognizes that they are concerned public servants, public relations campaigns will be successful.

Discussion Questions

1. What is the connection between public relations and community relations?
2. Discuss the concept and practice of public relations. Why is it important to emphasize both practice and policy in public relations programs?
3. What are some strategies and techniques which the police can employ in public relations campaigns?
4. Discuss the relationship between the media and the police in terms of public relations. How can this relationship be developed best by the police?
5. Why is the public skeptical of public relations efforts by any corporation or government agency? Should they be? What distinguishes good public relations from whitewash?
6. What incidents produce the most difficult public relations problems for the police? What can be done to minimize damage to the department's image on those occasions?

Endnotes

1. Wadman and Ziman. "Courtesy and Police Authority."; William Raspberry. 1991. "L.A. Beating Puts Spotlight on 'culture of violence.' " *Chicago Tribune* (March 18): sec. 1: 11; John Epke and Linda Davis. 1991. "Civil Rights Cases and Police Misconduct." *FBI Law Enforcement Bulletin* (August): 14–18; Victor E. Kappeler, Richard D. Sluder, and Geoffrey P. Alpert. 1994. *Forces of Deviance: Understanding the Dark Side of Policing.* Prospect Heights: Waveland Press.
2. Lawrence W. Nolte. 1979. *Fundamentals of Public Relations: Professional Guidelines. Concepts and Integrations.* 2ed. New York: Pergamon Press: Chapter 1.
3. Ibid.: 11–13.
4. Ibid.: 20.

5. Clifford E. Simonsen and Douglas Arnold. 1993. ''TQM: Is It Right for Law Enforcement?'' *The Police Chief* (December): 22; Geoffery P. Alpert and Roger G. Dunham. 1992. *Policing Urban America.* 2ed. Prospect Heights: Waveland Press: 198–199; Trojanowicz. 1990. ''Community Policing.''
6. Nolte. *Fundamentals of Public Relations.*: 13.
7. Ibid.: 63.
8. Wadman and Ziman. ''Courtesy and Police Authority.''; Kappeler, Sluder, and Alpert. *Forces of Deviance.*
9. Bouza. *The Police Mystique.*; 10–11; Alpert and Dunham. *Policing Urban America.*: 78–79; Langworthy and Travis. *Policing in America.*: 342; Sparrow, Moore, and Kennedy. ''Beyond 911.''': 33–37.
10. For an interesting discussion of the New York City experience with civilian review see Algernon D. Black. 1968. *The People and the Police.* New York: McGraw-Hill; Kappeler, Sluder, and Alpert. *Forces of Deviance.* 266–268.
11. Skolnick. *Justice Without Trial.*: 245; see also, Alan M. Webber. 1991. ''Crime and Management: An Interview with New York City Police Commissioner Lee P. Brown.'' *Harvard Business Review* (May–June): 111–126; D. Rudovsky. 1992. ''Police Abuse: Can the Violence Be Contained?'' *Harvard Civil Rights-Civil Liberties Law Review* 27(2): 467–501.
12. Edward Davis. 1978. *Staff One: A Perspective on Effective Police Management.* Englewood Cliffs, NJ: Prentice-Hall: 201.
13. Ibid.: 202.
14. Mark. *Policing a Perplexed Society.*: 50–51.
15. Ibid.: 123.
16. Ibid.: 124.
17. Robert Wolfgang. 1992. ''Working Together, Police and Media.'' *Law and Order* 40(2): 29–30.
18. James J. Onder, Jack Mahar, and Barry McLoughlin. 1994. ''Improving Your Image in the Media.'' *Police Chief* 61(5): 60–61.
19. Richard Weinblatt. 1992. ''The Police and the Media.'' *Law and Order* 40(2): 32.

Suggested Readings

Dunphy, Francis R. and Gerald W. Garner. 1992. ''A Guide to Effective Interaction with the News Media.'' *Police Chief* 59(4): 45–48.

Nehrbass, Arthur F. 1989. ''Promoting Effective Media Relations.'' *Police Chief* 56(1): 40–44.

Nolte, Lawrence W. 1979. *Fundamentals of Public Relations: Professional Guidelines, Concepts, and Integrations.* New York: Pergamon Press.

Onder, James J., Jack Mahar, and Barry McLoughlin. 1994. ''Improving Your Image in the Media.'' *Police Chief* 61(5): 60–61.

Weinblatt, Richard. 1992. ''The Police and the Media.'' *Law and Order* 40(2): 32–38.

Wolfgang, Robert. 1992. ''Working Together, Police and Media.'' *Law and Order* 40(2): 29–30.

Chapter 5

Youth and the Police

*A*mong the most rewarding and, at the same time, the most frustrating persons with whom the police interact in any community are children and adolescents. In this chapter some critical aspects of the relationships between the police and the youth of a community will be explored. Special attention will be given to the reasons for the sometimes difficult relationships between adolescents and the police.

Working with youth has two basic rewards for the police. First, officers are no less susceptible than are the rest of us to the innocence and charm of children or the curiosity and energy of adolescents. The opportunity to help create early (and at least potentially lasting) good impressions of the police and of the law which the police represent is likely to be both important and gratifying to one who has chosen a career in law enforcement. Second, to the extent that the police are successful in helping youth gain respect for the law, future adult careers in crime may be reduced. In fact, many believe that, while adult criminals are typically set in their patterns of illegal conduct, young people are more salvageable. Police officers want youth to develop an image of the officer, not just as a rule enforcer, but as a teacher and friend, as a source of help and protection in case of trouble. Visiting school classrooms, bicycle safety presentations, informal bantering with kids on the street, "Officer Friendly" programs, summer camps, "junior police" programs, and scout troops are a few of the police-sponsored programs and activities designed to create constructive contacts between youth and the police, and to reinforce a positive image of the police in the eyes of youth. Of course, police also provide direct assistance to youths who are lost, in danger, injured, or in need of other types of aid.

Indirect benefits also flow from direct contact between police and youth. The image that adults in a community have of the police is often influenced by the relationship that adults believe to exist between the police and youth. For example, the newspaper photo of a uniformed officer carrying a frightened and perhaps injured child away from danger may increase, at least temporarily, support for the police among adult citizens of the community. Furthermore,

when children report to their parents about an officer's visit to school, for example, parents have an opportunity to reinforce the friend, protector, and helper image the officer hoped to create in the child's mind. They also may use the occasion to emphasize the role of the officer as a rule enforcer, especially at times when parental authority seems to require support. Finally, when the police are successful in preventing youth from annoying or victimizing adults, support for the police can be enhanced.

Police frustrations with youth come from two related sources. First, relations between teenagers and the police are often strained because youth frequently feel harassed and may not demonstrate the deference to which officers feel entitled during encounters.[1] Lack of respect from youth is likely to be taken as especially serious by the police.[2] Although the law does not prohibit rude conduct vis-à-vis the police, officers may view such behaviors as indicators of improper socialization and harbingers of criminal misconduct. In short, from the police point of view, the basic moral order of society is at stake and they sometimes demand that youth show them some respect. Perhaps for that reason, the police approach to youth is often characterized as more moral than legal.[3] Unfortunately, these well-intentioned efforts to ''make'' teenagers engage in deference displays often only exacerbate youth-police tensions. Adding to the difficulties here are some of the dynamics of adolescence as a phase of life, which we will explore later in this chapter.

The second major source of police frustration with youth stems from the fact that youth (and young adult) crime rates, violent offenses included, are relatively high.[4] Hence youth are sometimes major contributors to a community's crime problem and are often viewed in this light by the police whether or not the perception is accurate. They are also overrepresented in victimization statistics.[5] It is certainly no easier for police officers than for other citizens to see young people's futures jeopardized either through victimization or criminal activities.

When there is trouble between the police and the youth of a community, it is most likely to involve older youth, usually ranging in age from twelve to nineteen, the group most often referred to as adolescents. Relationships between adolescents and law enforcement officers, especially the animosities which sometimes develop between the two groups, are probably better understood as functions of societal roles played by police and adolescents, rather than as enduring characteristics of the personalities of the police or the adolescents. The various components of the police officer's role have already been discussed. Adolescence in American society and some aspects of the adolescent role as they relate to the police officer's role are the topics of the next section.

Adolescence: A Period of Turmoil and Change

Adolescence is the transitional period between childhood and adulthood. It is a time of rapid physical, psychological, and social development. Identities are tried on and sorted through, while relationships with others undergo significant changes. Understanding some of these changes may shed some light on the nature of relationships between adolescents and the police. First, the propensity of many adolescents—especially males—to test their coordination, control, strength, and nerve is a widely recognized aspect of adolescence. Outlets for these activities, of course, vary greatly. Football or soccer fields, basketball, volleyball, racquetball or tennis courts, motorcycle or bicycle racing courses, and track and field events provide more or less legitimate arenas for testing physical prowess. Adventures which violate rules set by parents or societal authority ("the law") also often present an attractive combination of features for the adolescent testing his or her maturity. Considerable physical skill, careful planning, and quick wit are frequently required. There is the challenge of coping with unanticipated events. There is the risk of getting caught and the thrill of fleeing, as well as getting away with it (whatever *it* may be). There is also the opportunity to demonstrate to peers (and to oneself) where one belongs in one's peer society hierarchy.

Second, adolescence is characterized by very significant changes in mental ability. It is during adolescence, for example, that what Jean Piaget calls "formally operational intelligence" begins. Some of the properties of this formally operational intelligence are:

1. the capacity to reason in a formal way, to follow an argument and to draw appropriate conclusions from given premises
2. the capacity to identify all of the logically possible outcomes or consequences of a particular situation and to elaborate on and test each one to determine which is the more likely

3. the capacity to think through puzzles and problems and to arrive at reasonable solutions
4. the capacity to make complex moral analyses, taking into account extenuating circumstances and psychological motives when arriving at moral judgments[6]

Adolescents are inclined to practice and test cognitive skills just as they are their physical skills. Detailed fantasies about exploits of various sorts are common. The sense that almost anything is possible, comes without clear guides for distinguishing the possible from the likely, dangerous, illegal, or immoral. The confusion, anxiety, and stress that occur during adolescence may well be as much a function of this cognitive maturation as of the physiological maturation and hormonal changes which are the most often cited causes of adolescent turmoil.

Third, the adolescent's relationships with others change. Actually, several significant alterations are a part of this change. Relationships with parents are sometimes strained as the adolescent seeks to establish an identity clearly distinguishable from that conferred by his or her family membership. Perhaps the easiest way of doing this is to reject much of what the adolescent associates with family values, religious beliefs and practices, standards of dress, and conduct. Perhaps most important of all in the present context is the resistance of the adolescent to parental and other authority.

Accompanying these attempts to establish greater ''psychic'' distance from the family, are closer relationships with peers. The peer group often becomes a major, and sometimes a dominant force in shaping the adolescent's values, beliefs, and behavior. Adolescent peers often support each other in their efforts to establish independence from their respective families.

Typically, peer relationships with members of the opposite sex also emerge during this period. Such relationships involve the formation of simple companionship and intimacy of both a sexual and nonsexual nature. They may also involve a propensity to ''show off,'' or to ''prove'' something to one's partner (and to one's self) concerning one's knowledge, strength, or toughness.

As should be clear from the previous discussion, one theme in the personal and social changes that accompanies the emergence and development of adolescence is the conflict between authority and freedom, conformity and independence.[7] Police officers, because of the role they play in society, are perceived by many adolescents (not to mention adults) as representatives of societal authority—''law and order.'' Police officers sometimes see themselves in the role of societal parent and moral guide to youth, especially in circumstances where they perceive supervision and discipline to be lacking in the youths' home environment. Contacts between adolescents and police officers often support this perception. The reputations and perhaps the records of some young people make them highly visible to the police, and they are often watched carefully. Furthermore, whether roaming the streets at night in small groups or cruising city blocks in hopped-up cars, much adolescent activity, by its very public nature, is highly visible to the patrolling officer and may well be the

Johnny Boy . . .

12-Year-Old's Career in Crime Crashes to an End

By Robert Dvorchak

of the Associated Press

PHILADELPHIA—John Sullivan's lawless young life had already careened out of control by the time the 12-year-old struck and killed two people with a stolen car while trying to outrun the cops.

"I knew sooner or later there was going to be an accident," said Pauline Payne, the 72-year-old great-grandmother who raised the boy from infancy after his unwed parents abandoned him. "I knew he was going to do the wrong thing."

Now, she said, "There's nothing I can say but cry."

John L. Sullivan III, a wisp his family called Johnny Boy, admitted responsibility for the Oct. 24 deaths of a father of nine children and an 11-year-old girl. He's now serving four years at a maximum security lockup for juveniles in rural northeastern Pennsylvania.

Street-savvy at 10

He was a street-savvy career criminal before age 10, when his first arrest was recorded—for stealing $327 from under his great-grandmother's pillow. His family said he was stealing bicycles years before that.

His rap sheet includes 13 arrests, five for stealing cars, in the last two years. He escaped five times from minimum-security juvenile homes, committing more crimes every time he hit the streets.

Johnny Boy, who turned 13 on Dec. 12, was on the loose at the time of his fatal joy ride, although he was supposed to be under watch, awaiting placement in a secure state lockup that was too crowded to take him right away.

How could a boy so young get into so much trouble? Why didn't anybody stop him?

A litany of failure offers clues: a broken home, a guardian too old to keep up with Johnny Boy, lack of resources in a social services system that should have intervened before things got out of control, and an overcrowded juvenile justice system ill-equipped for criminals so young. . . .

Spreading Blame

Johnny Boy was charged with homicide by vehicle, involuntary manslaughter, aggravated assault, auto theft, unlawful use of an auto and conspiracy.

Because he is a juvenile, he was tried under the single charge of delinquency. In Pennsylvania, no one under 14 can be tried as an adult unless the charge is murder.

"There's more than enough blame to spread around," said Richard Schwartz, executive director of the Juvenile Law Center, an advocacy group.

"The solution is to build another major lockup for several million dollars we don't have or plan for a program to deal with the problem up front when juveniles first get into trouble," Schwartz said.

"It makes more sense to spend money to build a barn that works rather than spend money on locks for a door that's already open. You can't do patchwork repairs on a juvenile justice system."

object of an officer's efforts to reduce noise, enforce traffic laws, or otherwise restrain activities which adolescents themselves perceive as harmless fun or kicks. The adolescent's resentment of the police officer is often the result.

Because the police officer represents institutional authority and may in fact legitimately exercise power to physically restrain, he or she becomes an especially attractive focus for some adolescents' challenges. Among some peer groups, a great deal of prestige can be gained through both open and covert challenges to the police officer's authority, in part because they involve risk-taking which is often associated with the personal and interpersonal dynamics of adolescence.

It is important to remember that adolescence is not experienced in the same way by all teenagers. Not all adolescents have serious difficulty coping with parental or societal authority. Young adults vary remarkably in their willingness to take risks and to flaunt the law. Police relations with adolescents in many communities and subcommunities are quite positive. When youth is combined with ethnic minority status and poverty, however, the likelihood that police-youth relations will be tense seems to increase.

Delinquent Youth—A Dilemma for the Police

In all types of societies and throughout all ages, certain types of behavior of some young people have occasionally angered and frustrated adults. Authors and commentators from Plato's time to the present have lamented the licentiousness of youth, their disrespect for their elders, and the disturbances and destruction which they sometimes perpetrate. Often these complaints are accompanied by pleas for stronger family units, more discipline, and stricter law enforcement. If the persistent repetition of these laments and pleas are any indication, not much has changed in the general relationships between some adults and some youth over the last two thousand years. In short, troublesome youth have created a dilemma for their parents and other adults for a long time.

In American society, development of the juvenile justice network is one of the most recent and most fundamental manifestations of the ongoing struggle to solve the problem of troublesome youth. The basic idea that motivated court reformers was that juveniles who committed crimes should not be treated like adult criminals. Because of their relative immaturity and their potential for reform, the treatment of young persons should be more humane than that accorded adults; for youth, rehabilitation rather than punishment should be the principal objective. Hearings should be conducted in more informal settings governed by less formal rules of procedure. More dispositional alternatives should be available, so that the best interests of the youth may be served. Incarceration should be avoided whenever possible. If confinement was required, places of detention created specifically for youth and completely separated from the brutalizing effects of adult prisons should be established.

From the first Family Court in Illinois in 1899, the court reform movement spread rapidly through the nation. The wisdom of some of the reformers' principles and the effectiveness of certain juvenile court procedures have from time to time been questioned. In the past three decades, for example, more of the procedural safeguards employed in adult courts have been mandated for juvenile hearings and more teenagers accused of violent offenses are being treated as adults. Nevertheless, the basic concepts of the juvenile justice network have remained quite stable to the present day.[8]

The police have had an important if somewhat complex role to play in the juvenile justice network. In the case of juvenile offenders no less than adults, the police represent the long arm of the law, with the power to take persons into custody and, thereby, to initiate the judicial process. In some respects, as we shall see in the next section of this chapter, the police officer's exercise of discretion in dealing with juveniles is especially complex and critical. For the moment, however, we shall elaborate briefly on the phenomenon of juvenile delinquency itself.

Juvenile delinquency is a difficult concept to define in a practical manner. Perhaps the simplest technical definition is: a juvenile delinquent is a young person whom a court of law has declared to be a lawbreaker. To be declared a delinquent by the court, one must be: (a) of a certain age (i.e., under the age at which a person is considered an adult—seventeen or eighteen years of age in most jurisdictions), and (b) adjudicated a delinquent as a result of a hearing in a court specifically designed for handling the misbehavior of youth, that is, misbehavior, which if engaged in by an adult would be a crime (e.g., theft or assault) or misbehavior in the form of ''status offenses'' (in this case, offenses which can only be committed by someone who is not an adult, such as truancy or being a runaway).

For most laypeople, a juvenile delinquent is simply a youth who is a troublemaker, who fails to show respect to elders, who is annoying and mischievous, but ''old enough to know better.'' The ''violations'' committed by juveniles are often as much transgressions of manners, morals, and customs, as of formal laws.

The fundamental dilemma of delinquency for the police is essentially the same as for all of us: How can one best deal with youthful misbehavior so that, where necessary, the public is protected and the juvenile's objectionable behavior is discouraged without, in the process, increasing the likelihood that the youth will develop into a full-fledged adult criminal? It seems there are at present no easy answers to this question.

Literally hundreds of potential causes of delinquency have been proposed and investigated; these include broken homes, psychopathology, genetic factors, parent-child relationships, weaning time, etc. It seems fair to say that although some very interesting theoretical leads have emerged and some useful research strategies have been developed, at this point no single suggested cause (and no particular group of causes) of delinquency has received such convincing research support that we can confidently declare it (or them) as a major cause in most cases of delinquency. While such a conclusion may seem insignificant or unimportant, it teaches one valuable lesson: whatever our favorite personal explanation of why youth become delinquent, when it is subjected to careful observation and analysis, it does not seem as significant a factor in delinquency as we might have thought or hoped.

Consider, for example, what is perhaps the most frequently reported situational characteristic of delinquency—social class. In particular, researchers have repeatedly demonstrated that youth from poor families with little education, who live in lower-class neighborhoods, are more likely to be delinquent than those who have higher social status. The definition of delinquency used in most research of this type is the legalistic one: a delinquent is a person so declared by a court. When delinquency is defined in this way, the data are clear. Social class is linked to delinquency.

The question that arises in interpreting these studies is: What actually is being reflected in official delinquency statistics? Do poor youth from poor families in poor neighborhoods really engage in delinquent acts more often than middle-class or upper-class youth? Or do the statistics reflect something else? Perhaps lower-class youth are simply more likely to be caught than their middle-class counterparts. Or perhaps, once caught, there is a greater probability that lower-class youth will be referred to the court, while middle-class youth are more likely to be sent home with a scare and a warning. Or perhaps middle- and upper-class families mobilize their resources and provide a more rigorous defense of their offspring in the courts.

Furthermore, there is considerable evidence from other research projects that suggests that middle-class youth are just as likely to commit delinquent acts as are lower-class youth. These projects define delinquency as the commission of an act that is a violation of law, whether or not the actor was caught and adjudicated. In this type of research, for example, youth are assured of anonymity and asked to indicate which if any of a series of listed delinquent and nondelinquent acts they have engaged in. Most researchers employing this research methodology report that middle-class youth admit to as many delinquent acts as do their lower-class peers, although those reported by lower-class youth tend to be more serious violations. To the extent that these results are valid, the alternative explanations for the apparent relationship between social class and delinquency become more credible. At the very least, a final answer to this question has yet to be found.[9]

Another explanation frequently offered for delinquency is peer or gang pressure. According to this explanation, persons who associate with delinquents are more likely to become delinquents themselves. There is little doubt that this is true. This suggests that delinquency and the attitudes and values which support such behavior are learned, often from peers. It also implies that peers exert a very powerful influence on youth, an influence very difficult to counter.

A broad range of proposed "cures" for delinquency have made the rounds in the United States. Some advocate rigorous law enforcement and stiff penalties—sentences to juvenile detention centers.[10] As the number of violent offenses perpetrated by youth has increased, more calls are heard for treating young offenders as adults and trying them in adult courts. Others argue that incarceration only tends to harden youth and that they emerge from their institutional experiences more antisocial than when they entered.[11] These persons advocate diversionary strategies, like shunting troublesome youth into specially designed counseling, recreational, and social service programs. Still others believe that a good scare is what troublesome youth need. "Stationhouse adjustments," where officers take a youth to the police station, subject him or her to intense interrogation, perhaps confine the juvenile for a brief period, and often summon the youth's parents, are common examples of scare strategies. So also are the widely publicized "scared straight" programs. The idea here is to bring small groups of youth into a prison setting to be confronted by inmates who talk about prison life in very blunt and graphic terms, describe in very explicit language what is likely to happen to the youth, including homosexual victimization, if they end up in prison and, frequently, physically intimidate and humiliate one or more members of the ''target'' group of youth in the process. Finally, several jurisdictions have established quasi-military ''shock treatment'' boot camps where firm discipline, education, and hard physical labor are emphasized.

Again, there is no clear winner in this contest over how best to deal with delinquency or delinquents. Initial reports often praise the successes of these programs, but careful research using control groups lends very little support to any of these approaches as clearly superior to the others or to doing anything in terms of reducing recidivism. For the officer on the street, perhaps the most useful general observations are that delinquency apparently results from a host of different causes and that there is no single ''treatment'' of delinquency which holds much promise in most cases.

Gangs, Drugs, and Satanic Cults

Among the more visible forms of delinquency is that associated with gangs. The words ''juvenile gang'' evoke unsettling images: defiant, macho teenagers roaming ghetto streets; impulsive, wanton violence; garish graffiti declaring territorial ownership by groups with shocking names and logos; extortion of lunch money from defenseless seven-year-olds in the school yard; blind loyalty to the gang and its leaders; recruitment of new members through intimidation; destruction or theft of public and private property; the use and sale of drugs, etc.

Gangs

The origins of scholarly research on gangs is typically traced to Frederic Thrasher's Chicago studies in the 1920s.[12] Publications peaked in the 1950s and 1960s and then virtually disappeared until the mid 1980s, when interest in gangs was rekindled by escalating violence associated with cocaine and crack marketing.[13]

Researchers and other observers (including law enforcement officials) have always had difficulty clearly distinguishing between gangs and other teenage groups. Differences among groups designated as gangs may be quite dramatic and generalizations about them are risky.[14] But the most often cited defining characteristics of traditional gangs include their origins, size, gender, age, social class and ethnic composition, social structure and organization, subcultural values, and group activities.

Gangs originate ''spontaneously'' among the participants themselves—that is, they are neither created nor supervised by ''responsible'' adults or legitimate social agencies or institutions. Usually, they are relatively large groups (say, five or more members) of male adolescents (though female gangs are being reported with increasing frequency). Participants in a particular gang share ethnic and social class backgrounds as well as neighborhood residence. The gang has a collective identity (i.e., a group name, dress code, and logo), and

A Snitch's Tale: The Killer Gang

*Critical
Issue*

An Informer Tells about Life as an 'El Rukn'

By Patricia King

First came the bust. An army of federal and local police raided "The Fort," headquarters of the violent El Rukn drug gang on Chicago's South Side, and arrested 17 alleged members last Friday. Later in the day came the announcement of grand-jury indictments of 65 reputed gang members and their associates, many of whom were being picked up elsewhere in the city and in six other states. The charges, which included murder, drug trafficking, robbery and kidnapping, spanned the entire 24 years of the gang's existence. . . .

The crackdown was the climax of a six-year investigation of the gang and its multimillion-dollar cocaine and heroin operation. Former El Rukn Anthony (Sundown) Sumner, 36, helped make the day possible when he turned state's evidence in 1985. Fearing retribution from the gang, Sumner was moved to an out-of-state location by the government. In a recent exclusive interview with **NEWSWEEK** at his quiet suburban hideaway, Sumner recounted the murderous history of the El Rukns and their ruthless leader, Jeff Fort, 42. The gang started as a pack of adolescents who robbed for kicks. By the late 1960s, then named the Blackstone Rangers, the gang appeared to go straight: they performed protective and other public-service acts for the community— and became widely admired. . . .

In the late 1970s Fort changed the name to El Rukn—Arabic for "the foundation"—and the gang became what prosecutors call a paramilitary drug-trafficking network. Over the next decade it built its estimated membership to between 500 and 1,000, and even contracted as U.S. agents for Libyan terrorists. Until recently Fort, an illiterate, charismatic autocrat, masterminded the operation, usually from prison. "He said he was the King," says Sumner. If Fort said kill, Sumner says, no one asked why: "We was just evil people I guess. Had to be." . . .

at least some structure (i.e., group leaders recognized as such by group members, age-graded subgroups and some loyalty of members to the group and its leaders). Group values emphasize immediate (rather than delayed) gratification, being "street smart" and tough (rather than school smart and wimpy), defending the neighborhood turf from invasion, avenging insults to their individual or collective honor or manhood by similar but rival groups, and demonstrating disrespect for virtually all legitimate authority figures (e.g., parents, teachers, and the police) through offensive manners of speech and dress, truancy from school (though gangs are becoming a significant problem in schools, too), as well as through theft, vandalism, illegal drug use, and other delinquent activities.

As Klien and Maxson point out, few new theories concerning the origins or functions of gangs have emerged since the 1960s. Results from recently expanding research efforts are as yet too incomplete to assess confidently the extent of changes in gang activities or organization that may have occurred in the interim.[15] A few preliminary findings are worth noting, however. First, gangs are no longer exclusively a phenomenon of large urban areas; they have emerged in many cities with populations ranging from 100,000 to 500,000 as well. Second, while there is little evidence that gang membership has extended much into younger age groups, higher rates of participation have been reported for young adults (nineteen to twenty-four years of age). Third, while the vast majority of gangs remain African American or Hispanic in ethnic composition, many observers have noted the emergence of Asian American (principally Chinese and Vietnamese) as well as Jamaican groups in larger cities with concentrations of these ethnic populations. The Asian American groups are reportedly almost without turf concerns.

Finally, while gang violence remains quite rare overall, its frequency and lethality are apparently increasing, especially in certain ethnic underclass enclaves in the largest cities.[16] Referring to the gang wars in south central Los Angeles, in which he played a prominent role, Sanyika Shakur (a.k.a. Monster Cody of the Crips) says: "The soldiers are engaged in a 'civil war.' A war without terms. A war fought by any means necessary, with anything at their disposal. This conflict has lasted nine years longer than Vietnam. Though the setting is not jungle per se, its atmosphere is as dangerous and mysterious as any jungle in the world."[17]

The context of some gang violence has also changed. Some of the violence appears to be related to the illegal and unregulated business activities of the drug trade. The previous emphasis on defense of turf/territory has become, in some instances, a defense of (and efforts to expand) drug-selling areas and market share. It would not be too much of an exaggeration to say that some gangs are engaging in big (albeit illegal) business with enviable cash flows and expanding markets—in short, capitalistic competition and free enterprise run amuck. A reemergence of organized crime, integrating different generations in a network of illegal but highly profitable activities, seems to be in the making.[18]

Finally, the predominant modes of responding to gangs have altered in ways which reflect changes in the political ethos of the larger society. During the earlier, more liberal era, most intervention efforts were operated from neighborhood centers and other social service agencies. The guiding philosophy of these efforts emphasized working with gangs in order to direct members' values in more conventional directions. As the country turned more conservative in the 1980s, emphasis shifted to a law enforcement approach. Specialized gang intelligence and control units were created in many urban police departments. Strategies often included aggressive patrolling, deliberate harassment of gang members, and arresting gang leaders.[19]

Unfortunately, there is not much carefully gathered evidence upon which to base firm conclusions, but preliminary findings suggest that the latter strategies have been no more effective than the former ones in curtailing gangs or their criminal activities. In fact, both the earlier social work strategies and the law enforcement mode of response may have made things worse. The earlier intervention strategies, for example, sometimes had the effect of "legitimizing" the gang. Furthermore, the attention and rewards received by the groups, which were intended as inducements for change, helped gangs attract new members. Aggressive police tactics, on the other hand, sometimes make gangs more cohesive and provide concrete experiences that at once justify and magnify the antiestablishment attitudes of members. Then, too, gangs are typically not as well organized as is often supposed; their leadership has proven to be quite fluid and situational, making the strategy of targeting gang leadership almost futile.[20]

As with delinquency in general, no clear solutions for the "gang problem" have developed. It is unlikely that any will soon emerge, especially if gangs are a product, at least in part, of adolescence itself and of larger social problems such as deindustrialization, social inequality, racism, and inadequate employment opportunities for youth. It should also be noted that most adolescent gang members "mature out" of gang involvements as they grow older, get married, start families, and get a job, suggesting that the gang phenomenon does indeed have something to do with adolescence as a phase of life in our society. It is worth bearing in mind, too, that this maturing-out process takes place independent of law enforcement or social service agency intervention. Finally, Joan Moore summarizes well some good reasons for treating media, social worker, and police accounts of gangs with caution:

> Gang members are quite adept at telling social workers and policemen lies. Glib information is, in fact, a survival tool for many gang members. It is easy for outside people (and that is practically everybody) to believe social workers and policemen because they have direct contact with gang members. Yet this direct contact is often managed by the gang members themselves, sometimes for survival, sometimes even for self-glorifying exaggeration, and the police and gang workers also have some self-interest in the images they purvey.[21]

We might add that researchers are not immune from being misled by their informants, gang members or not.

Obviously, law enforcement has an important role in coping with violence and other illegal gang activities, but it is unlikely that the police can eliminate (or even much curtail) the gang phenomenon. Furthermore, it seems to us that, in the absence of clearly illegal conduct, police harassment tactics are more likely to aggravate than to alleviate gang problems.

Drugs

Closely associated with the gang phenomenon in recent years has been the drug problem, as we noted previously. Of course, drug sales and consumption are not confined to gangs, but much of the gang violence pervading the headlines in the late 1980s and early 1990s is drug related.[22] Interestingly, the portrayal of drug-associated violence seems to have shifted from an emphasis on the effects of consuming drugs (inducing mania in users, causing them to commit irrational and brutal offenses) to an emphasis on the establishment and defense of drug supplies and markets.[23] Here, too, as with gangs, the 1980s witnessed a shift to a more hard-line, conservative law enforcement strategy, aimed at deterrence and punishment on the demand side and disruption of international drug trafficking on the supply side. Stiffening local, state, and federal drug penalties, appointing a national drug czar, involving the military in drug supply interdiction efforts (including the military overthrow of Panamanian dictator Manuel Noriega), and playing up the devastating effects on the quality of community life have all been part of the ''get tough'' drug control strategy.

Much of this is, to say the least, controversial. As many observers have noted, this recent effort is hardly the first time our society has declared ''war'' on drugs; by some counts, in fact, it is the seventh such declaration in American history. The frequency with which such declarations have been made is evidence in itself that ''warring'' with drugs has limited utility. Some prominent scholars and civic leaders (a few federal judges, some mayors, etc.) have argued that drug-related violence is as much a result of our drug control policy as it is of drugs themselves. Legal prohibition, it is contended, creates the very lucrative black market for drugs, which, in turn, provides powerful incentives for recruiting new users, especially among the young, and engenders the violence that accompanies competition for a share of the market. They advocate a different approach to the drug problem, one which would treat both addiction and ''casual'' use as matters to be dealt with by public health rather than law enforcement agencies. Under this strategy, drug availability and use would be regulated, as tobacco and alcohol now are. Law enforcement would, of course, continue to be involved where criminal violence was involved. Critics of these proposals argue that regulation will be impossible, if the alcohol and tobacco examples are any guide, and that addiction rates will skyrocket.[24]

Clearly, there are substantial risks involved with the regulatory approach for at least some drugs, but just as clearly, law enforcement crackdowns don't hold much promise either. While the latter have succeeded in filling to over capacity our jails and prisons, their impact on general drug use and abuse patterns appears minimal at best. In fact, the available evidence suggests that, with the exception of cocaine and crack, illegal drug usage rates were going down well before all the current uproar over drugs began. In short, drug abuse may be best viewed as a cyclical phenomenon, whose vacillations are determined more by users' experiences and shifts in general cultural mores than by legislative or law enforcement activities. Furthermore, as the use of drugs popular at one point in time goes down, old ones return to favor and new ones emerge. It has been widely reported, for example, that as marihuana use has diminished, alcohol has become the drug of choice on high school and college campuses. A variety of ''designer drugs'' (so called because they are produced by slightly altering the chemistry of an existing synthetic drug) continually enter the drug supply networks. And, recent newspaper reports have highlighted the appearance in Hawaii of ''ice'' (a crystalline form of methamphetamine), hailed by users as the ultimate trip and condemned by public officials as the most dangerous and addictive drug ever to appear on the American scene.

As with the gang problem, effective solutions to the drug problem are elusive and promise to remain so. There are simply too many natural and synthetic substances with abuse potential too readily available from local and worldwide sources. Police officials occasionally declare a victory, as still another bust and new street value records for confiscated drugs are announced. But even the most optimistic of them, when they are honest, acknowledge that the impact even in the local arena is likely to be minor and short-lived. The devastation to individual and community life that drugs can bring is undeniable; so also is the futility of the efforts of the police, acting alone, to control them.[25] Citizen involvement—community members policing their own neighborhoods with the assistance of law enforcement officers—may help, as we shall see in Chapter Ten. It must be remembered, though, that without city or countywide efforts, the drug problem is simply shuffled from one area to another within a community and there is always the risk of vigilanteeism itself getting out of control. In any event, if the police are left to fight it alone, this new drug war, like those of the past, will almost certainly be lost. In that case, frustration for law enforcement officers and other citizens alike is the probable result.[26]

Satanic Cults

Satanism and satanic cults are potentially explosive topics because so many highly emotional issues may be linked to them. First, adolescents are sometimes attracted to nontraditional religious cults. Satanism's emphasis on secrecy, sexuality, immediate gratification, and ritual seem especially well-suited to typical adolescent interests. In general, satanism, sometimes referred to as devil worship, is perceived as the antithesis of Christianity. It has also been associated with the lyrics of some rebellious ''hard rock'' and ''heavy metal'' music, some music videos and computer games, and the fantasy role-playing game of ''Dungeons and Dragons,'' all of which are popular among some youth. In addition, witchcraft and the sexual abuse of children have been linked to these cults. When children, the dominant religion, basic social morals, and the work ethic are thought to be threatened, the potential for community arousal (and overreaction) is enormous.

That some such groups exist and that some illegal practices occur seem certain, but how well-organized and widespread they are is difficult to determine. Determining whether discovery of external trappings of satanism (e.g., symbols, charcoal fire remains, and ritual paraphernalia) represents adolescent experimentation or serious criminal activity is not an easy task. Many dramatic media reports of satanic symbols and cult activity have turned out on subsequent investigation to be relatively harmless and haphazard adolescent fooling around. Some incidents known to the police and the media, however, clearly have substance and some murders (whether sacrificial or occasioned by more common motives remains unclear) have been traced to satanic cults.

Law enforcement efforts to deal with reports of satanic cult activities have necessarily been circumspect. Because of the emotions that may be aroused, police want to avoid false alarms. Furthermore, satanism and witchcraft are constitutionally protected religions and there is nothing illegal about being a practicing satanist or witch, so long as criminal conduct is not involved.

Those who study delinquency, gangs, drugs, and cults are unable to reach consensus about the causes or appropriate control. It is small wonder that the police officer on the street is often confused, ambivalent, and frustrated about

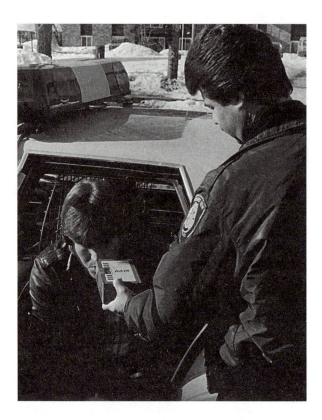

how to deal with these phenomena. Nor is it surprising that the exercise of discretion on the part of the officer is especially noticeable in encounters with juveniles.

Police-Juvenile Encounters—Discretion in Action

What actually happens when a police officer encounters a juvenile suspected of a crime? The simplest answer to that question is that the officer selects from several available alternative responses the action that seems best in the circumstances. In short, the officer exercises discretionary judgment. How does the officer decide whether or not to make an arrest? To answer this question it is necessary to examine several general aspects of police juvenile encounters and their results, and then to discuss certain variables which apparently influence an officer's discretionary decisions.

Although there is some variation from one jurisdiction to another, almost all practitioners and theorists agree that, while juveniles sometimes commit very serious offenses, the great majority of police contacts with juveniles involve relatively minor infractions of the law. Cox and Conrad concluded that the first half of the decade of the 1980s saw an actual decline in the involvement of juveniles in serious and violent crimes.[27] However, evidence indicates that as the 1980s came to a close and we entered the 1990s, violent crime by youth was becoming an increasingly serious problem.[28] Still, status offenses, (i.e., offenses which only a juvenile can commit such as curfew violations, truancy, or being a runaway) and other offenses such as disorderly conduct and petty theft predominate. Almost all observers also agree that the majority of police-juvenile contacts result in some action short of arrest; that is, officers choose an action which avoids introducing the juvenile into the formal juvenile justice system.

Among explanations which have been offered for this pattern of police behavior are:

1. the officer's belief that the outcome of a formal juvenile proceeding will be either too severe or too lenient a punishment
2. the officer's doubts about the efficacy and competency of the other actors in the juvenile justice system
3. the officer's reluctance to run the risk of having juvenile courts set the young person free, thereby seriously diminishing the juvenile's respect for the police and the law, while undermining an officer's position in future encounters with the juvenile
4. the officer's belief that through ''curbside justice'' (e.g., stern, on-the-spot reprimands), stationhouse adjustments (which involve the playing out of a drama in the police station designed to persuade the juvenile of the seriousness of his or her offense), embarrassing and frightening the juvenile, careful surveillance, and, in some cases, using tactics amounting to harassment, the officers themselves can do a better job of preventing crime and keeping the juveniles in line than can the formal justice system[29]

Finally, almost all of the available data suggest that the police are generally lenient in dealing with juveniles, often choosing not to make arrests when such action would clearly be justifiable. Estimates (and that is all they can be) range from 50 to 95 percent of all police juvenile contacts involving the police in their law enforcement role result in no formal action whatever by the police. If these estimates are accurate, then on those comparatively rare occasions when the law is invoked, what influences the officer to take official action?

There are several aspects or variables, involving not only the juvenile but also the officer and the situation in which the contact takes place, that have been shown to influence the officer's decision to invoke the formal justice process. Among the more important of these variables are: the presence and expressed desires of complainants; the officer's assessment of the ''character'' of the juvenile (influenced significantly by the juvenile's demeanor and dress during the encounter); the seriousness of the offense; the presence of physical evidence; and departmental policy.

There is considerable evidence to demonstrate that the police are strongly influenced by the wishes of citizens who have requested police assistance in dealing with juveniles. Black and Reiss and Roberts[30] note that in those circumstances where a complainant was present at some time during the contact between the juvenile and the officer, and when the complainant expressly indicated a preference for arrest, arrest was more likely to follow than in comparable situations where a complainant was not present. The research of Lundman, Sykes, and Clark[31] in large urban settings substantially confirms the findings of Black and Reiss. Both studies also indicate that when complainants urged against arrest, the police were likely to follow that course as well, even in cases where relatively serious offenses had been committed. Hence, the desires of a complainant who is present during the police-juvenile encounter manifestly affect the officer's decision about what to do with the juvenile.

Another variable which influences the officer's decision is his or her assessment of the juvenile's character, especially the young person's demeanor during the encounter—that is, how the juvenile behaves, and specifically the attitude which the juvenile displays toward the law, the officer, the offense, and the victim. Juveniles who are reasonably polite, respectful, cooperative, honest about their involvement, remorseful, and willing to offer something in the way of restitution are much less likely to be arrested than those who are belligerent, disrespectful, dishonest, and without remorse. It is interesting to note, however, that the juvenile's deferential and cooperative demeanor can be carried too far. For example, a juvenile who is, in the officer's judgment, too polite and too deferential, sometimes arouses the officer's suspicions to the point where formal action may be taken just because the officer is suspicious of being "conned." It is worth noting, too, that a "mouthy," disrespectful juvenile is not always arrested. Still, the evidence suggests that in some contexts, in the absence of a complainant seeking arrest, the juvenile's demeanor does substantially influence arrest decisions.[32]

The seriousness of the offense also influences the officer's decision to invoke the law, although it is apparently not as important as one might infer. Several studies have indicated that more serious offenses are more likely to lead to arrest; but the correlation between seriousness of the crime and the likelihood of arrest is not strong. Other variables, such as the desires of the complainant, the officer's confidence in the juvenile justice system and the particular circumstances surrounding the action, often outweigh the seriousness of the offense itself in determining whether or not an arrest will be made.

The presence or absence of physical evidence bearing upon an alleged offense also influences the officer's decision. Not surprisingly, where physical evidence exists, arrest is more likely. This may simply reflect the officer's judgment about the strength of the case against a juvenile. It may also be attributable to the visibility of the offense to others or, in some cases, to the fact that property damage has occurred and some form of restitution is possible. Whatever these conditions, juveniles encountered by the police in the presence of physical evidence of an offense are more likely to be arrested.

Finally, departmental policy influences the officer's decisions. In some cases, departmental policy tends to encourage formal processing, while in others such processing is discouraged.

Still another potentially influential factor in the exercise of police discretion is the presence of prejudice or racism on the part of the officer. Thus, several researchers have noted that black and other minority youth are more often arrested than white youth, and have suggested that this differential in arrest rates is attributable to racism.[33]

It is undeniable that racism has existed and continues to exist in American society. That some police officers, like some persons in every other occupation, are racists is also indisputable. Because police officers have considerable power in this society, racism in police work is especially insidious; accordingly, police officers and other citizens alike must be especially careful to minimize the influence of racism in the law enforcement context. Still, the data which have led some to identify prejudice and racism as primary factors in differential arrest rates may be construed in other ways. Such interpretations do not so much deny the influence of racism as explain that when racism is a factor, it often operates in a rather complex context. Black and Reiss as well as Lundman, Sykes, and Clark have found, for example, that although black young people were more likely to be arrested than white juveniles, it was also true that black complainants were more likely than white to insist on arrest of black juveniles, and the police were more likely to conform to the wishes of a black than a white complainant. Hence, the differential in arrest rates between black and white juveniles may be at least partly accounted for by the greater likelihood that more of the other factors tending to influence an officer's decision in the direction of arrest (such as the presence of a complainant who asks for arrest of the juvenile) are present in police encounters with blacks than in their encounters with whites. Another question implied in these findings is whether or not blacks are more likely to initiate contact with and request the intervention of the police than are whites. We are not aware of any convincing answer to this question, but it is worth investigating, since it has many implications for this whole issue of racism in law enforcement.

The police officer apparently weighs many factors in deciding whether to bring a juvenile suspect into the formal justice system, to divert the juvenile to an established diversion program where one is available, or to deal with the situation personally and informally. The assessment the officer makes and the decision reached are among the most visible forms of police discretion in action.

It should be evident from the preceding discussion that juvenile encounters present special problems for the police. Police who most frequently participate in these encounters (juvenile officers) require special training and an affinity for working with youth. Patience and understanding, as well as familiarity with juvenile codes are essential prerequisites for such work. Unfortunately, there has been a tendency to regard juvenile officers as "kiddie cops" and to overlook them at promotion time. The amount of training received by those officers who work with juveniles is, of course, subject to variation as training budgets fluctuate; and there is often a tendency to regard juvenile bureaus as more or less expendable when funds become tight. Finally, it is a rare department which attempts to provide more than superficial training to patrol officers for working with juveniles, even though these officers are usually the first representatives of the police department to encounter youth. Impressions left on both officers and adolescents during these initial encounters often determine the nature of future encounters.

Some elements of community policing hold promise for improving police relations with youth. Insofar as it emphasizes officers and civilians getting to know each other personally and creating avenues for citizens to express grievances about police conduct and vice versa, there is at least a possibility that some change in the human and public relations involving youth may change for the better. As we noted above, for example, youth—especially minority youth—often complain that police unjustly harass them when they are not engaged in illegal activity. Community policing would suggest creating lines of communication between the police and citizens—including youth—for airing grievances, exchanging interpretations of events occurring in the neighborhood, and soliciting suggestions about police procedures and activities. Not all difficulties in police-youth relations derive from misunderstandings, of course; the obligations and priorities of the two groups may be quite different. But some of these tensions are reducible through better communication and changes in the approach taken by police in many of their encounters with youth.

Summary

Police encounters with juveniles constitute a significant portion of police interactions with other citizens. Some of these encounters are part of a police department's efforts to demonstrate concern for and a willingness to work with youth. The ultimate aims of such programs are to build trust and respect for the law and the police officer in the community, and, by this means, to prevent crime and improve police community relations.

The role of youth in American society as a whole and the nature of adolescence as a biological, psychological, and social phenomenon add a special character to relationships between a community's police and its juvenile citizens. Most of these encounters are civil (i.e., characterized by a reasonable amount of mutual respect), even when the police officer is playing a law enforcement role. On occasion, however, the adolescent's struggle with authority and freedom as well as the youth's attempt to explore and master his or her physical, emotional, intellectual, and interpersonal capabilities which are maturing, combine to produce difficult situations. Drug abuse and the delinquent acts of individuals as well as youth involvement with gangs and cults diminish the quality of community life and present a significant challenge to the police. Unfortunately, there are no readily available, effective solutions to these problems.

The exercise of police discretion in the case of police-juvenile encounters often results in the officer's decision not to prefer formal charges, a decision which may reflect the ambivalence and uncertainty characteristic of many adults' dealings with teenagers. Here, as in other situations, factors like the demeanor and dress of the juvenile suspect, the expressed preferences of the complainant for dealing with the juvenile, departmental policy concerning the handling of juvenile offenders, and other aspects of the situation in which the encounter takes place clearly influence police officers' decisions.

Juveniles are important in the life of any community because they represent its future. An investment by the police department in building positive relations with the community's youth may well pay handsome dividends in the future. Even if we regard that prospect as an uncertainty, however, there is immediate justification for directing special attention to relationships with juveniles. A substantial portion of the police department resources, for example, are expended for juveniles, whether in planned community relations (e.g., "Officer Friendly" or DARE) programs or through law enforcement activities. Furthermore, juveniles are capable of committing and, not infrequently, do commit very serious crimes. Hence, it would seem wise to make efforts to improve police juvenile relations as a part of the crime prevention and community relations program, not only for future returns but because of what is happening now.

Discussion Questions

1. Should the police and the courts treat juvenile offenders differently from adult offenders? If so, how?
2. What factors influence an officer's decision to arrest a juvenile?
3. What is the reputation of the juvenile court and the social service agencies serving young offenders in your community? In what way, if any, does this reputation influence the way officers behave toward juveniles?
4. How do the roles of the adolescent and of the police officer conflict with each other? How do they complement each other?
5. What should the role of the police and law enforcement be in coping with the drug problem?
6. Should drugs be legalized? Why or why not?
7. What is the best strategy for dealing with gangs?
8. Why are cults (especially satanic cults) so frightening to the public and to law enforcement personnel? What is the appropriate role of the police in dealing with such groups?

Endnotes

1. Bouma. *Kids and Cops.* Albert R. Roberts. 1989. *Juvenile Justice: Policies, Programs, and Services.* Chicago: Dorsey Press: 95–98; Thomas J. Bernard. 1992. *The Cycle of Juvenile Justice.* New York: Oxford University Press: 171.
2. Irving Piliavin and Scott Briar. 1964. "Police Encounters with Juveniles." *American Journal of Sociology* 72(2): 206–214; A. J. Meehan. 1992. "I Don't Prevent Crime, I Prevent Calls: Policing as a Negotiated Order." Symbolic Interaction 15 (4): 361–368. Roberts. *Juvenile Justice.*
3. Ibid.
4. *Report to the Nation on Crime and Justice.* 2ed. 1988. U.S. Department of Justice. Washington D.C. : U.S. Government Printing Office; Deborah Nelson. 1992. "Juvenile Injustice: Cases Overwhelm Cook County's Courts." *Chicago Sun-Times* (March 22): 1.

5. Ibid.; Kevin Johnson. 1992. "For Kids, Nowhere to Hide: Gunfire Part of Life in Chicago Projects." *USA Today* (October 15): 3A.

6. See Jean Piaget. 1968. *Six Psychological Studies*. New York: Vintage Books: Part I; and Barbara Inhelder and Jean Piaget. 1958. *The Growth in Logical Thinking from Childhood to Adolescence*. New York: Basic Books.

7. Larry J. Siegal and Joseph J. Senna. 1991. *Juvenile Delinquency: Theory, Practice and Law*. 4th ed. St. Paul: West: 7–8.

8. For a discussion of the history and current status of the juvenile court network see Steven M. Cox and John J. Conrad. 1991. *Juvenile Justice: A Guide to Practice and Theory*. 3ed. Dubuque, IA: Wm. C. Brown.

9. Ibid.: 37–41.

10. A number of states, including New York, Washington, Minnesota, and Illinois have passed "get tough" laws to deal with the problem of chronic or violent offenders. See, for example, Bernard. *The Cycle of Juvenile Justice*. Sam Vincent Meddis. 1993. "Poll: Treat Juveniles the Same as Adult Offenders." *USA Today* (October 29): 1A.; Jay Livingston. 1992. *Crime and Criminology*. Englewood Cliffs, NJ: Prentice-Hall: 589–590.

11. Cox and Conrad. *Juvenile Justice.*: 172–173.

12. Frederic Thrasher. 1927. *The Gang*. Chicago: University of Chicago Press.

13. For a comprehensive review of the literature on gangs see J. C. Quicker. 1983. *Seven Decades of Gangs: What Has Been Learned, What Has Been Done and What Should Be Done*. Sacramento, CA: California Commission on Crime Control and Violence Prevention. See also James A. Inciardi, Ruth Horowitz, and Anne E. Potter. 1993. *Street Kids, Street Drugs, Street Crime: An Examination of Drug Use and Serious Delinquency in Miami*. Belmont, CA: Wadsworth.

14. Joan Moore. 1988. "Introduction" in John M. Hagedorn. *People and Folks: Gangs, Crime, and the Underclass in a Rustbelt City*. Chicago: Lake View Press: 3–17; Malcolm W. Klien and Cheryl Maxson. 1989. "Street Gang Violence" in Neil Alan Weiner and Marvin E. Wolfgang, eds. *Violent Crime, Violent Criminals*. Newbury Park, CA: Sage: 203–206.

15. Klien and Maxson. "Street Gang Violence." For an example of the new gang research, which is often ethnographic in nature, see Hagedorn. *People and Folks*. 16. Klien and Maxson. "Street Gang Violence.": 212–221. See also Cox and Conrad, *Juvenile Justice.*: ch. 12.

16. Sanyika Shakur. 1993. *Monster*. New York: Penguin Books USA: xi. See also William B. Sanders. 1994. *Gangbangs and Drive-bys*. Hawthorne, New York: Aldine de Gruyter.

17. Shakur. *Monster.*

18. Mark H. Moore and Mark A. R. Kleiman. 1988. "The Police and Drugs." *Perspectives on Policing* 11(September). U.S. Department of Justice and Harvard University. See also Carolyn Rebecca Block and Richard Block. 1993. "Street Gang Crime in Chicago." U.S. Department of Justice: National Institute of Justice Research in Brief: December.

19. Klien and Maxson. "Street Gang Violence."

20. Ibid.

21. Moore. in *People and Folks.*: 4.

22. "Juvenile Gangs: Crime and Drug Trafficking." 1988. Juvenile Justice Bulletin (September) Office of Juvenile Justice and Delinquency Prevention. Washington D.C.: U.S. Government Printing Office; Cheryl Carpenter, Barry Glasner, Bruce D. Johnson, and Julia Loughlin. 1988. *Kids, Drugs, and Crime*. Lexington, MA: Lexington Books.

23. See Paul J. Goldstein. 1989. "Drugs and Violent Crime" in Neil A. Weiner and Marvin E. Wolfgang, eds. *Pathways to Criminal Violence*. Newbury Park, CA: Sage: 16–48.

24. Erich Goode. 1989. *Drugs in American Society*. 3ed. New York: Alfred Knopf.

25. Moore and Kleiman. "The Police and Drugs."

26. Ibid.

27. Cox and Conrad, *Juvenile Justice.*: 216.

28. Jack E. Bynum and William E. Thompson. 1992. *Juvenile Delinquency: A Sociological Approach*. Boston: Allyn and Bacon: 83–84.

29. Siegal and Senna. *Juvenile Delinquency.*: 443–450; Cox and Conrad. *Juvenile Justice.*: 143–148.

30. D. Black and A. J. Reiss, Jr. 1970. ''Police Control of Juveniles.'' *American Sociological Review* 35: 63–77; Roberts. *Juvenile Justice.*: 96–97.

31. Richard J. Lundman, Richard E. Sykes, and John A. Clark. 1976. ''Police Control of Juveniles: A Replication.'' *Journal of Research in Crime and Delinquency* 15: 74–91.

32. Piliavin and Briar. ''Police Encounters.''; Richard J. Lundman. 1993. *Prevention and Control of Juvenile Delinquency.* 2ed. New York: Oxford University Press: 15.

33. See, for example, Piliavin and Briar. ''Police Encounters.''; Richard Quinney. 1977. ''Class, State, and Crime.'' New York: McKay; Kappeler, Sluder, and Alpert. *Forces of Deviance.*: 7; Gaines, Kappeler, and Vaughn. *Policing in America.*: 199.

Suggested Readings

Bassett, Adele. 1993. ''Community Oriented Gang Control.'' *Police Chief* 60: 20–23.

Cox, Steven M. and John J. Conrad. 1991. *Juvenile Justice: A Guide to Practice and Theory.* 3ed. Dubuque, IA: Wm. C. Brown.

Fadley, Jock L. and Virginia N. Hosler. 1979. *Confrontation in Adolescence.* St. Louis: Mosby.

Goode, Erich. 1989. *Drugs in American Society.* New York: Knopf.

Hagedorn, John M. 1988. *People and Folks: Gangs, Crime and the Underclass in a Rustbelt City.* Chicago: Lake View Press.

Klien, Malcolm W. and Cheryl L. Maxson. 1989. ''Street Gang Violence.'' In Weiner, Neil A. and Marvin E. Wolfgang. *Violent Crime, Violent Criminals.* Newbury Park, CA: Sage.

Sanders, William B. 1994. *Gangbangs and Drive-bys: Grounded Culture and Juvenile Gang Violence.* Hawthorne, New York: Aldine de Gruyter.

Shakur, Sanyika. 1993. *Monster: The Autobiography of an L.A. Gang Member.* New York: Penquin Books USA.

Thurman, Quint C., Andrew Giacomazzi, and Phil Bogen. 1993. ''Research Note; Cops, Kids, and Community Policing—an Assessment of a Community Policing Demonstration Project.'' *Crime and Delinquency* 39: 554–564.

Chapter 6

Crowds and the Police

C ivil unrest, in a variety of forms, has been a traditional part of the American scene. Demonstrations, labor protests and strikes, sit-ins, and nonviolent protests typically begin in peaceful fashion but may end in violence. Such unrest severely tests the ability of the police to maintain order while protecting the lives and property of all parties involved. Many of these situations are difficult to predict and, given the right combination of circumstances, may occur anywhere at any time when relatively large numbers of people are present. Yet there are often some warning signs which may be identified by the police in order to help them prepare to deal with possibly violent confrontations and some ways of dealing with crowds which may prevent or help minimize damage resulting from them.

People gather together in small and large assemblies in a variety of settings for many different reasons and with very different consequences. Some of these gatherings have no implications for police community relations, while others create relatively minor problems. A few present truly challenging situations, indeed confrontations where relations between community citizens and the police are severely strained. The purpose of this chapter is to review briefly several types of human gatherings and to explore the implications of these different types of gatherings for police community relations.

Collective Behavior—Patterns, Causes, and Consequences

Sometimes people assemble in large numbers simply because each individual, pursuing a private objective, is drawn to the same location. Such is the case, for example, when large numbers of people crowd a subway platform during rush hour, waiting for transportation home. Although the presence of each individual on the platform is purposeful, the collective presence of all of the individuals in the same place at the same time is not purposeful. Furthermore,

Table 6.1

Distinguishing Characteristics of Crowds

Types of Collectivity	Action Orientation	Stability of Membership	Self-consciousness of Participants as Members of a Group	Emotional Intensity	Duration of Assembly	Difficulty for the Police
Casual Crowd	very low to none	low	very low	very little	short	rarely
Conventionalized Crowd	moderate to high	moderate to very high	high	moderate to high	long	sometimes
Acting Crowds						
a. mobs, riots	very high	moderate to high	very high	very high	short to long	almost always
b. celebrational assemblies	moderate to low	low to moderate	moderate to high	moderate to very high	short to long	sometimes
c. civil disobedience	high	very high	very high	high to very high	long	sometimes
d. demonstrations or protest marches	high	high	very high	moderate to very high	long	somctimes

they rarely become conscious of each other as members of a collectivity. Gatherings of this type, where people continually and without deliberation join and leave the collectivity, where the existence of the gathering is without conscious intent and the members are without collective consciousness, assemblages which are not characterized by emotional expression and that are typically of short duration may be referred to as "casual crowds."[1]

As Table 6.1 indicates, casual crowds present very few problems for the community or the police. Occasionally, casual gatherings near public displays or other events or objects that attract the attention or the curiosity of passersby may create traffic flow problems. When police intervention is undertaken, it is typically polite and brief. Compliance of the public is usually quick and without resentment of the officers' assertions of authority. Finally, neither the members of the casual crowd nor the officers perceive themselves to be at risk in the situation.

A second type of human gathering is called a "conventionalized crowd." The most ubiquitous examples are groups of spectators at sporting events, rock concerts, or public addresses. One difference between the casual and the conventionalized crowd is the tendency of the latter to be a more stable gathering, in the sense that a smaller proportion of the participants come and go during the gathering. The conventionalized crowd also tends to be an assemblage of longer duration than that which characterizes the casual crowd. Typically, the participants in a conventionalized crowd also act together according to conventional social rules governing such audiences. For example, a touchdown will be cheered by a football team's fans, the audience will applaud at the end of a speech, and listeners may tap their feet or sway to and fro to a musical rhythm.

Furthermore, those in conventionalized crowds have a much stronger sense of themselves as a group with a common interest than do those in casual crowds. Finally, the potential for emotional arousal and the actual expression of emotions is likely to be greater in conventionalized than in casual crowds.

Sometimes on-duty police officers are assigned to events likely to attract conventionalized crowds. At other times, off-duty police officers or special security officers are hired. In either case, the duties are essentially the same: to help maintain order by guiding the flow of persons (and sometimes vehicles) into and away from the event; to provide some deterrence to those who might wish to exploit members of the crowd (pickpockets, muggers, etc.); to deal with relatively localized disputes involving small and isolated groups of persons in the crowd; to attempt to prevent members of the audience from taking too active a part in the performance (e.g., trying to keep fans off the playing field during a game, or off the stage and away from stars during concerts); to help protect the personal safety of politicians, rock stars, and others who for one reason or another may be physically vulnerable when they appear before a crowd.

Officers working with conventionalized crowds experience a wide range of situations that may present an equally diverse set of problems. In most cases and in most important respects, however, the problems which officers confront in dealing with conventionalized crowds are not substantially different from those presented by casual crowds or those which they encounter in routine patrol. The public is generally willing to comply with the requests and orders of officers attempting to facilitate human or vehicular traffic. Violent episodes which occur usually remain localized to the immediate disputants. These episodes typically create few problems for the police officers who deal with them.

There is, however, one very important exception. The officers' activities often take place in the sight of a large number of other persons who, if things do not go well, may be drawn into the affair. If extraneous persons become involved, then the entire situation may take a turn for the worse. Generally the police attempt to minimize the visibility and to maximize the civility of arrests or other types of intervention in the presence of conventionalized crowds.

Two other exceptions to the similarities emphasized previously deserve brief mention. First, officers working essentially as personal security officers in the context of a conventionalized crowd may be exposed to considerable physical danger because of their proximity to someone who is a target of some person or group in a conventionalized crowd. The grim reality of that danger to police officers has been vividly illustrated in the events surrounding attempts to assassinate important political figures which often lead to injury or death for those charged with protecting the target.

Second, conventionalized crowds, because their participants have a stronger sense of collective identity than members of casual crowds and their members sometimes act in concert (though usually in conventional ways), have a greater potential for turning from an assemblage of spectators into a group of performers. When audiences become actors, very challenging situations may emerge, both for the officers involved and for police community relations in general.

The Angry Protector

By Roger Simon

He has been a Chicago policeman for 11 years. He has been commended dozens of times and injured a few. It is his job to protect all the citizens all the time. He is not allowed to pick and choose.

These days, those citizens include a small group of Nazis who already have held two rallies and are planning more.

Policemen already have been injured at the rallies, usually by being hit with hurled objects that were intended for the Nazis. Getting injured does not upset the policeman as much as whom he is getting injured for.

"I can't believe that I am putting my butt on the line to protect the Nazis," he said. "It is unbelievable. I am sworn to uphold the law. I have to protect them. But I'd like to bash them, instead. I really would.

"I just don't understand the courts today. Did you know that in Germany it's against the law to be a Nazi? That's right. It's against the law. Yet, we, here, allow it.

"These people advocate the overthrow of the government and we allow it. I tell you. I don't blame the Jewish people who oppose them. Look what they did to that group of people. The same can happen to any group. 'Gas the Jews, kill the niggers.' It can happen to any group.

"You know, I work with some racists on the force. And I say to them, I hope there's reincarnation, that's what I hope. And I hope they come back as a black or a Jew.

"Where are the parents of those kids out there? Where are the parents of those kids who were in Marquette Park beating up on the blacks? If those people are so peace-loving, why didn't they keep their kids at home?

"I'll tell you, blacks are more complacent than you think. They are not as united as the whites. They only unite in crisis. The only time blacks come out in masses is when they are angry. This Nazi stuff on the Southwest Side is doing it.

"We are concerned about peace. I am a law enforcement officer. A peace officer. I love peace more than the world. But the thugs are destroying it. The news media build them up and give them a platform.

"I know you have to cover the news. I know we need press freedom. But you should blank out these Nazis' words."

As a matter of fact, many news organs did blank out the words of Frank Collin and his supporters during their rally last Sunday. The Sun-Times did not quote Collin except in its first edition and the Tribune quoted him, but avoided using his most provocative statements.

But it was the very nature of his words that is creating some confusion over just what the limits of free speech are in America.

The policeman is an educated man. He has a college degree and yet he, like many others, cannot understand why people are allowed to preach hatred, death and murder on the streets.

Contrary to some belief, free speech is not absolute, not even in America. There are limits. One limit, fixed by Supreme Court decision, says that speech advocating violence or law breaking cannot be forbidden unless it is directed to inciting or producing imminent lawless action and is likely to produce such action.

Boiled down, that means speech can be forbidden when:

- It is purposefully directed at causing violence or law breaking.
- It is likely to cause immediate violence or law breaking.

Continued

The third basic type of gathering to be discussed here is the "acting crowd." The principal defining characteristic of an "acting crowd" is its focused, purposeful, and emotion-charged collective behavior. Planned and relatively orderly demonstrations and protests are examples of acting crowds. So too are more or less spontaneous rioting mobs. Before discussing the nature of acting crowds and the challenge they present to police and to the community, a brief discussion of the role of conflict in human communities and the circumstances that seem to contribute to the formation of acting crowds of various types is in order.

- The violence or law breaking will be produced as a direct and imminent result of the speech.

But that leaves a great deal of room, as it was intended to. ACLU lawyer David Goldberger once was asked if Nazis should be allowed to demonstrate in Skokie if they carried signs saying ''Kill a Jew Today.''

Goldberger responded that they should be. In his opinion, and probably in the opinion of the courts, that sign is not likely to cause imminent violence.

But the words at the Nazi rally were even more direct. The New York Times quoted Michael Allen, a St. Louis Nazi leader, as saying to the crowd, which included protesting Jews:

''Do you want us to put you in the ovens? We will. . . .

We say one more time, all you Jews are going to get it.''

According to a Sun-Times reporter on the scene, Frank Collin said:

''Jews deserved what happened in the 1940s just like they're going to deserve it this time. We want the final destruction of world Jewry.''

According to Goldberger, this, too, is protected by the First Amendment. Even though Collin and Allen advocated murder, and advocated murder in a crowd that had been worked up, their words lacked a *specific* call to murder of a *specific* individual.

Had Collin pointed to a specific Jew in the crowd and asked his supporters to murder that man there, and the supporters had immediately done so, then probably Collin would not be protected by the First Amendment and might be held responsible for the crime.

But for all that has been printed about the constitutional issues involved in the Nazi controversy, many are either unable or unwilling to believe that a free country could allow such speech. To many, including the policeman, the Supreme Court has drawn a very fine line and a line that may someday be crossed.

''I can understand those people who throw those bricks and bottles at us,'' the policeman said. ''I really can. When I go out to these rallies it is like a big knot balled up in my stomach.

''When these men get up and say kill a nigger, kill a Jew, let's say there's a riot and people are killed. Are you telling me that's free speech? We've gone way beyond free speech. And if anyone gets hurt, I think we should charge the Nazis with inciting a riot and mob violence.''

''There has got to be a limit. I mean this man is advocating gassing and killing. We have to comprehend that he is advocating murder.

''I have a terrible time understanding the ACLU. I believe in rights. I know we have to protect the unpopular so that all of us can be free. But when they talk about extermination, I just don't know.

''I'll tell you honest. I don't blame the groups for wanting to attack the Nazis physically. I don't blame them. I'm going to stop them, I'm going to uphold the law, but can you blame these people? After what they have been through? I mean they've been put in ovens!

''I believe in free speech, but when speeches advocate violence, is that right? Are we going to allow our parks to become platforms for death and violence.''

The unpleasant answer is that, yes, we are. And we are because the law says we are. And the policeman may not like it, and the rest of us may not like it, but we will live with it. And we will live with it because we choose to live with the law.

And, that, perhaps is one of the things that makes us different from the Nazis.

© Chicago Sun-Times, *1978. Reprinted with permission.*

Community Conflict

As we have noted throughout this book, American society is complex and diverse. Within the boundaries of the nation as a whole and within the limits of many of the nation's cities, there exist groups of citizens with very different cultures, values, norms and behavioral patterns, not to mention differences in wealth and power. In view of this diversity, it is not surprising that open conflicts among groups within our society are frequent. Although it is less obvious, such conflicts may be not only traumatic but also healthy for the body politic.

Open conflict is traumatic because in a heterogeneous society like ours, it is evidence that a piece of the social fabric has been torn, and this seems to threaten the integrity of the whole social cloth. For all of us to some extent, and to a great extent for some, enforcement of the law and preservation of order by the police seems the only bastion against total social disintegration and anarchy. Yet it is essential for all of us—general public and police alike—to recognize that conflict is a universal social phenomenon.

Even in primitive societies, instances of social conflict abound. In both primitive and modern communities there are disputes over territory and possessions; there are struggles for power and contests for prestige; there are lovers' quarrels which usually result in or are caused by kinship group disagreements. And there are always those who cannot seem to lose gracefully or to play by the rules and abide by the social conventions. By their behavior, they threaten the community's sociocultural structure and processes. In fact no human community is so perfectly organized, with such clearly defined and harmoniously integrated social norms and individual personalities, that community life subsists without social conflict. Hence, for any group, including the police, to have as a goal the total elimination of social conflict is to engage in a hopeless pursuit.[2]

In many instances conflict is also a necessary social phenomenon. It is often healthy for a community, in that it contributes to, and in many cases constitutes the primary mechanism of social change. Communities that do not change die. That is not to assert that all changes or all conflicts are beneficial, that they contribute to the community's survival. But conflict, change, and survival seem to be interrelated. Among other effects, conflicts help to define important social issues, provide an opportunity for the community to confront these issues, and provide periodic tests of the relative strength of various groups or ideas within a society.[3] Sometimes, as a result of a conflict, new definitions of values, roles, and social structures emerge, definitions that are better adapted to existing conditions. It is a mistake, therefore, to believe that social conflict is an unmitigated evil. In fact, the evidence indicates that conflict is both necessary and at least potentially beneficial to the growth of a society and its culture.

In the previous paragraphs, we have discussed conflict as a general concept. Obviously, even if one believes that conflict is inevitable and potentially beneficial, it does not follow that one should simply stand by and watch groups tear each other and the community apart. Although individual citizens may stand on the sidelines during the battles, the police are not so privileged. The officers' oath to enforce the laws and to help preserve order in a community, as well as the police department's role in the community's social structure, involve the police in community conflicts. In one role or another, whatever the particular circumstances of conflict, intervention by the police may be as inevitable as social conflict itself. It seems best, therefore, to view the police, not as officials who prevent community conflict, but rather as mediators and managers of such interaction.

Sometimes police find themselves both literally and figuratively between conflicting groups, essentially fulfilling their obligation of preserving the order by "managing" the conflict in a way which prevents it from becoming physically violent. In effect, they are buying time for other forces or processes to resolve or reduce the conflict. When police lines form between American Nazis and members of the Jewish Defense League, or between a group of Ku Klux Klansmen and members of the Southern Christian Leadership Conference, the role of the police as conflict managers becomes obvious.

Although participants from all sides in the conflict may criticize the police role in such situations, they are often quite thankful that the police stand between them and their adversaries. The police presence provides an excuse, as it were, not to be as physically active as the group's rhetoric would imply, resorting to actual open combat. In fact, it is probably correct to state that conflicting groups sometimes count on the police to contain the conflict, despite verbal protestations to the contrary.

Of course, in such situations the police may, in fact, be caught in a cross fire of bricks, bottles, stones, and, occasionally, bullets. Moreover, there is always the possibility that the police barrier between the groups will be breached, resulting in a very dangerous situation for the police as well as the combatants.

Essentially, when police function as barriers between contending groups, the community tends to focus attention, not on the police, but on the groups in conflict. There are few who even recognize, or appreciate, the critical role of the police on these occasions. Yet in a democracy which values freedom of expression and tolerance of diversity, it is in precisely such situations that the police role is vital and deserves the respect of the community. It is necessary to note that this type of police intervention does not prevent or eliminate expression of the conflict. Rather, if the police intervention is successful, the conflict is contained within certain channels and is manageable.

Another role which the police sometimes play in conflict situations is that of the aggressor, actively going after and attempting to capture, subdue, or rout a group engaged in activity believed to be a serious threat to the community, or to some important institution in the community. The police attack on the demonstrators at the 1968 Democratic National Convention in Chicago, the assault on the hideout of remnants of the Symbionese Liberation Army, and the march up the hillside on the campus at Kent State University are examples of this type of police intervention in conflict situations.

When playing the more active and aggressive role, the police become very visible. They are likely to be perceived by almost everyone, participants and observers alike, as taking sides in the conflict. As a consequence, the police are likely to be denounced as oppressors and enemies by some parties to the conflict, but cheered as guardians of "right" and heroes of the community by other parties to the conflict. Because of this more active role, the partisan image of the police (derived from the origins and early history of the American police as employees of the wealthy), and the public's continuing perception of the police as often acting in the interests of the powerful and the wealthy—that is, the "establishment"—find contemporary expression.

Crowds in Action: Protests and Demonstrations

One of the ways in which social conflict may manifest itself is in the formation and behavior of an "acting crowd." A crowd in action is a collectivity—usually a very large collectivity—with the following characteristics: (a) the participants perceive themselves as members of the collectivity; (b) they are in immediate proximity to each other; (c) their attention is focused on a particular object or issue; (d) they are acting collectively (i.e., they are pursuing some goal or purpose as a group); and (e) the emotional tension among the participants as they act is usually quite high. Riots, demonstrations, and protests of various types are familiar examples of acting crowds.

The development of an acting crowd in a particular place at a particular time indicates that certain general social conditions are present in that particular community and that certain events have already occurred there. A brief, selective review of some of these conditions and events which have been identified by researchers will help us understand the complexity of the situations when the police interact with acting crowds.

Before beginning this discussion, however, it should be recalled that because of the nature and spontaneity of acting crowds, it is virtually impossible to make precise, controlled studies, either of the crowds themselves or of the particular conditions which precede their formation. Hence, generalizations about crowds and crowd behavior must be regarded as tentative and subject to numerous exceptions. There are, nevertheless, some observations which appear to be useful in understanding most acting crowds and their social concomitants.

The general societal conditions from which acting crowds emerge have been described by Blumer[4] and by Smelser.[5] The major research projects whose results are relevant to Blumer's "interactionist's" theory and to Smelser's "value added" theory of collective behavior have been reviewed by Perry and Pugh.[6] Following are the more important general social conditions of communities where acting crowds emerge.

First, major social or cultural differences exist within the community—differences in the norms, values, or behavior patterns of various subcultures or subgroups which make up the community. These differences may be traced to variations in the cultural traditions of the community's citizens (e.g., different ethnic subcultures), or to differences in the pace or rate of social changes occurring among different groups in the community (e.g., the emergence of a generation gap), or to differences in the prestige, wealth, or power of the community's subgroups (e.g., when one ethnic group holds virtually all the powerful political and financial positions in the community, while another holds almost none). When all three of these types of difference converge in one subgroup of a community (as they have, for example, in many of our cities where there are relatively large, poor, powerless black or Hispanic ghettos), the perception and sense of difference among those affected is likely to be significantly enhanced.

Such appears to have been the case in Los Angeles with respect to animosities between blacks and Koreans which surfaced in violence after the original Rodney King verdict had been handed down.

The existence of differences does not by itself mean that the community is experiencing conflict. Citizens may perceive the differences which exist as interesting, useful, and healthy. But when there is at least one significant subgroup of the community which perceives the differences which exist as undesirable and which desires, either overtly or covertly, to remove them this is a second general social condition conducive to the emergence of an acting crowd.

Those differences which are most likely to be considered unacceptable are almost always variations or distinctions in wealth and/or power. The subgroups most likely to perceive these differences as unacceptable are those whose members are relatively poor and powerless. Often these conditions are combined with a common ethnic origin. In these instances it is relatively easy for members of the subgroup to interpret their lack of wealth and power as a product of long-standing patterns of social discrimination with its concomitant economic oppression and political repression.

In this context it is useful to recognize that it is not absolute but relative material deprivation that is conducive to the emergence of crowds in action. In other words, it is not so much how little one has in an absolute sense, but how little one has compared with how much one wants to have or how much others possess, that engenders the personal frustration and social tension related to outbreaks of collective behavior.

For example, the results of Project Star show clearly that a "lack of progress in key areas, such as equal pay for comparable work and excessively high unemployment for black youth," plus an increasing "concentration of more black teenagers and young adults aged fifteen to twenty-four in urban slums," cause social strains and inconsistencies which may manifest themselves in criminal activity or other forms of deviant behavior.[7]

It is also significant that periods of rising but as yet unfulfilled expectations of greater wealth and power, of a better standard of living, and of general upward social mobility are likely to be punctuated by the emergence of acting crowds. Although theorists are not very explicit in their explanations, perhaps this tendency is related to the influence of relative as opposed to absolute deprivation which was discussed above. It may not be the anticipated gains themselves but rather the progress being made as compared with those who are perceived as better off that produces special tension during such periods.

The third general social condition which is characteristic of communities where acting crowds form is the existence of interaction and communication networks. Whatever its source, persons experiencing social strain must be in position to interact with each other and to express and communicate their sense of malaise and tension. An active rumor process concerned with current events is also a contributing factor. For example, when persons likely to be exposed to social strain are gathered together in relatively large numbers in urban neighborhoods or on college campuses, communication is clearly facilitated. In such

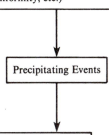

Predisposing Social Conditions:

  a. Social or cultural differences especially in relative wealth or power or rates of social mobility

  b. The definition of the differences as unacceptable or intolerable by at least one segment of the community

  c. Well-established networks of interaction and communication

  d. A social structure conducive to group formation and mobilization (e.g., leadership structure, cultural or ethnic uniformity, etc.)

Precipitating Events

Major Stages in the Life History of the Acting Crowd

  a. Gathering of people

  b. Milling and social contagion

  c. Emergence of leaders

  d. Identification of the target or focus

  e. Attempted action against the target

  f. Dissolution of the crowd

Figure 6.1 The development of acting crowds.

social settings there exists at least an incipient community whose collective attention and hostile action may be focused quite rapidly.

Finally, there must be a structural environment conducive to crowd formation and action. Both very strong and very weak community leadership may contribute to the creation of structural conditions leading to the formation of acting crowds. Strong community leaders have the power to restrain those who are under great social pressure, but they also have the power to deliberately create or foment acting crowds. Weak community leadership results in a reduction of local restraint, with greater tendency to violent collective outbursts once people are aroused. Thus, concentrations of economically or politically disadvantaged persons, with other (e.g., ethnic) similarities, in distinct neighborhoods is another example of a structural condition conducive to the formation of acting crowds.

The four factors discussed here provide the general sociocultural environment in which crowds in action are likely to develop. Whether they actually develop at a particular time in a specific place depends on several other factors more proximate to the emergence of the crowd. Often there is at least one precipitating event—an incident or episode which occurs in a "public" place within view of several people and which attracts and holds the attention of potential crowd members.[8] It may be a fist fight between "one of us" and "one of them,'' a forceful (perhaps unnecessarily forceful) arrest of ''one of our own'' by the police, an assault by an ''establishment'' storekeeper on a customer who is ''one of us,'' or the verdict in a jury trial. Whatever their specific nature, precipitating events attract a number of interested spectators who quickly become partisans and interpret what they see as ''just another example of a larger pattern of malicious and evil deeds perpetrated on us relatively helpless and powerless victims.'' In short, a particular event comes to symbolize a whole series of past grievances and humiliations.

Once the precipitating event has occurred and a crowd begins to assemble, there ensues, according to Blumer, a ''milling'' process characterized by ''social contagion.'' More and more people, attracted by a growing crowd or the sights and sounds of squad cars, sirens, or shouting, converge on the scene. Information (often distorted by rumor) is exchanged, and emotions rise. The level of excitement and emotional agitation of the members mounts quickly, as the emotional fervor of one member creates increased emotional intensity in another, and this, in turn, may reflect on the originator. Actually, emotional and social excitement are contagious. Both emotional and cognitive definitions of the situation are being formed in this process, but more in an emotional than in a cognitive sense.

The next stage in the development of the acting crowd is the emergence of a common ''target,'' objective, or purpose. Sometimes a leader is present or emerges from the crowd, speaks to them, and defines for the others the nature of the evil which has been committed, the larger significance of the evil, as well as who or what is responsible for it. Occasionally there appears to be no recognized leader. The more or less spontaneous hostile behavior of one or more persons in the crowd (e.g., throwing a stone or bottle at a particular target or carrying items out of stores) is quickly imitated by other members of the crowd. Actions may range from lynching or extensive property destruction to mass movement to a particular location, followed by verbal or physical aggression. It is at this stage that the crowd presents the most danger to other members of the community and to police officers attempting to ''control'' the crowd.

The final stage is the dispersal of the crowd. The discharge of the crowd's energy may be gradual or sudden. Having accomplished the purpose defined in the latter stages of the crowd's development through a violent, destructive outburst, for example, the participants may leave the scene rapidly, often in order to avoid detection and arrest. Sometimes, the crowd's agitation is such that a spokesperson may be able to initiate a dialogue (of sorts) with the crowd. In such cases the crowd may remain intact for a relatively long period of time, while its more violent tendencies are deterred and its energies are gradually dissipated. In still other instances, where large numbers of people are involved, the emotional arousal is very high and the behavior of the crowd extends over a relatively large area. This makes it virtually impossible for police officers to restrain the crowd, which may remain violent and destructive for many hours. Frequently, riots accompanied by looting in urban ethnic ghettos conform to this pattern, especially when the difficulties either begin during, or extend into, the night, a time when behavior is more difficult to observe and participants can more easily maintain anonymity.

Dealing with Crowds in Action

Acting crowds present both challenges and opportunities for police in their relationships with the community. Since this is not a training manual, we will not attempt to comment on the full range of specific strategies and tactics which may be used by law enforcement agencies in attempting to deal with acting crowds. But general observations will be made about different types of acting crowds, and comments will be offered about the police community relations involved in some of the tactics which have been used in dealing with crowds in action.

Perhaps the most difficult and dangerous acting crowd is the "mob." A mob consists of a large and densely packed group of individuals who have temporarily submerged their own identities in the crowd, who are responding almost exclusively to what is happening in their immediate environs, and whose emotions, typically hate and/or anger, are highly aroused. If and when a target emerges, the group becomes a focused mob whose emotional energies converge upon that object. Riots consist of mobs whose collective behavior has turned to violence, destruction, and mayhem.

Once a mob has focused its attention and people have begun to move en masse, it becomes extremely difficult to control. Where it is possible to do so, the construction of physical barriers in carefully chosen locations may help contain the crowd and thus restrict destructive behavior to a particular geographic area. In certain circumstances police lines may also be effective, especially when they are used to shift the direction of a crowd's movement. But once a large mob is on the move, a "thin blue line" in the direct path of approach to the crowd's objective will seldom suffice to halt them. The use of force by the police against an attacking crowd is usually ineffective. In the writers' judgment, coercive physical action involving either nightsticks or guns should only be used as a very last resort, and then only to protect the lives of the police themselves and the others who may be present. The reason for avoiding physical force is simple: it does not usually have any appreciable effect on the crowd except to increase its anger and hostility. Further, it often has a serious detrimental impact on subsequent police community relations.

Perhaps a more effective strategy seeks to confine the crowd to as small an area as possible, until its energies are exhausted. Another possibility is to surprise the crowd and divert its attention, not to the police themselves, of course, but rather to some other object or sensation. Actions which tend to increase the visibility of individual members of the crowd (such as directing bright lights onto a crowd at night) are sometimes effective. Another tactic is to divide the mob into smaller groups, reducing the individual sense of anonymity and immersion in the crowd.

Another type of acting crowd is what might be called a "celebrational assembly." This category would include fan rallies after sports team victories, exuberant assemblies with nonsensical themes such as the New Year's Eve crowds in Times Square, and religiously based events, such as the Mardi Gras of New Orleans. Small, planned celebrations present relatively few difficulties, but large, spontaneous assemblies may be another matter.

One of the authors was present during several ''Pogo for President'' rallies which occurred in Cambridge, Massachusetts, in the early 1960s. Usually these demonstrations were large (four or five hundred) but relatively peaceful gatherings filled with the springtime youthful exuberance of college students (often enhanced by alcohol) and their adolescent town counterparts. On one occasion, however, a group much larger and more vocal than usual assembled near Harvard Square. Through the late afternoon and early evening hours the crowd grew gradually, eventually comprising an estimated 2,000–3,000 young people. They moved into the streets and took over several major intersections, completely shutting off all vehicular traffic. The assembly was not especially emotion-charged, but the people were in high spirits. Occasionally, ''Pogo for President'' slogans were chanted by small groups within the crowd. The general atmosphere was more one of silliness than of hostility; and apparently there was no shared collective purpose, except perhaps ''to have a good time and blow off a little steam.''

However, the crowd presented a very serious problem for the Cambridge police, since major traffic arteries were blocked during rush hour. The general life of the larger community had been disrupted by the sheer numbers of people assembled, as well as the noise and general commotion which accompanied their presence. The first approach of the Cambridge police observed by the author consisted of a few officers in standard duty uniform using bullhorns at different points on the periphery of the crowd, asking the young people to clear the streets in order to permit traffic to resume. While the officers' requests were generally ignored by the crowd, there was no apparent hostility directed toward the officers.

The next approach was the slow movement of a clearly marked police van into the center of the crowd. The crowd made way for the van, again with no apparent hostility. Once the center of the intersection was reached, two officers, in standard duty uniform, emerged and walked toward the rear of the van and opened the rear door. Shortly, from the back of the van there appeared two German shepherd police dogs, unmuzzled but on leash.

It is difficult to describe exactly what happened next, but there was a remarkably quick and almost palpable change in the feeling of the crowd—an illustration of the emotional contagion phenomenon discussed earlier. Suddenly things became very tense and hostile. To the credit of the officers, who must have sensed this change, they quickly returned the dogs to the van, and slowly drove it out of the crowd, to the cheers of the assemblage.

The successful dispersion of the crowd was finally accomplished with fire hoses. Two fire trucks pulled up on the periphery of the crowd opposite the direction the police wished to move them. The hoses were turned on and pointed at an angle into the air, presumably so that no one would receive the full blast of water and be knocked down or injured. The assembled people cheered in exuberance as the cold sensation captured their attention. In a short time, the crowd dispersed, in a good mood, thoroughly soaked and somewhat exhausted.

This example illustrates several general points. First, in some cases assemblies of people celebrating may not be very receptive to attempts by the police to interrupt their "fun." The choice of strategies and tactics in such circumstances is extremely important. The wrong tactic (in this case the use of police dogs) can turn an annoying but relatively harmless crowd into a hostile, dangerous mob. Tactics which do not attempt to confront or coerce the crowd but which divert the attention of the participants and arouse new and different sensations (such as a good dousing with cold water) often succeed in breaking the crowd's spirit as a mob and direct individuals to something else, as, for example, getting dry and warm.

Thus far, our comments have assumed that the police are, as it were, "third parties" to the ongoing events. Sometimes, unfortunately, the police themselves may become the target of an angry crowd, either as a result of some specific action attributed to them or because the police are the most visible symbols of the dominant group in the community. These are very difficult and often dangerous occasions for the police. They also may have far-reaching implications for the police community relations.

The most effective strategy for dealing with these situations is to minimize their frequency by means of preventive measures. Among the most important preventive techniques is the establishment of reliable communication networks between the police and those segments of the community most likely to be suspicious of the police. These channels can be used to discourage the spread of false rumors, and to air community grievances about police conduct and police grievances about citizen conduct. They may be used to clarify the ground rules for planned protests and demonstrations. They may also serve to inform the community when action has been taken in response to complaints that were found to be justified. Furthermore, the very existence of communication channels may help create and define moderate leadership in those communities. Other useful techniques which help to prevent police from becoming objects of hostility include police discretion in dealing with community citizens, civility in police encounters with other citizens, and the issuance of permits for large assembles based on planning involving the police and those seeking to assemble.

If preventive measures fail and the police become objects of a crowd's verbal and physical hostility, it is desirable to give a professional, controlled response. Usually this will pay substantial dividends, not only at the time, but also in the future, by fostering constructive police community relations. Courage and self-discipline in refusing to respond in kind to verbal abuse, and the appropriate choice between discretion and valor, are much more likely to make the next encounter easier to deal with than is uncontrolled and indiscriminate use of force. It should be emphasized, however, that all of this is much easier said than done. There are no simple rules of conduct which are applicable to all situations where the police themselves are under attack. It should also be noted that the need to make an arrest in a crowd situation focuses attention on the police; if the arrest is not properly carried out, this may turn a relatively harmless crowd into an acting mob determined to vent their anger on the police. In general, it is preferable that the police should make such an arrest after the crowd has dispersed. This is particularly true if the offender is known and can be followed or easily located later. But if an immediate arrest is necessary to protect other citizens, or the police themselves, this should be done as swiftly and inconspicuously as possible. Once the arrest has been made, both the arrested party and the arresting officers who have this person in their custody should leave the crowd scene quickly and quietly. Use of these tactics seldom allows crowd members sufficient time to direct the attention of the crowd to the parties involved in the arrest.

Another type of acting crowd which presents difficulties for police involves collective acts of civil disobedience. Sit-ins, stand-ins, and sleep-ins, combined with passive resistance, place the police in a difficult position. Typically, laws are being violated and demands are being made by other community citizens that the law be enforced. The behavior (or perhaps more appropriately the presence) of the crowd attracts attention. Attempts to remove protesting citizens arouse even more attention, putting the police and their conduct squarely in the spotlight, and perhaps on the TV evening news. Unless the intervention of the police is carefully planned and executed, this may inflict great damage by eroding community respect for the police. Pictures of a policeman punching, clubbing, or pinning down a passive resistor may serve only to increase other people's sympathy for the passive resistor and his or her cause, and may decrease public respect for their community's police. Again, use of minimum force and maximum civility in dealing with the resistors appears to be the best way to enforce the law while projecting a relatively positive image of the police.

The last type of acting crowd to be considered here is the "active protest" or demonstration, for example, a citizens' march for equal rights in housing, a picket line of striking union member employees in front of a plant. America has a long history of active protests and demonstrations. Citizens have a right to express their views collectively and to urge remedial action in a public way, provided that in doing so they abide by rules which the Constitution and the community establish for such activities. So long as active protests and demonstrations are planned with the cooperation of civil authorities and adequate resources are available to the police department, few problems are likely to occur and police and police community relations are not likely to be affected.

If protesters and demonstrators abide by the established rules, the role of the police in these circumstances is limited to protecting the freedom of expression of the protesting groups. Sometimes police are stationed at key spots along the route of a protest march in order to discourage inadvertent or deliberate interference with marchers. A motorized escort may be provided for the front ranks of a marching group, while officers on foot and motorcycles may move along with the marchers, providing a physical boundary between them and spectators.

Although public protests and demonstrations seldom present serious difficulties for the police, or for the maintenance of satisfactory police community relations, such activities are designed to focus the community's attention, usually on some controversial issue. As a result it is not uncommon for the demonstration to attract some spectators who take a position opposite to that espoused by the demonstrators. When this occurs, difficulties may arise, especially if those opposed to the marchers show up in significant numbers and engage in collective vocal opposition to the marchers.

As has been noted previously in this chapter, in such situations the police are sometimes called upon to maintain a line of demarcation and to contain or limit conflict (both physical and verbal) between the contending groups. This is not an easy role for the police. It exposes them to the verbal abuse from both sides and occasionally to physical danger as well. But in our society it is very important that the police play such a role, preserving constitutional freedoms and protecting contending groups.

Spontaneous, unapproved, and unplanned (at least insofar as the police were not involved in the planning) marches and demonstrations may present even more difficulties. They are often technically illegal; and the mobilization of appropriate police resources in sufficient time to control the situation effectively is in some circumstances virtually impossible. It seems reasonable to assume, also, that unplanned police intervention in response to spontaneous demonstrations is likely to be inappropriate. Careful handling of spontaneous demonstrations may prevent the formation of a larger, more hostile and destructive mob.

A discussion of crowds and the police would not be complete without some reference to social movements. Like certain types of acting crowds, social movements are usually advocating social changes. A social movement is different from an acting crowd, however, primarily in that a crowd of any type seldom persists for more than a few hours, but a social movement often extends over several years or more. A social movement also has a much more elaborate ideology and typically is represented in many different communities at the same time, with adherents of the movement conscious of their participation in a broadly based social phenomenon. A crowd in a particular community may be perceived by others, and its participants may perceive themselves, as part of a much larger effort to change society. This connection with a larger sociocultural phenomenon often provides special impetus to a particular crowd in a particular community and lends greater significance to its actions.

A significant characteristic of social movements for police community relations in most cities and towns is that the core leaders of the movement may be citizens of other communities. Thus, activities which take place in a particular community are often initiated and sometimes planned by persons outside the community. Frequently circumstance complicates the establishment and maintenance of communication channels which are so essential to preventing a deterioration in the relations between the community and its police.

It should be noted, too, that the police themselves are often in a position to make or influence the decision as to whether or not a crowd will be allowed

A Welcome 'Challenge' in L.A.

Police Get a Determined New Leader

By Sally Ann Stewart

USA TODAY

LOS ANGELES—After 16 months of beatings, riots and tensions, southern California may not be prepared for Willie Williams.

But after love-him or hate-him Daryl Gates, there's no way things will be the same.

Williams, who replaced Gates Friday as this battered city's new police chief, already sounds different.

"We've got to stop being afraid of each other. We have to begin to reach out and hold hands and talk to each other and support each other," said Williams in an interview. "Say hello to each other, and we'll all have a better day."

It's clear the former Philadelphia police commissioner plans to spend as much time healing as he does fixing, and it's a role that comes naturally.

But words, even kind words, are unlikely to be enough as Williams grapples with what may be this city's and police force's biggest fix-it job.

"It's going to be tough," says the American Civil Liberties Union's Ramona Ripston. "The city wanted anybody but Gates, so everyone has hailed Willie Williams, almost making him a savior and it's not going to be that easy."

Even cops says it won't be a snap. "Not everything is going to be different when we wake up the day after Willie Williams comes in," says police spokesman Lt. John Dunkin.

The department has fewer than 8,000 officers now, because of budget cuts and officers driven to early retirement by the tension. Moreover, the city's budget deficit makes it virtually certain Williams will have even fewer officers to do the job.

And he faces a department that has been unswervingly loyal to Gates.

"There's tremendous pride in the LAPD . . . and that pride has been bruised badly," says Dallas Police Chief William Rathburn, who served with the department for 27 years.

"I think an outsider coming in is going to hurt that pride even more. Chief Williams, first of all, has got to develop 'followership' in the LAPD. You can't lead if you don't have followers."

Williams faced similar problems as part of the team that revamped the embattled Philadelphia Police Department in the 1980s.

"I'm looking forward to the challenge to take a police department whose morale is below rock bottom," he said.

"If I do a good job and show loyalty to the men and women of the LAPD, they'll show loyalty to the chief's office and then to Willie Williams as an individual," he added.

And Williams says he thinks "history long-term will be a lot kinder on Daryl Gates when you put the (past) 16 months in relationship to his 14 years."

Williams, who can serve no more than two five-year terms, plans to move quickly, first by meeting with command officers and uniformed police "just one-on-one."

"You have to empower people . . . below the level of chief and deputy chiefs to make decisions," Williams says. "And if they make mistakes along the way, as long as they're not major and critically intentional, you allow those mistakes to be made and you view those as growing points."

Police aren't the only ones he plans to empower. "You look at community policing the same way the private sector looks at doing business," he says. "We've got to be customer-oriented."

One hurdle that may not be so hard to jump: making the personal adjustment from Philadelphia to Los Angeles. His family has settled into a 2,000-square-foot condo in Hancock Park, an ethnically-mixed neighborhood where many of this city's power brokers live.

And if Angelenos don't like what he's doing, Williams wants to hear about it.

"None of us is without a boss," Williams says. "I have a boss, which is the Police Commission and also the citizens of this city here.

"If I'm not doing my job then let those folks who hire and fire me, let them know."

to form, and they may recommend the rules within which the crowd may legitimately operate. Often parade and demonstration permits are required for these events; and the police, by working closely with political officials who decide whether or not to issue such a permit, can sometimes help to avoid situations which may become explosive.

As was suggested earlier, the media play a very important role in shaping the public's attitudes and images of the police and of relations between the police and the community. One context in which the media are especially significant is their treatment of encounters between the police and acting crowds. Heavy media coverage can help transform a neighborhood disturbance or protest into a citywide or national phenomenon and, in the process this escalates a local issue into a national crisis. Decisions by media executives not to cover or to discontinue coverage of a demonstration severely restrict the extent to which others may become aware of or involved in the event. For most people not directly involved in the event, the public's images and impressions of the participants in an acting crowd, of the issues involved, and the police ''working'' the crowd are shaped by the media. Because press, radio, and television to some degree select the events, the people, and the issues to be covered, and since these are the principal sources of information about what is happening in the community or in the nation as a whole, the media are recognized as very powerful forces. As we have noted previously, they clearly affect and sometimes determine police community relations.

It may be useful to distinguish between two different functions of the media in their coverage of community conflicts. On the one hand, when covering crowds in action the media have a responsibility to the community they serve: to observe with as much objectivity and to report with as much neutrality as possible. In order to fulfill this responsibility, the media actively seek to discover what is going on in the community and why, then to inform their readers, viewers, and listeners about their observations. In this aspect of their role, when covering community disputes and acting crowds, the media may provide background information, including the opportunity for those involved to explain their positions, air their views, and account for their behavior. It is essential that the police be aware of this aspect of the media's role. When appropriate, a department spokesperson should be available to furnish information about the role, obligations, and conduct of the police in the situations being discussed.

On the other hand, groups involved in a community dispute, being fully aware of the power of the media to shape public opinion, may view such observers and reporters as forces to be manipulated to their own ends. In this phase, the media become the object of other people's actions. In certain cases groups deliberately stage events in order to attract the attention of the press or television cameramen. In some of these instances, calculated attempts are made to provoke extreme, inappropriate responses from the police so as to undermine their reputation and authority. In this way, groups may seek to engage the sympathy of media audiences for themselves and for the cause they espouse. When the police are deceived by such provocations and respond by using excessive force, these reactions may very seriously impair police community relations. In addition, there is the physical harm inflicted on those who are objects of such treatment. Pictures of uniformed officers wielding nightsticks on crouched or prone civilians are vivid in the memories of many American citizens. It is precisely when the temptation for the police officer to retaliate in a very personal, violent way is greatest that it is essential to respond with minimum necessary force. This is characteristic of a well-trained and disciplined professional police officer.

The police should regard difficult situations as valuable opportunities to demonstrate their ability to "keep their cool," to function well under stressful conditions. They should take advantage of opportunities provided, in order to display the professional care and skill with which they discharge their obligations. Thus they can keep the public informed about police behavior during such events.

In the final analysis, in spite of accusations of bias in coverage and their potential for abusing the public's trust, the presence of the media in the various arenas of community conflict appears to be in the best interests of both the police and the public. Besides functioning as reporters of community events, the fact that media observers are present, that they have the ability to communicate their observations quickly to many others, in most circumstances tends to discourage extreme behavior in all parties to a conflict. Furthermore, in a democracy, exposure to public scrutiny is a salutary experience for all powerful forces, including the police.

Summary

Crowds are a universal human phenomenon; so also are conflicts within human communities. Sometimes, social conflicts are expressed through collective behavior in the form of crowd action. Crowds resorting to violence are most likely to emerge in communities where social stress exists, where communications networks have been established, where people perceive themselves as disadvantaged compared with others in the community, and where the social structure is conducive to crowd formation.

Although social conflict may be injurious to a society, it is also quite necessary. Actually, such conflict is one of the primary mechanisms by which diverse and rapidly changing societies like ours survive. These confrontations sometimes become difficult challenges to the police and to police community relations. Recognition of the importance of police actions which may precipitate events leading to the formation of hostile acting crowds is the first step in examining the implications of police actions for crowd behavior. Maximizing civility and minimizing force are the two strategies most likely to limit negative implications of police intervention in crowds for police community relations.

Different types of acting crowds present diverse challenges to the police. Rioting mobs are the most difficult to control; well-planned and organized active protests and demonstrations usually present few situations requiring police intervention. Civil disobedience, especially when accompanied by passive resistance to police intervention, places police behavior in the spotlight; police conduct—especially the human relations demonstrated in these situations—may have a very dramatic positive or negative impact on police public relations.

The role of the police as conflict managers is vital in American society. It is important to all of us that they play this role effectively. In order to do this, the social service function of the police should be allocated as much resources as the law enforcement function; communication links between the police and all types of persons and groups must be established, and police riot control, when necessary, must be highly disciplined. When the police are successful, the conflict is either contained, minimizing personal injury to citizens and the police and perhaps preventing unnecessary, irreparable damage to the society, or the attention and action are channeled into other areas where the conflict may be resolved.

Discussion Questions

1. How is social conflict related to social change?
2. What is the difference between viewing the police as conflict managers and perceiving them as conflict suppressors?
3. Identify some occurrences which might transform a conventional crowd into a mob.
4. What are some of the important differences between a rioting mob and a planned demonstration? What are some implications of those differences for police community relations?
5. What new or distinctive implications for police community relations exist when an episode of collective behavior (e.g., a mass demonstration) is a part of a social movement rather than an action limited to the local community?

Endnotes

1. The discussion of crowds in this section is based on a typology developed by Herbert Blumer. See, Herbert Blumer. 1975. ''Outline of Collective Behavior'' in Robert Evans, ed. *Readings in Collective Behavior*. Chicago: Rand McNally: 22–45.
2. Nigel Fielding. 1991. *The Police and Social Conflict: Rhetoric and Reality*. Atlantic Highlands, NJ: Athlone Press.
3. For an interesting discussion of the role of conflict in human societies see Lewis Coser. 1956. *The Functions of Social Conflict*. New York: Free Press.
4. Blumer. ''Outline of Collective Behavior.''
5. Neal Smelser. 1951. *Theory of Collective Behavior*. New York: The Free Press.
6. Joseph B. Perry, Jr. and M. D. Pugh. 1978. *Collective Behavior: Response to Social Stress*. St. Paul: West Publishing Co.
7. See Project Star. 1976. *The Impact of Social Trends on Crime and Criminal Justice*. Cincinnati: Anderson/Davis: 333; and Clark McPhail. 1973. ''Civil Disorder Participation: A Critical Examination of Recent Research.'' *American Sociological Review*. 38: 721–735.

8. The data concerning 24 riots gathered by the National Advisory Commission on Civil Disorders (Washington, D.C.: U.S. Government Printing Office, 1968), indicate that in each case there were at least 3 precipitating events and that 40 percent of those were police actions.

Suggested Readings

Coser, Lewis. 1956. *The Functions of Social Conflict.* New York: Free Press.

Cox, Steven M. 1989. ''Crowd/Riot Control'' in Bailey, William G., ed. *The Encyclopedia of Police Science.* New York: Garland Publishing: 121–125.

Fielding, Nigel. 1991. *The Police and Social Conflict: Rhetoric and Reality.* Atlantic Highlands, NJ: Athlone Press.

Kornhauser, William. 1959. *Politics of Mass Society.* New York: Free Press.

National Commission on the Causes and Prevention of Violence. 1969. *Rights in Conflict.* Washington, D.C.: U.S. Government Printing Office.

Perry, Joseph B. and M. D. Pugh. 1978. *Collective Behavior: Response to Social Stress.* St. Paul: West.

Police Foundation. 1994. *Civil Disorder: What Do We Know? How Should We Prepare?* Washington, D.C.

U.S. Community Relations Service. 1993. *Principles of Good Policing: Avoiding Conflict Between Police and Citizens.* Washington, D.C.: U.S. Government Printing Office.

Community Policing and Police Community Relations

W e have mentioned on several occasions in earlier chapters the significance, or potential significance, of community policing as we approach the end of the twentieth century. In this chapter we will discuss community policing and its relationship to problem-oriented policing. We will also discuss the differences between community policing and police community relations and the relationship between community policing and policing in rural areas.

Community Policing

Community policing is a philosophy which proposes to alter the relationship between the police and other citizens by addressing community problems and improving the quality of life.[1] While the idea has roots as far back as Sir Robert Peel (1829), the concept was rediscovered, modified, and reintroduced in the 1980s and has become the single most often repeated ''buzzword'' in police circles. Still, defining exactly what the term community policing, or community-oriented policing, means is difficult, since it refers to a variety of initiatives tailored to specific communities. As Bayley noted: ''Although widely, almost universally, said to be important, it means different things to different people— public relations campaigns, shopfronts and mini-stations, rescaled patrol beats, liaison with ethnic groups, permission for rank-and-file to speak to the press, Neighborhood Watch, foot patrols, patrol-detective teams, and door-to-door visits by police officers.''[2]

While all of these initiatives and others are covered under the rubric of community policing, the approach is actually a response to the recognition that traditional policing has failed to live up to the expectations of either the police or other citizens. Brown believes this is so because of two key tenets of traditional policing. First, police officers traditionally respond to calls for service from the public. Although they do occasionally initiate action themselves, they

119

The Case for Community Policing

By Chief Richard Overman

Delray Beach Police Department, Florida

There is a quiet crisis occurring in American policing today, and I believe it can be illustrated in a few words.

What is the role of the police?

Have we as chief administrators helped our people redefine the role of a police officer based on the changes in society, circumstances and expectations?

Have we embraced the idea of change ourselves?

These questions must be asked and answered if we are to exercise good leadership and provide sound guidance for our officers in the future. It is absolutely essential that we both help our people understand how and why their jobs are changing, and emphasize that failure to face the future will spell serious consequences. It is equally essential, however, that this notion of changing the way we do business, setting our priorities and measuring success must be sold to—rather than forced on—our people.

Traditionally, we in law enforcement have set our own priorities, with little regard to community input. Murder, rape, robbery, etc., were always at the top of our list; little attention was paid to nuisance problems such as loud music, loitering, petty theft, traffic, etc.—mainly because these matters get little attention in the judicial arena.

Herein lies the problem: the latter list has more impact on neighborhoods and quality-of-life issues than all the murders, rapes and robberies we will ever investigate. Of course, we cannot ignore these serious felonies; I am suggesting only that people feel the frustration generated by those problems that hit them where they live, work and raise their children. We must begin to listen to the people we serve and prioritize our efforts based on quality-of-life issues. This is where community policing begins.

However, community policing will fail should you make the mistake of mandating it before you can convince the majority of your employees trying a different approach is called for.

The arguments for change are obviously linked to our past. The first question we must ask ourselves is, "Are the streets safer than they were 20 years ago?" The obvious answer to this question is "No."

"Have we won the war on drugs?" Again, the answer is "No."

"If, in fact, we have more professional, better-educated, -paid and -equipped officers who receive the latest in technical training, then why aren't the streets safer?" The answer to this question is more complex, involving economics, demographics, politics and the strains on the criminal justice system, among other factors.

We have traditionally measured our success or failure based on statistics: number of arrests, number of summonses, etc. Based on such statistical criteria, it would be hard to say we have not been successful; indeed, we are probably the most efficient component of the justice system. But perhaps we have been measuring the wrong things. The average citizen really does not care whether you made five or 50 arrests on his corner for crack cocaine sales; what he cares about is whether it is still possible to buy cocaine on the corner. We must go beyond the traditional approaches and begin to judge our effectiveness by the condition of the corner rather than by the number of arrests.

If we are to be successful in taking back our streets, we must also be able to define our responsibilities as a police department. For the past quarter-century, we have been telling citizens that if they would lock their windows, put deadbolts on their doors and install alarm systems, we would take care of them. But while we thought we could take care of them, the truth is that we can't—and I'm not sure we ever could. In Delray Beach, where 50,000 citizens live in a 17-square-mile area, 130 police officers work 24 hours a day, 7 days a week, 365 days a year—and still can't be everything to everybody.

I am convinced that we must mobilize our communities to protect and help themselves. We can no longer allow them to abdicate the responsibility for their own well-being and quality of life. Although we have helped foster this unrealistic expectation for years, we must now offer a more pragmatic standard with which to measure our performance. We should be judged on our responsiveness to their needs and our willingness to facilitate, mobilize and work with them to solve the problems within each neighborhood. The key, of course, is the active input and participation of the citizens. They must take ownership and have a stake in the outcome in order to ensure success.

We must open up the police fraternity for scrutiny and help shed the mystique surrounding law enforcement. It is amazing how perceptions begin to change once people have an opportunity to see the law enforcement operation firsthand.

Of course, tremendous courage is required to embrace change. If ever there were a challenge for a chief today, holding and maintaining a vision for community policing is it. Many police officers are not only not interested in change, but will actively resist what they consider a gimmick in favor of maintaining the status quo. That is why the best strategy for implementing community policing is selling it first.

The Case for Community Policing *(Continued)*

Based on my experiences implementing community policing in the Orlando and Delray Beach police departments, I recommend making a personal study of the problems facing law enforcement until you are convinced of the need for change. If you are not convinced yourself, there is no point in trying to convince others. Study the national, state and local demographics. Examine the political issues, study jail overcrowding and review Supreme Court decisions that limit the power of the police. You must get a handle on the future.

Our troops know the difference between token commitment and the real thing. They must believe you are willing to pursue change no matter what it costs, including your job. Obviously, however, you must balance this with patience; the all-or-nothing approach will not work. Remember, you may have some outstanding officers who will never fully accept this change, and you cannot afford to discount their contributions to the department.

Your commitment can be demonstrated as follows:

- Be prepared to withstand resistance, criticism, flagging morale and lack of support from some of your command staff when you begin to press for the change.

- Communicate your reasons for implementing community policing, and gain the support of your command staff.

- Involve your people in the plan. Ownership in the plan is the key to success, and all must be part of the process in order to achieve this. Of course, you will have to compromise in some of the ''how-to'' areas, but as long as this does not get in the way of the overall objective, it is a small price to pay.

- Start a citizens' police academy in order to (1) signal the community that you intend to open the doors and allow them to see what we really do, (2) demonstrate to the officers who teach in the academy that there are people who care enough to get involved and (3) let citizens know specifically what they can do to help you when they ask.

- Explore opportunities for your employees to participate in community activities—such as civic organizations—that are not directly related to police work. This will give them a different perspective than they are used to seeing during the course of their duties.

- Hold regular community meetings and listen to what people are saying about what troubles them. Of course, none of us likes criticism, but it is essential if we are to respond to constituents' needs. Use these meetings also to present the truth about crime and your ability to deal with it without their help. Count on the first meeting to turn into a ''gripe session''; once you are past this, however, the positive response you will get from most citizens can be very encouraging.

- Commit yourself to decentralization, to the extent possible. Substations, storefronts and neighborhood offices are outward, concrete signs of your commitment.

- Get officers out of their cars and closer to the people they serve. Some may insist that calls for service will prevent them from working in this mode, and you will likely have to reexamine current operations and eliminate or modify some steps. An alternative-response committee, comprised of both civilian and sworn practitioners, can help solve the time and resource problem.

- Finally, be results-oriented. If you commit to a course of action, make it happen. Credibility is everything in community policing. No matter how difficult things become, don't bow out with excuses. A community with an historical distrust of the police is not likely to change its perceptions overnight.

What we know for sure is that to ignore the future is the worst alternative of all. Since that's where we're all headed, we must dedicate our maximum effort to affect it positively for our communities' sake as well as our own. While it is not without risk, we—as leaders—must take the first step. The future depends on it.

basically operate in reactive fashion. Second, they spend a good deal of their time on random patrol in the belief that they are deterring crime. In fact, random patrol (whatever that may mean) appears not to make any difference in crime rates.[3] We would add a third feature of traditional policing: officers respond repeatedly to calls for service from the same persons or involving the same problems in the same geographic areas. In fact, in traditional policing, officers today are responding to the same types of calls, originating from the same areas, often involving the same complainants and alleged offenders, as the previous generation of officers in their communities. Further, the next generation of officers will follow suit. This is true because traditional policing deals with treating symptoms, not solving underlying problems. Finally, the police typically perform these traditional duties from a patrol car which serves as a means of transportation, a communications center, and office. Unfortunately, it also often serves to isolate the officers involved from the citizens they serve so that neither knows the other very well. As a result, mutual suspicion and downright fear may develop, making cooperation difficult if not impossible. Whatever its form, community policing is an attempt to confront these problems that have characterized traditional policing in the United States.

It is interesting to note what has happened to the patrol officer in the course of traditional policing. While traditional police officers do maintain a good deal of discretion, they are largely at the mercy of forces beyond their control. First, they cannot, by and large, control the timing or type of calls which they receive. Second, their alternatives in dealing with problem cases are limited. They can take official action in the form of a citation or an arrest. They can issue informal warnings. But they seldom see themselves as capable of solving the problems which lead to the incidents to which they repeatedly respond. This in itself is frustrating and may contribute to job burnout and cynicism which may lead to further alienation and problematic encounters with other citizens. This sense of frustration is heightened by the recognition that even if they do possess problem-solving skills, they are not encouraged to use them or rewarded when they do. In fact, in most departments, in order to ''get ahead,'' they must either leave the rank of patrol officer to become a supervisor or transfer to some other specialty within the department (such as the investigative division). Community policing attempts to address these issues as well by ''empowering'' police officers. This empowerment comes in part through the use of techniques first spelled out in problem-oriented policing.

Problem-Oriented Policing

The term problem-oriented policing originated in the works of Herman Goldstein.[4] Goldstein recognized that solving problems is the essence of police work and that law enforcement is only one part of policing. Yet traditional departments often assess the effectiveness of their personnel by counting the number of arrests made, citations written, or the time lapse between receiving and responding to a service request. If problem solving is the core of police work, these traditional measures are inadequate in determining the success of officers.

Instead, police effectiveness ought to be determined, according to Goldstein, by assessing the extent to which officers identify and develop solutions to the problems which are responsible for the incidents to which they continually respond. In other words, the incidents may be viewed as symptoms of underlying problems.[5] From this point of view, the basic unit of police work becomes a problem as opposed to a call or an incident. Incidents or calls which form patterns are regarded as problems, which affect both the police and other citizens. In order to solve problems, the police, in partnership with other citizens, must identify them and propose solutions. Often the solutions proposed are beyond the ability of the police alone to implement. Thus the requirement for meaningful partnerships, that are an important part of community policing, between the police and other citizens.

In order to participate effectively in solving problems, police officers in general, and patrol officers in particular, must be given considerable discretion, must be rewarded for demonstrating ingenuity, and must be encouraged to persist in attempting to solve problems even when their solutions fail. Innovation and the ability to work with others to develop solutions to problems must be encouraged. All of this flies in the face of traditional police wisdom which encourages officers not to ''rock the boat,'' which often frowns upon and sometimes punishes attempts at innovation, and which requires police officers to be suspicious of other citizens (''outsiders''). It also requires a change from a reactive to a proactive stance on behalf of the police. And, it requires that the police admit that they are not the only experts in enforcing laws and maintaining order. Such changes are not easily made, but are essential if the police and other citizens are to work together to improve the quality of life in the community.

The Elements of Community Policing

Community policing is not a particular program within a police agency, but a department-wide philosophy and an organizational strategy.[6] The philosophy is based upon commitments to crime prevention, police accountability and openness to the public, customized or personalized police service, and community organization. The strategy is expected to lead to greater citizen support, shared responsibility for dealing with crime in the community, and greater job satisfaction for police officers. It is not a strategy which is ''soft on crime,'' but one which includes a variety of police responses, including arrest and personalized police services. Ideally, community residents would be less hesitant to call the police with problems because each resident would have a ''personal'' police officer, the community police officer responsible for the resident's neighborhood, who could be called to relay questions or information.

Once the philosophy has been accepted by police personnel, police officers are assigned to permanent or long-term beats in a specific geographic area and are given responsibility for developing community ties which will lead to a reduction in crime and improvement in the quality of life in the area, beat, or neighborhood in question. The entire approach is both dependent upon, and designed to improve, relationships between the police and other members of

Table 7.1

Differences Between Community Policing and Police Community Relations

Community Policing	Police Community Relations
1. Goal is to solve problems	Goal is to change attitudes; project positive image
2. Line officers regularly contact citizens	Staff officers irregularly contact citizens
3. Citizens identify problems, participate in setting police agenda	Blue ribbon committees identify problems
4. Police are accountable to citizens served	Police are accountable to civilian review boards and police supervisors
5. Real organizational change occurs (selection, training, evaluation)	Organization doesn't change, some new programs are added
6. Requires department-wide acceptance of philosophy	Isolated acceptance, often only in PCR unit
7. Influence is from bottom up (including other citizens)	Influence is from top down, experts make decisions
8. Officers are always accessible in decentralized locations	Intermittent contact through central headquarters
9. Officers encourage citizen participation in problem solving	Citizens encouraged to volunteer, but also to request more government services
10. Success determined by improved quality of life	Success determined by crime rates and other traditional measures

Adapted from Trojanowicz (1990).

the community. Police community relations and community policing, however, are not one and the same, as the late Robert Trojanowicz (1990) pointed out.

Differences Between Community Policing and Police Community Relations

Many believe that community policing is simply the latest version of police community relations. According to Trojanowicz, however, the differences shown in Table 7.1 exist.[7]

As can be seen from the table, while community policing and police community relations are compatible, they are not the same. In fact, it can be argued that the former includes the latter as part of its philosophy. There are those, however, who continue to believe that community policing is simply another community relations program which can be implemented within the framework of traditional policing, as well as those who believe that community policing amounts to little more than social work. Hunter and Barker conclude that there is a disturbing lack of substance in many so-called community policing efforts.[8] And, not all departments that have begun the transition from traditional to community policing are convinced that the effort should continue as the Critical Issue box indicates.

Cops, Not Social Workers
NYPD to Rethink Community Policing

New York Mayor Rudolph Giuliani plans to re-examine the Police Department's nascent community policing effort with an eye toward refocusing the initiative away from its ''social service aspects,'' following the disclosure of internal police memos that question the effort's effectiveness.

Giuliani on Jan. 25 ordered the city's Department of Investigation to look into possible criminal allegations raised in the memos by then-Assistant Chief Aaron Rosenthal, who had been assigned by former Police Commissioner Raymond Kelly to assess the community policing program. In a series of memos prepared last year, Rosenthal said the effort had been hampered by mismanagement and staffed by officers who worked ''banker's hours'' and who made no appreciable arrests at night or on weekends.

Giuliani stressed that the department remains committed to the program, which was instituted in 1990 by then-Commissioner Lee P. Brown, but that the focus may shift.

''Police officers have to play the role primarily of preventing crime,'' said Giuliani, a former Federal prosecutor. ''Social service aspects that were kind of added on to community policing, some of that has to be done but can't become a primary focus of all the police aspects in the neighborhood. The police officer's there to make sure the burglary doesn't take place, the robbery doesn't take place, a person can walk along the street safely.''

Giuliani added that the philosophy of the program had shifted from getting more officers on walking beats to ''a complex, convoluted academic science, training police officers in assessing social services'' and in other duties ''inconsistent with the role of police.''

Rosenthal found ''major discrepancies'' in the amounts of time beat officer spent on the street and what was claimed in records. Officers were given the flexibility to fashion their work schedules in a way that could best confront problems on their beats. But Rosenthal found that officers often were not on duty when the problems were most likely to fester, such as nights or weekends. In an evaluation undertaken last May, Rosenthal studied the records of five officers and a supervisor in each of nine precincts, and found that 78 percent of the officers were off on Sundays and 61 percent were off on Saturdays.

A high turnover rate among community police officers was also noted by Rosenthal, which he said may be due to the lack of incentives offered to those who stay in the units.

Rosenthal also determined that undercover narcotics officers did not work Sundays and made few arrests after 6 P.M., and pointed out that the hours do not reflect residents' concerns about drug activity occurring at night and on weekends.

In-service training program for community police officers was described by Rosenthal as a ''dismal failure.'' He said the training is sabotaged by ''an overall blasé attitude on the part of management which has filtered down to the attendees.'' Drawing his conclusions from visits he and his staff made to several precincts to monitor training sessions, Rosenthal wrote that ''precinct-level in-service training is frequently conducted in a haphazard and perfunctory manner.'' [See LEN, March 15, 1993.]

While a central objective of community policing is to coordinate the efforts of officers with those of other police units and social service agencies to attack a persistent neighborhood problem, Rosenthal found that wasn't happening in many instances.

Six precincts identified traffic congestion and illegal parking as a constant problem, but did not work with city traffic agents to solve it, Rosenthal said in a report last August. Six other precincts identified prostitution as a big problem, but community police officers did not work late at night when the prostitutes most often appeared, and made few of the prostitution arrests that occurred within their precincts. Most arrests were made by other uniformed officers or members of the public morals division, he said.

Giuliani campaigned last fall on a law-and-order platform, arguing that the ''quality of life'' had eroded because police no longer made arrests for such crimes as panhandling, street-level drug sales and prostitution. He has seized upon the ''secret'' memos, which were detailed by the New York Daily News, as evidence a department paralyzed by bureaucracy and moribund leadership.

Former Police Commissioner Kelly, who with Brown played a major role in organizing and implementing the community policing program, responded to the swirling debate by saying that he directed Rosenthal to undertake the assessment of the program so that problems could be identified and solved. Kelly said he had ordered an immediate review of the Rosenthal's findings, particularly those that involved staffing, and that many problems had been addressed.

Kelly charged that many of the criticisms leveled by the Giuliani Administration against the Police Department are politically motivated—a case of ''blaming all of the problems of the world on the past administration.'' Giuliani's attack on the department's community policing effort, Kelly said, suggested that the Mayor was ''trying to put some sort of his own stamp—hardline stamp—on this program.''

''He clearly doesn't understand community policing,'' Kelly told The New York Times. ''We are not doing social work.''

Continued

Cops, Not Social Workers
NYPD to Rethink Community Policing (Continued)

Police Commissioner William Bratton, who undertook a major shakeup of the department's top echelons late this month, hinted at still more changes to come that will directly affect beat officers. Appearing on a TV news program a few days before the high-level shakeup, Bratton pointedly lamented the complacency exhibited by some beat officers.

"There are some cops who I want to give a kick in the butt," said the former Boston police commissioner. "Police are paid to try to prevent crime, and to act—not just drive by—when they encounter a situation, whether it be the squeegee person or drug dealing. Nothing discourages me more than when I see a cop moping around his post, hands in his pocket, hat on the back of his head, literally looking bored to tears. There's

enough on any beat in the city to keep that cop busy and to have the public see him—him or her—constantly busy."

In a related development, Giuliani on Jan. 25 appointed a panel to determine whether the Police Department was deploying the number of officers required by the "Safe Streets, Safe City" anticrime program, which has swelled the NYPD's ranks by thousands of new officers in the past three years.

The program, which was approved by state legislators in February 1991, authorized $1.8 billion over five years from a special property tax and a surcharge on income taxes for the expansion of the city's three police departments. The city agreed to adopt a strict timetable for deploying the new officers to meet a goal

of 38,310 by the end of the 1995 fiscal year.

The panel will include Adam Walinsky, a prominent attorney and advocate of a national police corps; Richard Koehler, a former Chief of Personnel for the Police Department, and Richard Mark, Deputy Commissioner of the Department of Investigation.

City Council Speaker Peter F. Vallone, who will chair the hearings, said the committee will look into why the department had about 350 fewer officers on patrol each day than was projected when its budget was adopted last year. Giuliani said the numbers are in dispute, but could be as high as 800 officers.

Reprinted with permission from Law Enforcement News, *John Jay College of Criminal Justice, NYC, Vol. 20, No. 394: 1.*

Still others believe that community policing is just another term for a particular style of policing that always existed, particularly in rural areas.

Community Policing and Policing in Rural Areas

Most research and writing concerning the police focuses on urban areas, while the problems of rural police and rural crime have been largely neglected. However, understanding small town and rural police is important since departments with ten or fewer officers comprise the vast majority of police departments in the United States.

For our purposes rural areas include towns with a population of less than 2,500, and the unincorporated areas surrounding these towns or adjacent to larger cities. The decade of the 1980s saw an outward migration from rural communities, diminishing the tax base in these areas and resulting in funding difficulties for many rural police agencies. Some rural sheriffs, for example, had to make staff cuts and many feel they cannot attract well-qualified candidates because of the relatively low salaries they can offer. These financial difficulties are occurring at the same time as the demand for services and crime

*A small rural police
department.*

Courtesy of the Galena Gazette

rates are increasing, leading some rural communities which formerly supported their own police agencies to contract for services with the county sheriff or some other larger department. This typically means giving up some degree of local control, which, as we have noted elsewhere in this book, is an important cornerstone of American policing.

Styles of Policing and Rural Communities

James Q. Wilson has developed a typology of policing styles which may serve as a starting point for understanding rural police and their relationships with members of the communities in which they operate. Specifically, Wilson identified three types or styles of policing.

1. ''Legalistic style'' departments tend to be composed of officers who: issue traffic tickets at a high rate, detain and arrest a high proportion of juvenile offenders, act vigorously against illicit enterprises, and make a large number of misdemeanor arrests even when, as with petty larceny, the public order has not been breached.[9]

    Pressure to ''produce'' tickets and arrests, a law enforcement rather than familial view of their jobs, and technical efficiency are emphasized in legalistic departments. College-educated police officers, new buildings, computer capabilities, relatively high salaries, and elaborate training courses further characterize such departments.[10]

2. In "service style" police departments, the police intervene frequently but not formally in daily activities. Public education and a community relations orientation characterize such departments. When possible, arrests for minor infractions are avoided, and informal sanctions are used in such cases.[11]

3. "Watchman style" police departments "use the law more as a means of maintaining order than regulating conduct."[12] Circumstances of person and condition are taken into account in all cases, violations by well-known community figures are often overlooked because they have influence, and violations by "outsiders" (minority group members, for example) may either lead to arrest or be ignored depending upon the circumstances. Officers are allowed to follow the path of least resistance, and often encouraged to keep their "noses clean" and "not to rock the boat." Little emphasis is placed on the appearance or demeanor of officers, educational requirements are minimal, officers are selected from the community, learning results from on-the-job training, and salaries are low.[13]

The "watchman style" police officer operates under what Klonski and Mendelsohn call the "communal system" of criminal justice.[14] This system does not aspire to be professional. The police lack even minimal training and are drawn from the local community.

> The outputs of the system will be biased, but the basis of the bias will be community rather than class. Members of the community in-groups will be protected and served by the legal subsystem, while out-groups will find the system hostile and even punitive.[15]

Out-group members may live outside the area or may be otherwise set apart by race or ethnicity, or both. Thus, local community standards rather than actual behavior determine who will and who will not be subject to arrest and prosecution except in very serious cases. To some observers, this means that a partnership between the police and community residents exists in many rural areas, constituting a kind of community policing. Of course, community policing may be practiced by police agencies utilizing any of the styles discussed above, not just the watchman style. In fact, it might be argued that the service style is easier to adapt to community policing than the watchman style which often seeks to exclude certain citizens (outsiders) from the police-community partnership.

Both watchman style policing and communal justice systems are likely to be found in basically conservative communities. Numerous researchers have noted that the smaller the community size, the more traditional or conservative the community tends to be.[16] In rural areas, informal rules of conduct tend to be shared by members of the community, and traditional institutions such as family, school, and church tend to receive more emphasis than in urban areas.[17]

The qualities of openness, hospitality, trust, and desire for untroubled living, with the underlying capacity for rather violent conflict resolution have always characterized the rural ethos.[18]

Local Control of the Police

Another characteristic of rural America has always been a strong desire for local control, including local control of police operations. Most departments in these areas are small, and for the most part, they operate independently of one another. As Horgan, Smith, and others have noted, local control has led to a number of difficulties in law enforcement.[19] The winning party in an election often believes that its members should be immune from arrest (except in very serious cases), or be given special promotions, or be allowed to pursue vendettas against political opponents.[20] Further, "Since most departments were small, they were notably slow in adopting technological devices to assist them in their battle against crime.[21] Vollmer concluded that local control often has led to the use of amateurs in law enforcement, as well as to a lack of coordination among police agencies.[22] In addition, territorial or jurisdictional jealousies often prevent cooperation between local agencies and better-equipped state and federal agencies. Still, there is little doubt that in rural areas police officers and their clientele are more likely to know one another personally than in more urban settings. This phenomenon, too, has sometimes been considered an indicator that rural officers are, almost by definition, involved in community policing.

The Role of the Sheriff in Rural Law Enforcement

The sheriff's department is the rural police agency that frequently epitomizes the watchman style of policing and the problems resulting from local control of rural police. The office of sheriff exists in forty-nine of the fifty states, and in the majority of these states it is an elective office.[23] Since political appeal and party support rather than law enforcement expertise are the basic requirements for being elected to office, we might expect (and indeed we actually find) great differences in professionalism and efficiency among sheriffs within any given state. Research indicates that sheriffs in urbanized counties are more likely to be professional law enforcement agents than their rural counterparts, who tend to be more politically inclined.[24] Still, the fact that the position is an elected one means that sheriffs are required to get to know a significant proportion of the population within their jurisdictions in order to get elected to office. Prior to election at least, they are likely to be accessible to voters who have interests in policing and community problems and to make promises that they will attempt to resolve crime-related problems once elected. And, in order to be re-elected, they may have to confront some of the issues raised by voters during the campaign and keep themselves informed of public opinion concerning key issues. Similarly, those who voted for the sheriff may feel free to discuss their problems with him/her and not uncommonly expect favors from the sheriff.

Among the functions frequently performed by sheriffs is assistance to small town police. Numerous one- or two-person "departments" comprised of full- and/or part-time constables, marshals, and police officers exist throughout rural America. Many of these police officers have little or no training and have little or none of the equipment (except personal weapons) employed by municipal police as a matter of routine in more urban areas. Radios, speed checking equipment, properly equipped patrol vehicles, and assistance in emergencies are often available only through the county sheriff, and then sometimes only when the sheriff's department is relatively large in size. Nevertheless, rural law enforcement described in the preceding discussion continues to predominate in many areas, in part at least, as a result of the expectations and desires of rural residents with respect to law enforcement. Whether or not community policing characterizes a particular jurisdiction depends more upon the extent to which the philosophy is understood and accepted than the size of the community involved.

Police Community Relations in Rural Areas

Police community relations in rural environments are often very different from those in urban areas. The sheriff is an elected official, and town constables or marshals are often hired and fired at the whim of locally powerful political leaders. In many cases, there are no unions, merit boards, or fire and police commissions to insure that rural police officers are protected by means of formalized grievance procedures. We are aware of one community in which citizens have been so opposed to paying for the training of police officers that they have hired officers, employed them on the streets for the maximum allowable time before training is required by the state, then terminated them, and started the cycle over again with new officers.

Similarly, in talking to a number of county sheriffs and other rural police officers we have noted that many share in common this law enforcement philosophy: enforce traffic laws only when necessary and only against persons who do not reside in the county or who are defined by influential county residents as "troublemakers"; don't overemphasize the need for professional law enforcement in rural areas, especially if a tax increase is required to support such improvement; don't alienate political allies if you seek reelection/reappointment. All these policies and procedures are predictable, in view of our earlier discussions of watchman style policing and the communal system of criminal justice. To the extent that they reflect policies understood and supported by members of the community, they may be said to reflect community policing.

Frequently the concerns of urban police officers are not shared by rural police officials. For example, alienation of minorities and outsiders is often viewed not as a violation of civil rights, but as a responsibility of rural police.

Henry County Sheriff Asks Farmers to Help Eradicate Wild 'Pot'

By William C. Cole
Correspondent

CAMBRIDGE—Henry County Sheriff Gilbert ''Gib'' Cady is asking farmers to spray wild marijuana plants growing on their land, especially if the plants can be seen from a road.

For the last few years, illegal harvesting of the plants has caused a law enforcement nightmare for the sheriff's department and has cost the county a small fortune to incarcerate and prosecute the pot pickers. These costs involve not only the sheriff's department, but the state's attorney's office and other court-related departments.

And 1990 was the worst year ever.

Starting in August, 47 people were arrested in the county for harvesting wild marijuana, a plant that has grown in abundance for many years throughout the area. Most of those arrested were from outside the county, and many were from out-of-state.

A marijuana shortage throughout the nation contributed to the high number of pickers, according to Cady. This, coupled with skyrocketing marijuana street prices, made the wild marijuana found in the county attractive enough for dealers and processors to harvest.

The wild variety of the plant is relatively weak, Cady explained, but can still produce a mild ''high.''

''The sheriff's department can make the arrests, of course,'' said Cady, ''but we don't see the real solution as a law enforcement program. We want to get rid of the plants.''

Cady added that the Illinois Department of Transportation should get involved in the eradication, too, wherever the plants grow on highway rights-of-way.

Meeting on the problem last week in Cambridge were Cady, Chuck Spencer, manager of the county Farm Bureau office; Assistant Henry County State's Attorney Ted Hamer; Illinois State Trooper Stanley Talbot; Woodhull Police Chief Jim Bethell; county agricultural extension advisor Dean Oswald; and Dick Strandberg, of the Henry Service Company.

Talbot said state troopers have been contacting farmers when they spot marijuana growing on private property.

Spencer said the Farm Bureau has surveyed county farmers and found that many are interested in the eradication program.

''We are finding that a strong majority are willing to participate,'' said Spencer. ''In fact, while a few of the farmers said they would need financial help to take part, the majority said they'd help out at their own expense.''

Spencer said farmers were asked if they would need funds but it hasn't been determined if those funds are available.

''I'd say, based on the survey results so far, that cost-share funds are not going to be a consideration in this program,'' he said.

Cady and other officials agreed that the first priority is to knock out plants that are visible from highways.

''The next priority would be to kill those plants visible from county and township roads. Most of the pickers don't really know where to look, so they drive around until they see some marijuana growing. Then they just stop and go get it.''

''The ideal time to kill these plants with herbicide is when they are germinating, and that happens when they are from three to five inches tall,'' Spencer said.

The marijuana plants germinate about the same time corn is emerging, Spencer said. If the plants can't be killed then, they could be mowed later in the summer. Still, ''The best way to kill the plants is spring spraying,'' he said.

Equal opportunity employment may be considered only with respect to individuals born and raised in the community. Education and training are often viewed as unnecessary and unnecessarily costly for rural law enforcement personnel. Knowing who to get along with is sometimes perceived to be more important than knowing the law, knowing how to conduct an investigation, or how to write a good report. In many respects, rural residents know their police better and have more direct control over their police than city dwellers. The compilation of information which characterizes many police-citizen encounters in urban areas is often unnecessary in rural settings where police officer and citizen may have known each other all their lives or at least recognize almost immediately each other's status in the community.

In some ways rural and small town police do have an advantage when it comes to community relations. As Sims notes: "Reoccurring interaction for nonpolice reasons between small town and rural officers and community members integrates the police and the community in a fashion unknown in larger cities. Bureaucratic principles work to separate the police from the community while small-group principles function to blend people and police in an inseparable mixture of self policing."[25]

Rural police, then, are a mixed lot. While they frequently suffer from lack of resources and too much political control, they are, at the same time, in a better position to understand the other citizens with whom they work on a regular basis than are most police officers in larger communities. In addition, there are indications that change is occurring in rural law enforcement. The National Sheriffs' Association and similar state organizations are working to publicize and overcome some of the difficulties mentioned earlier. Increasing crime rates in rural areas have led some rural citizens to recognize the need for better training for rural officers, and to demand it. Rural police officers themselves often recognize the need for education and training. Some years ago, we conducted a lengthy training school for rural officers who had previously received no training at all. Some of the participants drove 150 miles round trip two nights a week for several weeks just to take advantage of the opportunity to participate in training. Merit boards are replacing the traditional "live and die by the election" positions of sheriffs' deputies in many areas. Attempts at consolidation are being made and many states now require training for all law enforcement officers. These and other changes indicate that some of the routine concerns of police in more densely populated areas may soon be addressed in rural areas as well.

In the meantime, community relations programs aimed at protecting farm equipment and livestock, and programs intended to help rural residents who may live some distance from their nearest neighbors protect their persons and homes, are increasingly characteristic of rural law enforcement agencies. To the extent that police and other citizens jointly develop and implement such programs in an attempt to be proactive and improve the overall quality of life in the community, we can say that community policing exists.

Summary

Community policing has become the buzzword of the 1990s in policing circles. However, there is evidence that many who verbally support the approach cling to traditional policing styles, substituting programs for philosophical change.

The problem-oriented policing strategy developed in the 1980s indicated to police administrators that traditional policing techniques which rely upon random patrol, sporadic community relations programs, and quantitative arrest and citation data to assess police performance have been less effective than they would like to believe. Problem-solving techniques, empowerment of police officers, evaluations based upon outcomes rather than traditional measures, and the need to be proactive have become increasingly popular topics of conversation. The outcome has been a trend toward community policing.

Community policing has roots as far back as the early nineteenth century, but has come to the fore again in the middle 1980s. Based upon a philosophy that focuses upon empowerment of police officers who are permanently assigned in decentralized areas, and that emphasizes partnerships with community residents in an attempt to improve quality of life, community policing has garnered a good deal of verbal support among police personnel. Whether or not the philosophy has been understood and the extent to which it is being put into practice are empirical questions.

Although rural and small town police agencies typify policing in the United States, they are often neglected by police researchers. Most police departments employ fewer than ten officers who often work with equipment that is less than state of the art and for salaries that are less than desirable. Budgetary cutbacks and lack of interest in consolidation, direct political control, and shortages of training and trained personnel have all hampered rural policing efforts.

In spite of these difficulties, however, there is a good deal that is positive about rural and small town policing. Close contact with community residents and a growing interest in training and education both reflect positively on opportunities for developing and maintaining good police community relations in rural areas.

Discussion Questions

1. Discuss community policing as a philosophy. How readily do you think most patrol officers would accept the philosophy? Most police administrators?
2. What is the relationship between problem-oriented policing and community policing? What is the role of the public in each?
3. It is often said that "the public gets the type of police services they deserve." To what extent and in what ways do you believe this is true in rural areas?
4. Are there any advantages for rural residents and rural police officers derived from watchman style policing and communal justice systems? Disadvantages?
5. Is it likely that the position of sheriff will disappear from the American scene in the foreseeable future? Why or why not?
6. Are human relations as important for rural police community relations as for similar relations in urban areas? Public relations? Do you see any major differences in human or public relations between rural and urban police and the communities they serve?
7. To what extent do rural and small town police typify the American scene? What steps are they currently taking to overcome some of the problems discussed in this chapter?
8. Are all rural police departments community policing agencies?

Endnotes

1. John E. Eck and Dennis P. Rosenbaum. 1994. "The New Police Order: Effectiveness, Equity, and Efficiency in Community Policing" in Dennis P. Rosenbaum, ed. *The Challenge of Community Policing: Testing the Promises.* Thousand Oaks: Sage: 3–23.

2. David H. Bayley. 1988. "Community Policing: A Report from the Devil's Advocate" in Jack R. Greene and S. D. Mastrofski, eds. *Community Policing: Rhetoric or Reality?* New York: Praeger: 225.

3. Alan M. Webber. 1991. "Crime and Management: An Interview with New York City Police Commissioner Lee P. Brown." *Harvard Business Review* (May–June): 111–126.

4. Herman Goldstein. 1979. "Improving Police: A Problem-Oriented Approach." *Crime and Delinquency* 25: 236–258. See also, the same author. 1990. *Problem-Oriented Policing.* New York: McGraw-Hill.

5. Hans Toch and J. Douglas Grant. 1991. *Police as Problem Solvers.* New York: Plenum Press.

6. Lee P. Brown. 1989. "Community Policing: A Practical Guide for Police Officials." *Perspectives on Policing.* (September). Washington, D.C.: U.S. Department of Justice; Robert Trojanowicz and Bonnie Bucqueroux. 1990. *Community Policing: A Contemporary Perspective.* Cincinnati: Anderson.

7. Robert C. Trojanowicz. 1990. "Community-Policing Is Not Police-Community Relations." *FBI Law Enforcement Bulletin* (October): 6–11.

8. Ronald D. Hunter and Thomas Barker. 1993. "BS and Buzzwords: The New Police Operational Style." *American Journal of Police* 12(3): 157–168.

9. James Q. Wilson. 1968. *Varieties of Police Behavior: The Management of Law and Order in Eight Communities.* Cambridge: Harvard University Press: 172.

10. Ibid.: 185–187.

11. Ibid.: 200–205.

12. Ibid.: 140.

13. Ibid.: 144–152.

14. James R. Klonski and Robert I. Mendelsohn. 1970. *The Politics of Local Justice.* Boston: Little, Brown and Co.: I7.

15. Ibid.: l7.

16. See, for example, G. Lowe and C. Peek. 1974. "Location and Lifestyle: The Comparative Explanatory Ability of Urbanism and Rurality." *Rural Sociology* 29: 392–420: or W. Glenn and L. Hill. "Rural-Urban Differences in Attitudes and Behavior in the United States." 1977. *Journal of the American Academy of Political and Social Sciences* 429: 36–50.

17. Robert Richard Lyerly and James K. Skipper, Jr. 1981. "Differential Rates of Rural-Urban Delinquency: A Social Control Approach." *Criminology* 19(3): 385–399.

18. Jay David Jamieson. 1980. "Understanding the Rural-Urban Dichotomy." Paper presented at the Annual Meeting of the Academy of Criminal Justice Sciences in Oklahoma City.

19. William P. Horgan. 1980. "A Look at Local Control and Efforts Toward Consolidation of Police Services." *Journal of Police Science and Administration* 8(1): 1–4; and Bruce Smith. 1960. *Police Systems in the United States.* 2ed. New York: Harper and Row.

20. Ibid.: 1.

21. Horgan. "Local Control.": 1.

22. August Vollmer. 1971. *The Police in Modern Society.* Montclair, NJ: Patterson Smith: 4.

23. Bruce L. Berg. 1992. *Law Enforcement: An Introduction to Police in Society.* Boston: Allyn and Bacon: 45.

24. Ibid.: 278.

25. Victor H. Sims. 1988. *Small Town and Rural Police.* Springfield, IL: Charles C Thomas: 195–196.

Clark, Jacob R. 1994. ''Does Community Policing Add Up?'' *Law Enforcement News* 20(399): 1, 8.

Decker, Scott H. and Steven M. Ward. 1989. ''Rural Law Enforcement'' in Bailey, William G., ed. *The Encyclopedia of Police Science*. New York: Garland: 561–564.

Hoffman, John. 1992. ''Rural Policing.'' *Law and Order* 40(6): 20–24.

Rachlin, Harvey. 1992. ''Small Town Training.'' *Law and Order* 40(6): 38–40.

Rosenbaum, Dennis P. 1994. *The Challenge of Community Policing: Testing the Promises*. Thousand Oaks: Sage.

Sims, Victor H. 1988. *Small Town and Rural Police*. Springfield, IL: Charles C Thomas.

Toch, Hans and J. Douglas Grant. 1991. *Police As Problem Solvers*. New York: Plenum Press.

Trojanowicz, Robert and Bonnie Bucqueroux. 1990. *Community Policing: A Contemporary Perspective*. Cincinnati: Anderson.

Walters, Paul M. 1993. ''Community-Oriented Policing: A Blend of Strategies.'' *FBI Law Enforcement Bulletin* 62(11): 20–23.

Policing Diversity

U ndoubtedly, one of the most visible and often problematic areas of policing involves encounters with members of culturally diverse groups. Such groups include racial and ethnic minorities, homosexuals, persons with disabilities, the homeless, the elderly, and many others. The police themselves are becoming increasingly diverse with members of racial and ethnic minorities and homosexuals, among others, joining their ranks. In this chapter we will examine policing in a diverse setting and in the next diversity among the police.

Policing Diversity

One of the most difficult and controversial aspects of police community relations involves police contacts with members of racial and ethnic minorities. Police encounters with other culturally diverse groups are also sometimes difficult and controversial, but we will focus here on relationships with racial and ethnic minorities since they contain all of the elements which make such encounters challenging.

Although much attention has focused on relationships between blacks and the police, it should be noted that similar problems frequently characterize relationships between the police and Mexican Americans, Cubans, Puerto Ricans, American Indians, some Asian Americans, as well as other minority groups.

A minority group consists of people who receive unequal treatment from dominant members of the social unit, in the form of prejudice and/or discrimination; they are relatively easy to identify because they have physical and/or cultural characteristics different from those of the dominant group.[1] This definition is sufficiently general to permit us to identify minorities on the basis of occupation, age, social class, gender, race, ethnicity, religion, or disability. To some extent the police themselves may be viewed as a minority group. They also are frequently the objects of prejudice and discrimination from the nonpolice majority; moreover, the police subculture emphasizes certain characteristics to a greater degree than does the larger society—for example, masculinity, aggressiveness, suspicion, authority, and use of physical force. Unlike members of racial or ethnic minorities, however, membership in the police minority is voluntary.

In our society, racial groups are commonly defined by skin color, while ethnic groups can be identified because they share a common culture and/or language which differs from that of the dominant group.[2] Though there is considerable disagreement among scientists concerning the most appropriate criteria for determining race, there is no doubt that the public make such distinctions. Further, the belief that racial and ethnic minority group members are inferior or not to be trusted is fairly widespread among members of the dominant group (and also among members of each minority group with respect to other minority groups and the dominant group). Since police officers are selected from the public, it is not surprising that they frequently share these attitudes. In addition, the police may develop additional prejudices or forms of discrimination, since they themselves are often viewed as outsiders who share a common language, style of dress, as well as subcultural values, because of the nature of police work and their encounters with minority group members, and as a result of "occupational discrimination" that leads some officers to verbally and physically abuse minority group members in order to be accepted in the police subculture.

In a world composed of many minority groups, we often tend to think in terms of "we and they."[3] "We" includes other people with whom we share racial, ethnic, and cultural characteristics; "they" includes everybody else. Generally speaking, we tend to trust and support members of the "we" group, but to distrust and sometimes oppose members of "they" groups. In the case of the police, the distinction between "we" and "they" can be extremely complex. Although they are often viewed as outsiders by both minority and dominant group members, the majority of police officers in our society, because they are white, identify to some extent with the dominant racial group. Total identification with this majority, however, is impaired by the very nature of some police work, which involves sharing secrets only with other members of the police subculture. The police, then, very often see "we" as consisting of other police officers, and are often perceived as "they" by both minority and dominant group members. Nonetheless, in part perhaps because of the tendency of most police officers to identify with the dominant racial group, the police often express prejudice toward nonwhite and ethnic minorities and sometimes act in discriminatory fashion toward members of these groups.

It is important to note that difficulties in police minority relations are not a thing of the past in our society as the Critical Issue box indicates. Further evidence of the persistent nature of difficulties in police encounters with members of racial and ethnic minorities is provided by the Rodney King incident that occurred in Los Angeles and the riots that occurred in the aftermath of the acquittal of some of the police officers involved.[4]

L.A. Police Beating Puts Spotlight on 'Culture of Violence'

William Raspberry

WASHINGTON—But for technology and luck, the recent police beating of a black Los Angeles motorist might not have triggered a full-scale investigation even by the local NAACP. But because George Holliday had a video camera and a lucky view of the scene, the Justice Department is now looking at police brutality cases from around the country.

Atty. Gen. Dick Thornburgh ordered the review following a Thursday morning breakfast meeting with two black congressmen, John Conyers (D-Mich.) and Edolphus Towns (D-N.Y.), after the head of the FBI had refused their request for an investigation of brutality allegations.

Under ordinary circumstances, Rodney King—even with his smashed skull, broken leg, concussion and burns from an electric stun gun—might have been a poor case on which to demand federal action. It might have been obvious that he was a victim of excessive force, but a lot of people would have believed that the 25-year-old King, who had served time for robbery, brought it on himself: leading police on a wild, high-speed chase and then attacking them like a crazy man after he was caught.

Civil-rights activists might have believed him but still might have found it prudent to wait for a "good case": a prominent minister, a business executive, someone of sterling character and reputation. If it comes down to the word of the victim against the police, the victim has to be credible. Indeed, had his injuries been less severe, King might not have filed an official complaint on his own behalf.

That's the thing about police brutality. It seldom happens to people whose manner and appearance suggest the possibility that they could make trouble for abusive officers. And because "good cases" are so rare, complaints are treated with skepticism by those unfamiliar with police behavior.

That's why a half dozen members of Congress decided to take advantage of Holliday's videotape to press for a federal investigation. "We know that a lot of cases go unreported, because many black and Hispanic victims think that's just how some police officers behave," Towns said Thursday. "They know it's usually a matter of your word against theirs, and the tendency is to believe the officers. But inasmuch as this case was so thoroughly documented, we decided to ask FBI Director William Sessions to do an in-depth study of the problem.

"When Sessions said he was prepared to prosecute cases where the evidence was clear, but not to look for systemic problems, Conyers and I decided to take it to Thornburgh."

The attorney general, to his credit, bought the suggestion. He agreed to order an investigation by the department's civil-rights division into six years' worth of brutality complaints from across the country—at least 22 cases—looking for what Conyers called "a culture of violence."

"Those engaged in law enforcement must be among the first to assume the observance of the civil rights and civil liberties of all citizens," Thornburgh said after the breakfast meeting.

Towns is thrilled at the decision. "A lot of people are already coming forward to confirm what we already know: that there is still a lot of police brutality going on," he said. "What will come of it? Several things. To begin with, the fact of police brutality will be proven if we have hearings across the country. Second, there's the hope that we can look at police training, particularly with regard to sensitivity to blacks and Hispanics. In addition, we may come to understand more about the tensions of police work. That's an important factor, and it may be helpful to think about rotating officers from area to area, just to relieve some of that tension.

"But the main thing is that it should help the credibility of law enforcement officers. Blacks and Hispanics, who may need the police more than most people, are the most likely to be victims of police misconduct. With any luck, this investigation will do for other police departments what [Police Commissioner] Lee Brown has done for New York: help make them more responsive to the communities they serve."

Meanwhile, Los Angeles Police Chief Daryl Gates has apologized "to the members of other departments because we have brought shame and dishonor to the profession. It is a unanimous opinion of this department that that kind of conduct was wrong. It was humiliating.

"One of the failures of this organization is that we bring in police officers from the human race. And human beings fail." It may be little more than an attempt to resist demands for his resignation, but the words, at least, are right.

Police officers are members of the human race. But so are the people they serve, including those they sometimes have to arrest.

Some cops—not all, nor even most, but some—forget this fundamental fact of police work, preferring to see themselves as occupying forces rather than servants of the people. And that's why that videotaped beating, though unarguably worse than most, is far from the isolated incident Gates would have us believe it is.

Prejudice, Discrimination, and Stereotypes

An important distinction needs to be made at this point between *prejudice* and *discrimination*. Combining parts of definitions used by Allport[5] and Schaefer,[6] we will define *prejudice* as a feeling, favorable or unfavorable "based upon faulty and inflexible generalization," which may be "directed toward a group as a whole, or toward an individual because he is a member of that group."[7] Prejudice involves attitudes, thoughts, and beliefs, not actions.[8] Although both Allport and Schaefer stress the negative aspects of prejudice, and while we will be concentrating here mostly on these negative aspects, it is important to note that prejudice also may involve faulty or inflexibly favorable bias. As a result, many minority group members feel that other members of their group must be right in confrontations with the police, and many police officers assume that members of the police force must be right in confrontations with minority group members, regardless of the facts of the specific confrontation. Thus, members of both groups may support fellow group members whether they are right or wrong as a result of both negative feelings toward the other group and their positive attitudes toward members of their own groups. It is observed that such feelings can be very intense and difficult to change.

Prejudice may or may not result in *discrimination;* which "is the denial of opportunities and equal rights to individuals and groups because of prejudice or other arbitrary reasons."[9] We note that discrimination may also involve behavior which concedes to all members of a group certain rights, opportunities, or privileges. Thus, one police officer may grant another the right to abuse or harass minority group members because he is a fellow police officer. Similarly, minority group members may support the harassment of police officers by other minority group members because they are fellow minority group members. In considering police minority relations, then, it is essential to be aware of both the positive and negative aspects of prejudice and discrimination, since both may be present in any given encounter.

While prejudice and discrimination do not always occur together, the presence or suspected presence of either is often enough to produce difficulties in police minority interaction. Evidence indicates that many white police officers (and some black police officers) have negative attitudes toward blacks.[10] While this prejudice may result in certain forms of discrimination, the evidence as to whether prejudice is the basis for determining whether or not to take official police action is mixed.[11] The various forms of discriminatory harassment which do occur may be extremely demeaning to minority group members, whether or not they reflect actual prejudice on the part of the police officer. Such discrimination results in loss of face and dignity. Human relations manifestly suffer, and since human relations are the foundation of community relations, the latter also are adversely affected.

There is little doubt that many minority group members believe that such harassment occurs frequently; that the police treat minority and dominant group members inequitably. As a consequence, they resent the presence of the police, partly at least, because of these beliefs.[12] Since discriminatory action of this type also occurs in reverse, that is, minority group members harass the police, both sides often enter encounters with prejudices against one another. It is essential to realize that prejudice and discrimination are not limited to the police or to the dominant group. Members of racial and ethnic minorities also harbor prejudices and act in discriminatory fashion. Thus, improvement in relationships involving the police, dominant group members, and minority group members is not likely to be accomplished by reducing or eliminating prejudice and/or discrimination in any one group. So long as one of the conflicting groups continues to act in discriminatory fashion, or to openly profess prejudices, certain acts or expressions in one faction will perpetuate negative feelings and actions toward the others.

Underlying much prejudice and discrimination are *stereotypes,* which are "exaggerated images of the characteristics of a particular group."[13] We all employ stereotypes in day-to-day life, but when stereotypes convey largely negative or distorted images of other people, they may create serious problems. Research indicates that the stereotypes or perceptions the dominant group in the U.S. hold concerning some racial and ethnic minorities and women frequently convey such negative information.[14] Our own observations and conversations with police officers over the past decade indicate that the police share many of these negative attitudes, and perhaps exaggerate them even more than does the general public. For instance, a young police officer observed, "These young blacks are trouble. They've all got the comb in the hair, jive talk, and pimp walk. They all think they're real bad actors. The old ones are different. They show a little respect. But the young ones—." There is little doubt that many minority group members also have negative stereotypes of both dominant group members and police officers. In dealing with people who do not belong to the "we" group, there may be a tendency to resort to these stereotypes. Thus, we have heard police officers say, "Blacks are all alike. You can't trust any of them." Similarly, minority group members often feel that "All cops are pigs. They're all out to harass us. They're all scared of us. They're all out for what they can get."

At one level, both police officers and blacks know that these attitudes are inaccurate. This is clearly indicated by comments from members of both groups about "exceptions," members of the "they" group who do not fit the stereotype. However, to the extent that individual differences are ignored and negative stereotypes employed in encounters, human relations and community relations suffer. Further, improvement in intergroup relationships is impeded because of a belief that positive interactions are exceptional, that is, not really representative of typical intergroup encounters.

The "Establishment," the Police, and the "People"

As we have indicated, police officers may be viewed as being members of a "marginal group," one which doesn't quite fit into either minority or dominant group status.[15] Nonetheless, the police are most often perceived by members of racial and ethnic minorities as representing the power and wealth of the "establishment" or government, which is controlled by the dominant sector in the interests of that group.[16] Herein lies much difficulty in police minority relations, and such a view is certainly not without foundation. As Alex points out, a major function of the police in the United States (and, we might point out, in every other society) is to serve as a buffer between the dominant group and potentially disruptive minorities.[17] As agents of the establishment, police officers are assumed to share the values of the dominant group, which include keeping minorities "in their place." The black population, of course, has several centuries of historical reasons for viewing the police with suspicion, resentment, and contempt. As Sykes points out, "In a democratic social order, the police are expected to be fair in their enforcement of the law and accountable to those who are policed. They are not to be an alien force imposed on a community, an autonomous body ruling by coercion, or agents of a tyrannical state, but servants of society maintaining a commonly accepted body of law in evenhanded fashion."[18]

The police have been the alien force Sykes mentions, far more frequently than the evenhanded servants of society, when they are dealing with blacks and other minority groups. Until the 1950s, in the South by law (*de jure*) and in the North by fact (*de facto*), nonwhites were considered by most whites to be second-class citizens, and treated as such. In the South, it was the police who enforced laws making nonwhites second-class citizens, and in the North, in spite of the law, many police officers acted as though nonwhites were second-class citizens. It is in this historical context (which will be expanded in the following section) that police minority relations must be viewed if they are to be understood.

Contemporary evidence demonstrates that the police expend a disproportionate amount of their resources in minority neighborhoods. Although minority group members often interpret this distribution of police resources as discriminatory, the dominant group supports this use of law enforcement resources. Further, the police justify the special attention given to minority group members on the grounds that these individuals are most likely to commit or be victims of crimes. As Sykes indicates, the police are probably correct in arguing that minority group members have high conventional crime rates and that such statistics are not simply the result of police prejudice or expanded surveillance.[19] In fact, the police "bias" in such cases may have more to do with social class than with race or ethnicity. Sykes argues, however, "But even if discriminatory tactics do allow the police to detect more crimes and apprehend more criminals, such practices cannot therefore be declared acceptable. The exercise of police power in a specific situation must, in theory, be based upon specific present knowledge and not statistical generalizations, even though such generalizations are a valid summary of similar events."[20]

Believing these policing practices are evidence of discrimination on behalf of the establishment, carried out by their agents, the police, many minority group members react with suspicion and hostility to police-initiated

Crimes of Bigotry Are More Violent Than Believed

By Arlene Levinson
of the Associated Press

BOSTON—Crimes motivated by bigotry are more violent than previously assumed, according to a study released Monday by Northeastern University.

"The idea that a civil rights violation consists of kids painting graffiti on a church or throwing a rock through a window does not describe the type of incidents reported to the Boston police," Professor Jack McDevitt wrote in his study for the Center for Applied Social Research at Northeastern University.

"More than 50 percent of the incidents of racial violence identified in our study are acts of a very serious and potentially injury-resulting character."

The study examined 452 crimes reported from 1983 to 1987 and identified by the Boston Police Community Disorders Unit as motivated by bigotry.

The crimes included whites assaulting a white boyfriend of a black female, bricks thrown through windows, a swastika painted on a synagogue and assaults on homosexuals.

Fifty-three percent of the crimes were categorized as physical assaults, and 47 percent as property damage.

Howard J. Ehrlich, research director of the National Institute Against Prejudice and Violence, an independent organization in Baltimore, called the Northeastern study "the first really decent analysis of hard data."

Such research reinforces findings of the Baltimore institute that one out of four or five minority persons will be victimized during the course of a year, he said.

"It's very underreported," McDevitt said. "Victims fear retaliation. And victims will deny it's a hate crime. If you feel you're a victim because of your religion or your color, then each time you step out the door (you fear) you're going to be attacked."

Among the findings:

- Sixty-three percent of the racial incidents were perpetrated by whites, 33 percent by blacks. Four percent of such offenses were committed by people of Hispanic or Asian origin.

- The largest percentage of victims—35 percent—were white, followed by blacks, 32 percent; Vietnamese, 12 percent, other Asian, 11 percent; Hispanics, including Portuguese, 7 percent; and Jews, 1 percent.

- In 30 percent of the cases, victims were told they were being attacked because they "did not belong" in a neighborhood.

---

encounters. Both well-meaning police officers and minority group members may be caught up in such suspicions and hostilities, and the cycle of poor community relations in minority areas continues.

Police Relations with Blacks

In the last five decades there have been a number of changes in American society which have influenced the nature of police minority relations. The decision of the U.S. Supreme Court in 1954 that separate educational facilities are inherently unequal, the use of civil disobedience and nonviolent resistance in the 1950s and 1960s, the passage of the Civil Rights Act in 1964, the establishment of the Equal Employment Opportunity Commission, the 1972 Amendment to the Civil Rights Act, and the Civil Rights Act of 1991 are among these changes.[21] Collectively, these actions prohibited discrimination in education, hiring and promotion, voting, use of public accommodations, etc. The urban violence of the years 1965–68 revealed that many minority group members were willing to take direct, sometimes violent action to bring about a change in the status quo. In the 1970s busing programs introduced to produce integration of schools resulted in white "backlash" and more interracial conflict. In the 1980s and 1990s, affirmative action programs have led to charges of reverse discrimination and more white backlash.

The police have been involved in all of these changes. At times, the police have been used to prevent minority group members from demonstrating on behalf of civil rights, and on occasion they have been extremely violent in dealing with protesting minority group members. At other times, the police have acted to protect these same demonstrating minorities from the wrath of the dominant group and from other minority group members who opposed such demonstrations. During the urban violence of the 1960s, the police were often contributors to the incidents which directly preceded such violence. In short, the types of encounters which have occurred between the police and minority group members have led to, as well as resulted from, the alienation of the groups from one another. Thus members of both groups enter encounters with one another with a good deal of "baggage" based upon what they have heard and seen with respect to such encounters. Police officers expect passive resistance, verbal abuse, claims of racism, and so on from members of minority groups who, in turn, expect that the police will harass them verbally and/or physically and harbor prejudices with respect to them.

Events occurring between 1960 and 1970 are of particular significance in analyzing the current state of police minority relations. In fact, it might be argued that these events and the investigations which followed have served to point out just how critical police minority relations are to society as a whole. Though it is true that police minority encounters were not the only, and perhaps not even the major, cause of violence resulting from or incident to racial protest, they were frequently the immediate precipitators of such violence.[22] Harlem, Watts, Newark, and Detroit were all scenes of major racial outbursts in the 1960s, and in each case the outburst was precipitated by arrests of blacks by white police officers.[23] Analysis of the results of seventy-five civil disorders occurring in 1967 involving blacks and the police shows at least eighty-three people killed, mostly black citizens. In addition, a number of police and fire department personnel were killed or injured. Estimates of property damage related to these disorders involved hundreds of millions of dollars.[24] Millions of Americans watched on television as blacks looted and burned in Watts, Chicago, and other locations, while the police looked on helplessly. In 1987, three black males were attacked by a group of whites in Howard Beach in New York. One was killed and another seriously injured as a result of the encounter.[25] In 1989, two black teenagers were picked up by Chicago police officers and dropped off in a largely white neighborhood where they were later beaten by whites.[26] And, in 1992, after the announcement of the verdict in the trial of officers accused of beating Rodney King in Los Angeles, the police were again helpless to stop the looting and burning which resulted in millions of dollars in damage, the severe beating of white truck driver Reginald Denny, and countless other injuries.[27] In the aftermath of each of these tragedies, observers were left with the same questions: Why? How?

Investigations following the protests of the 1960s disclosed that very few police departments had formalized policies for maintaining or improving relations with minority groups. Few had initiated measures to collect information concerning the attitudes and concerns of minorities with respect to the police (or for that matter, in regard to anything else), and this remains true in many cases as we approach the middle of the 1990s. The fact that many police officers expressed prejudice against blacks was widely known, but the extent to which these prejudices appeared as forms of psychological and physical harassment was unknown and apparently considered to be of little importance. As a result, civil disorders involving blacks in many cities throughout the United States caught the police largely off guard and unprepared.[28] National Guard units, state militia, and state police agencies were called in to assist local authorities, but the damage had been done.

For some time following the riots of 1967, police administrators voiced support for and concern about police minority relations. Numerous programs were developed and implemented to improve these relations. Some programs were relatively successful, others were merely devices employed to cover up the fact that nothing had really changed.

More than a quarter of a century later, we see clear evidence that the unpleasant memories of the 1960s have receded into the backs of the minds of some police administrators; the same appears to be true of the general public. There is little doubt, however, that the same tensions that found temporary release on the streets of the urban centers of our country in the 1960s, 1980s, and early 1990s still exist. The growing ''underclass'' represents a real and present problem which we cannot afford to ignore. Well-thought-out, well-planned programs to address the issue of policing in diverse settings are essential if the mistakes which led to earlier minority and police violence are not to be repeated. Although such programs cannot by themselves correct the underlying conditions that arouse the frustration and hostility of black and other minority Americans, they may well reduce the likelihood that the police will unwittingly precipitate racial outbursts.[29] Still, there is always the danger that the gap between expectations of minority group members and the reality they experience in the workplace, in schools, and in society in general will keep frustration levels high. Though the frustration may be directed primarily at the establishment, the target of the frustration is often the police who are the visible representatives of that establishment.[30] As Meddis notes, a vicious cycle begins with a host of inner-city problems—chronic unemployment, poor education, drug addiction, and broken homes—that often lead to crime. The police increase their presence in the inner city, to deal with that crime, leading to closer scrutiny of local residents, which in turn leads to higher arrest rates. This leads blacks to distrust the police and the police to look on blacks as enemies.[31]

None of these considerations indicates that police minority encounters are likely to be free of problems. Considering the fact that there are more than 30 million blacks in the United States, such encounters are common. In addition, increasing awareness of black political power, as indicated by the election of increasing numbers of black politicians, clearly demonstrates the need for greater understanding and better working relationships on both the societal and public service levels. Nonetheless, there is clear evidence that uncivil encounters between black Americans and the police continue to occur on an all-too-frequent basis.[32]

Police Relations with Hispanics

There are more than 20 million Hispanics in the United States. The term Hispanic covers a diverse population sharing a common language—Chicanos or Mexican Americans, Puerto Ricans, Cubans, and others. The largest group consists of Chicanos, who number over 13 million. Hispanics are located in different areas of the country—most Chicanos reside in the Southwest, most Puerto Ricans in the Northeast, and most Cubans in Florida. There has, in the last decade, been some movement away from these traditional areas, however. Like blacks, Hispanics have historically been victims of prejudice and discrimination in the United States.[33]

The vast majority of Hispanics live in urban areas, with about one-fourth existing at or near the poverty level.[34] Language problems handicap many Hispanics, and poor educational backgrounds are common among Chicanos and Puerto Ricans. Stacey reports that in 1.6 million Hispanic households in the United States, no one above the age of fourteen speaks English fluently.[35] In addition, many Hispanics are in this country illegally, which often leads to contact with the police. Hispanic gang activity has also created serious problems in several urban areas. According to Brantley and DiRosa: "In some areas, gang membership has become a family tradition. Hispanic gang members in East Los Angeles typically reveal in interviews that cousins, brothers, or other family members also actively participate in gangs."[36]

Puerto Ricans are even less well-off economically than Hispanics in general, with one-third at or near the poverty level.[37] A number of studies have indicated that Puerto Ricans in New York City are hostile toward the police, in part because of police tactics.[38]

Refugees have come from Cuba in several waves following Fidel Castro's assumption of power, and their presence is especially evident in the Miami, Florida, area, where they account for about half of the population. Overall, Cubans have fared well compared to other Hispanic immigrants in the United States. Many are reasonably well-educated and/or possess skills which they use to their advantage here. However, recent waves of immigrants have included a number of hard-core criminals who have caused serious problems for Miami and Dade County officials. Following anti-Castro protests in the streets of

Havana in 1994, Florida officials petitioned the federal government for assistance in planning for and financing an anticipated renewal of Cuban refugees.

As this brief discussion indicates, encounters between Hispanics and the police share many of the same characteristics of those discussed in the preceding section. Racial and ethnic differences may be further complicated by language barriers, but barrios and black ghettos share many common characteristics. Police response to these two minority groups has been similar in that more officers of each group have been hired in recent years, police resources are disproportionately allocated to both types of neighborhoods, and officers policing these neighborhoods are more often culturally and linguistically similar to area residents. One major difference between the two groups is in crime rates. Hispanics have crime rates more similar to Caucasians, at least in the area of violent crimes.[39]

Police Relations with Asian Americans

Asian Americans are a diverse group and the fastest-growing racial minority in the United States, numbering over 7 million.[40] Asian Americans have been held up as a model minority group because of their successes in the educational and employment fields, and some, specifically the Japanese, are involved in more mixed race marriages than within race marriages.[41] Not all members of the Asian American community have fared so well, however, and many are uncertain when it comes to dealing with the police. Many fear the police and as a result fail to call for help when crimes are committed.[42] At the same time, Asian American gangs who commit violent crimes are increasing in number, both in the United States and elsewhere, creating serious problems for the police.[43]

Although they do not represent all Asian American groups in the United States, perhaps a look at Chinese and Vietnamese immigrant's attitudes toward American police can provide some insights into police relations with Asian Americans.

Song[44] conducted a study in the Los Angeles area of Vietnamese refugees and Chinese immigrants with respect to their attitudes toward the police. He found that both groups listed fear of crime as a major concern. Additionally, the Vietnamese felt that poor communication with the police and gang activities were important problems, while the Chinese perceived police prejudice to be a major problem. Song concludes: "I believe that police-Asian community relations present new challenges to law enforcement in America. Language differences may generate more problems in dealing with the police for Asians than for blacks; cultural differences may generate different problems for Asians than for blacks or Hispanics."

It is clear that relationships between the police and members of racial and ethnic minority groups have been and remain problematic. What has been said about racial and ethnic minorities is basically true with respect to many other minorities as well, including, for example, the homeless, those with religious beliefs outside the mainstream, those with AIDS, homosexuals, and so on. What, if anything, can be done to improve the quality of these relationships?

Improving Police Relationships with Racial and Ethnic Minorities

Before discussing specific methods for improving police relationships with racial and ethnic minorities, a few general observations should be made. First, any lasting improvement in these relationships will require changes among members of all groups involved. Legomsky concludes: "The United States has two venerable traditions. One is to admit immigrants. The other is to complain vigorously about whatever immigrant group is most visible at the time. Irish, German, Jewish, Chinese, Japanese, Eastern European, Southern European, and, more recently, Mexican immigrants have all been targets at first. Successive generations all proved their detractors wrong. If we are patient, they will do so again."[45]

Second, although public relations programs may be used to help improve police minority relations, they are likely to fail if they are not based upon sincere and fundamental changes in human relations. Third, police minority relations will not be trouble-free while race and ethnicity remain bases for discrimination in the society at large. Recent events occurring in Wedowee, AL indicate that prejudice and discrimination remain alive and well. In this small southern town, a high school principal threatened to cancel the high school prom rather than permit interracial couples at the dance. He referred to a mixed race student as a "mistake." And in August of 1994, the high school serving the community was burned as a result of arson. "For some whites, it [the high school arson] means their quaint, friendly community, where the races 'always got along,' has been branded by 'outsiders' as a backwater steeped in racism. For some blacks, it means that the years of silent suffering at the hands of the high school principal and other whites in this town of 908 finally might be over. And for the entire region, it means being forced, yet again, to publicly examine prejudices that still divide blacks and whites in the New South—a place that in thirty years was supposed to have moved to tolerance from bigotry." (Watson and Stone, 1994.)[46]

We do not claim to furnish guaranteed or perfect solutions to these problems. However, progress anywhere along this front is important. Partial solutions and experimental programs must be tried if we do not wish to witness continually deteriorating police minority relations.

The brief historical overview we have presented indicates that the police, minority groups, and the dominant group all have somewhat negative images of each other. Each of these groups brings certain expectations to encounters. Some of these expectations are based on fact, others on prejudices formed over many years. For example, one police officer responding to a call in a largely black, low-income housing project reflected, "These people are nothin' but trouble. What the hell do you expect? They take the scum of the city and put 'em into half a dozen high-rise apartment buildings what do you expect? You watch, I'm gonna have to fight a couple of these bastards!" Or, a black woman explaining why she hadn't called the police to investigate the theft of a stereo worth over $1,000: "Call the police? What the hell for? They can't do nothin'.

They come down here, if they come at all, write down a bunch of crap on a piece of paper, go back downtown and throw the paper in the shitcan. They don't do nothin.'' All participants in such encounters, then, are subject to misperception and misinterpretation of one another's actions and intentions.

The patrol car in the ghetto may be perceived by members of racial and ethnic minorities as a form of police harassment, while the police may believe they are acting in the best interests of the minorities by providing as many personnel as possible in the areas where citizens are most likely to commit and be victims of crime. Similarly, the presence of a patrol car in a quiet, middle-class neighborhood may indicate trouble to residents, while the police may simply be performing routine patrol. Alternatively, young black, Asian, or Hispanic males who use the slang and dress of their subculture may be perceived by the police as troublemakers challenging their authority. Or the middle-class citizen who is upset with himself for being apprehended for a traffic violation may be perceived by the police officer who stops him as a threat to his prestige. The perception of all police as ''honky bastards'' is no more accurate than the perception of all blacks as ''lazy niggers.'' Such negative stereotypes are clearly inaccurate, and their persistence makes it difficult if not impossible to share a definition of the situation or reach a mutual understanding. In these circumstances, most encounters are threatening to the ''face'' of all parties involved. If police minority relations are to improve, these negative stereotypes will have to be replaced by more accurate portraits. Let us now look at some of the ways in which this goal may be achieved.

A major objective of integrated education is to provide equal educational opportunities to all individuals. If and when this is accomplished, members of minority and dominant groups should be equally well-qualified for the job market. Equal Employment Opportunity and Affirmative Action programs are designed to insure that race, ethnicity, gender, disability, and religion will not affect one's chances of being hired or promoted, unless there is some bona fide reason for selection based on one or more of these characteristics. As a consequence of these programs, intergroup contact will increase, and traditional attitudes which are inaccurate may be altered or eliminated where qualified minority group members demonstrate their abilities to perform competently the tasks assigned them. The results of such intergroup contact, among individuals of equal status who are convinced that one group's gain will not result in another group's loss, appear to indicate a positive change in attitudes, although the evidence is not clear-cut.[47] In terms of police encounters with members of racial and ethnic minorities, the condition of equal status is often lacking at the outset, and parties to the encounters may believe they will lose face or authority if they allow one another to share equal status. A great deal of effort will be required to convince participants in these encounters that everyone gains face and authority is less likely to be challenged when encounters are conducted in a civil fashion, where each participant respects the other's rights. This is clearly one goal of community policing in which all participants are engaged in improving the quality of life in the community or neighborhood. Chief Willie Williams of the Los Angeles Police Department believes the best way to accomplish this task is for police officers to view other citizens as customers rather than as enemies.[48]

The police are public officials whose job is to serve the public without regard to race or ethnicity. It must be made clear to police officers that it is the behavior of an individual, not his or her race or ethnicity, that should determine whether or not police intervention occurs. Although certain behaviors violate the law, race, ethnicity, and beliefs or preferences are not offenses. At the same time, minority group members should realize that if the police are to treat them civilly and as individuals, they must reciprocate.

Hiring and promotional policies implemented by police agencies are essential to bring about positive changes. Equal employment and promotional opportunity have several beneficial effects. First, when hiring and promotion are based on standards other than race, ethnicity, or gender, one of the criteria for bringing about positive change through intergroup contact is satisfied. Second, such practices show that the police no longer consist exclusively of dominant group personnel, with minority members not allowed to share the "secrets" of the establishment. Although the police may still be regarded by some as oppressive, or "puppets" of the establishment, it becomes increasingly difficult to characterize them as racist. It should be noted here that both hiring and promotional practices must provide equal opportunity if positive results are to be realized. It is not enough to simply change hiring practices, as many police departments have done. Both minority group members who are hired and minority group citizens at large are likely to believe that the "real power" still resides with dominant-group members if few or no minority personnel are involved in decision making. This may be interpreted to indicate that minority group members are acceptable as workers, but not as decision makers. Memories of the days when slaves or servants did all the work but made none of the decisions are easily revived, and such recollections can have only negative effects for police minority relations.

The hiring of minority group members by police departments does not mean that blacks should police only blacks, Hispanics only Hispanics, and so on. In fact, there is evidence to indicate that police minority relations suffer when these practices are implemented, since minority officers are often more strict with members of their group than dominant officers in similar situations. In addition, minority officers are frequently regarded by members of their own racial or ethnic groups not only as "cops" but also as "traitors."[49]

Equal employment opportunity and promotional practices provide opportunity for police officers who work with members of different races and nationalities to discover that they have common interests, needs, motives, and desires. In addition, along with some of the other measures we have discussed, these practices allow members of the public, irrespective of race, ethnicity, gender, or religion, to observe that individuals of all races, all ethnic groups/religions, and both genders can be relied upon to perform police functions. It is the behavior and competence of the individual officer that count, not the color of his or her skin.

In practice, equal opportunities for hiring and promotion are not always easy to arrange, primarily because of the second criterion we mentioned earlier with respect to intergroup contact—the fear that gains of minority groups will lead to losses among members of the dominant group. This apprehension is especially great, and to some extent justified, when different standards are set for hiring and promoting members of two groups. If well-qualified applicants are rejected and less-qualified applicants accepted in order to correct ''racial imbalances,'' members of the group considered to be more qualified will be angry, hostile, and frustrated. To say that minority group members have experienced such feelings over many years and that the shoe is now on the other foot does little to alter these reactions, even though it may be true. In addition, such practices violate the intention of the Equal Opportunity Act as we understand it. Nonetheless, we know of many police departments in which most dominant group members believe such practices exist, and some in which the evidence supports this belief. These beliefs and practices, where they exist, almost certainly will lead to intergroup hostilities.

Some of this resentment may carry over into police public encounters, because they create situations in which one group's gains will be another group's losses, and the outcome of such situations will not be based on behavior, but upon race, gender, or ethnicity. Since these are the very complaints that minorities have made for years, it is evident that such practices will not improve police minority relations. Though it may be difficult for dominant group police officers to accept minority officers as equals, it is certain that they will not do so if the standards for minority personnel are lower than those for members of the dominant group. Equal employment and promotion based upon equal qualifications, with race, ethnicity, and gender excluded from consideration, provide the best opportunity to modify traditional stereotypes.

Improving police training in the area of human relations is another important factor in ameliorating police minority relations. Many police departments have raised educational requirements for recruits, and have encouraged their recruits as well as in-service officers to take courses in the social sciences, in order to make them more aware of the nature and problems of human interaction. To the extent that these courses make students aware of the nature of human interaction in general and police public encounters in particular, they may help improve police minority relations. In most instances, whether or not an encounter between a police officer and another citizen occurs depends upon the officer. Thus, for example, the officer should realize the importance of beginning with a civil greeting, which may make it possible for both parties to interact with a minimum loss of face.

The officer's goals of obtaining information, assuming control, and resolving difficult situations may best be achieved without resorting to discriminatory words or actions. At the same time, minority group members need to be aware that antagonizing words or deeds on their part are likely to be interpreted as a challenge to the authority or prestige of the police officer, and thus may provoke the officer to assert greater authority, perhaps including the use of force, an action that makes civil or courteous conduct of an encounter difficult. Both parties should be aware of the importance of both verbal and nonverbal communications and make determined efforts to interact without serious altercation.

One major impediment to achieving mutual cooperation should be mentioned here. Although police departments can require police officers to take courses in the social sciences and participate in training seminars dealing with human and public relations, it is not possible to require minority group members in society at large to do the same. Of course, there are those officers who are required to participate in such seminars who do not benefit from them, who scoff at them, and who view being sensitive to and tolerant of diversity as unbecoming ''real cops.'' One of the authors who frequently facilitates seminars on diversity encounters such officers fairly frequently, and in some departments many, if not most officers, even in the mid 1990s, continue to hold this view. The influence of these officers on recruits is extremely difficult to overcome as a result of the pressures of the police subculture.

Nonetheless, the police must take the initiative in improving police minority relations. The desired improvements will only be achieved, however, if minority group members respond positively to police efforts, and if police officers realize that some encounters will be unpleasant despite their best attempts. Also, minority group members who attempt to improve police minority relations may be faced with uncivil or uncooperative police officers. Nevertheless, improvement can be made, as we have seen, even though the participants in the encounter do not like each other and have conflicting goals. It will be most difficult to ameliorate conditions or reconcile differences if neither party understands the need for mutual respect and concern in human relationships.

Police departments employ a variety of public relations activities to help improve relations with minority groups. The establishment of reasonable, well-publicized grievance procedures for citizens with complaints against the police is one such strategy. Another is to hold public meetings with any interested group to confront and attempt to resolve issues disturbing the parties involved. And there are other useful strategies—opening the police department to public inspection, providing opportunities for interested citizens to ride with patrol officers, establishing citizen police academies in which citizens learn more about police work, issuing clear public explanations for changes in policies and procedures, inviting the public to participate in policy making, and taking prompt public disciplinary action against officers who violate the law. Publication in the media of the goals and programs of police departments, and unbiased coverage of issues relevant to police minority relations, often have positive results. Programs designed to recruit minority officers, promote youth activities, acquaint neighborhood residents with the police, and cooperate with them in making their neighborhoods better places to live have also met with success. So, too, have programs aimed at increasing bicultural understanding and communication.[50]

Another step that must be taken by the police to improve relations with minority groups is to deal with officers who indicate by their behavior that they have no respect for minority group members. Though it is impossible to exclude from police work all those who harbor prejudices against one group or another, it certainly is possible to eliminate from the ranks of the police those who discriminate against members of racial and ethnic groups. There is, unfortunately, considerable evidence that the police have not been vigilant enough in weeding out officers who are involved in brutality complaints, let alone officers who use racial slurs or *ethnophaulisms*. In Los Angeles, for example, "two of the four officers indicted in the Rodney King beating had suspension records; one had been removed for 66 days in 1987 for beating and kicking a suspect. In a Miami incident that ultimately sparked disturbances last December, several of a group of six policemen allegedly beat Leonardo Mercado, a Puerto Rican drug dealer, to death. All had remained on patrol duty despite the fact that five of the six had previously shown up on the Miami Police Department's 'early warning list' for their violent behavior and three had been counseled for stress in the months before the incident. Among them, they had 'forcibly controlled' suspects a total of 38 times in three years. All were cleared of civil rights violations."[51]

Using racial slurs, using an individual's first name when courtesy would call for a surname, and questioning and frisking under circumstances that do not warrant such action are some of the more common forms of derogatory behavior. In one instance, for example, a police officer called to a young black male walking with some friends, "Hey, J. B. (Jungle Bunny). Get your black ass over here." To one of the authors he explained, "You gotta let 'em know where they stand right away." Officers who discriminate against minority group members using these techniques should be removed from the police ranks, for several reasons. First, they do irreparable harm to all police minority relations. Second, directly or indirectly, they increase to some unknown extent the danger and suspicion latent in every police minority encounter. Third, if such persons are allowed to continue as police officers, they are likely, without legitimate cause, to injure or kill a citizen (as we saw in the preceding paragraph), or to be injured or killed themselves.

In conclusion, it should be noted that a basic misunderstanding exists concerning the nature of police community, and therefore, minority relations. In order to impress upon the individual police officer the importance of these relations, we have stressed the fact that courteous, considerate relations are the responsibility of every police officer, not just the community relations officer or unit. Although this is quite obvious, it has been interpreted to mean that there is no need to have a community relations program under a supervisor who evaluates, develops, and plans the improvement of relations with the community. Without evaluation, development, and planning, many police administrators muddle along, assuming that police community relations are as good as could be expected, or that there is no problem. Experience reveals that this is very often not the case, that it is becoming less and less likely to be the case as the "underclass" in our society continues to grow, and that police departments would benefit from having someone assigned to make certain that every officer is aware of his or her responsibility for relations with the community.

In practice, then, it is essential for the police, minority groups, and the dominant group to recognize that police minority relations can be improved only when there is mutual concern, understanding, and respect. Only in these circumstances can contemporary difficulties, which have deep historical roots, be overcome, so that today's police minority relations may serve as the basis for positive attitudes in future encounters.

The police, of course, are not the only representatives of the criminal justice network who experience difficulties in relating to minority groups. Prejudice and discrimination are also found among court and correctional personnel, and, in general, minority group members do not believe they receive fair, unbiased treatment from these agents of justice. The fact that the majority of inmates in most state and federal prisons are nonwhite is interpreted (with some justification) as evidence that equal treatment in the criminal justice network is more a myth than a reality. It will require more than police minority relations programs to change minority perceptions; to expect the police alone to accomplish this change is unrealistic. Determined, coordinated efforts on the part of all members of the criminal justice network might reduce the strains encountered in dealing with members of minority groups, but only a change in prejudicial attitudes and discrimination at the societal level can be expected to alter significantly the basic nature of relationships between criminal justice representatives and members of minority groups.

Summary

For many years, police minority relations have been the most controversial area in police community relations. Racial and ethnic minorities, as well as other minorities, have been the objects of a great deal of prejudice and discrimination on the part of the dominant group and the police. The police themselves constitute a sort of minority group and are often regarded and treated as such by members of racial and ethnic minorities and, to some extent, by the general population.

Dividing the world into those who share the characteristics of our own group (''we'') and those who do not (''they'') often arouses feelings of suspicion and distrust that may lead to open hostilities.

An important distinction between prejudice and discrimination is that the former reflects feelings, attitudes, and beliefs, while the latter is expressed in actions. Problems in police minority relations result from negative feelings and actions on the part of members of different groups interacting with one another, and positive feelings and actions toward in-group members. All groups, including minorities, harbor feelings of prejudice and have their own ways of discriminating against outsiders.

The persistence of negative stereotypes hampers efforts to improve police minority relations. So, also, does the belief among some minority group members that the police are simply a ''tool of the establishment'' used to suppress the people. Feelings about unemployment, housing, health care, and other social issues, which should be directed at those in the establishment who are responsible for these matters, are often expressed as hostility toward the police, who are, in most instances, the most visible representative of the establishment.

The fact that police departments assign more personnel to heavily minority areas than to other areas often engenders negative feelings among residents of these areas. Some members of the minority group may view these practices as discriminatory and a form of harassment. The dominant group typically supports such police practices, and the police may consider such assignments appropriate, enabling them to apprehend more offenders, provide better services, and aid victims of crime.

Mutual resentment, contempt, and distrust between the police and minority groups have deep historical roots. Changes occurring in the past four decades have placed the police in the position of instigator of minority violence, protector of minority rights, and antagonist with respect to both dominant and minority groups. These changes are still going on, and problems of prejudice and discrimination remain unsolved. Any lasting solution will require the participation of all groups involved, and this is one of the goals of community policing efforts. Concern and respect for individuals, regardless of race or ethnicity, are the foundations of sound human relations, upon which positive community relations are based. Eliminating distorted stereotypes by means of education will help. Similarly, intergroup contact based on equal status of participants and fair standards for hiring and promotion should be developed, as they provide the opportunity to deal with misleading stereotypes. Improving police training in the area of human relations, using honest public-relations techniques, weeding out police officers who discriminate against other citizens, and providing for evaluation, development, and planning of police community relations efforts should also help improve police minority relations.

Discussion Questions

1. What is the difference between prejudice and discrimination, and why is this difference important in understanding and improving police minority relations?
2. List and discuss as many stereotypes involving minority groups, including the police, as you can think of. How accurate are these stereotypes? What are some of the implications of these stereotypes for police minority relations?
3. What are some of the historical reasons for distrust between the police and minority groups? What are some of the more recent changes or incidents that have complicated police minority relations?
4. What steps can the police take to improve their relations with minority groups? What actions on behalf of minority and dominant group members will be necessary if these improvement are to be made?
5. What is the relationship between community policing and police minority relations?

1. Richard T. Schaefer. 1993. *Racial and Ethnic Groups*. 5ed. New York: HarperCollins.
2. Ibid.: Chapter 1.
3. Gordon W. Allport. 1954. *The Nature of Prejudice*. Cambridge, MA: Addison-Wesley: Chapters 3 and 4.
4. George J. Church. 1992. ''The Fire This Time.'' *Time* (May 1): 19–25; David Ellis. 1992. ''L.A. Lawless.'' *Time* (May 1): 26–29.
5. Allport. *The Nature of Prejudice.*: 6–9.
6. Schaefer. *Racial and Ethnic Groups.*: 38–55.
7. Allport. *The Nature of Prejudice.*: 6, 9.
8. Schaefer. *Racial and Ethnic Groups.*: 38–55.
9. Ibid.: 67.
10. David H. Bayley and Harold Mendelsohn. 1969. *Minorities and the Police*. New York: Free Press: 144–147; Nicholas Alex. 1969. *Black in Blue*. New York: Appleton-Century-Crofts; Andrew J. Hacker. 1992. *Two Nations: Black and White, Separate, Hostile, and Unequal*. New York: Charles Scribner's Sons; Bouza. *The Police Mystique.*: 142.
11. Albert J. Reiss. 1970. ''Police Brutality: Answers to Key Questions'' in Michael Lipsky, ed. *Police Encounters*. Chicago: Aldine: 57–83; Gaines, Kappeler, and Vaughn. *Policing in America.*: 199–200; Langworthy and Travis. *Policing in America.*: 225.
12. See National Advisory Commission on Civil Disorders. 1968. *Report*. New York: Bantam.
13. Schaefer. *Racial and Ethnic Groups.*: 35.
14. Ibid.: 46–47.
15. Alex. *Black in Blue.*; Bouza. *The Police Mystique.*: 70–72; Langworthy and Travis. *Policing in America.*: 209–220.
16. Hacker. *Two Nations.*; Church. ''The Fire This Time.'' Ellis. ''L.A. Lawless.''
17. Alex. *Black in Blue.*; Bouza. *The Police Mystique.*: 4–5.
18. Gresham M. Sykes. 1978. *Criminology*. New York: Harcourt Brace Jovanovich: 395.
19. Ibid.: 388.
20. Ibid.: 388–389. For further discussion of this issue see Livingston. *Crime and Criminology*. 125–133; Roberg and Kuykendall. *Police and Society.*: 231 or William A. Geller and M. S. Scott. 1991. ''Deadly Force: What We Know'' in C. B. Klockars and S. D. Mastrofski, eds. *Thinking About the Police*. 2ed. New York: McGraw-Hill: 446–476.
21. Schaefer. *Racial and Ethnic Groups.*: Chapter 8.
22. See, for example, Hacker. *Two Nations.*; National Advisory Commission on Civil Disorders. *Report.*; Allen D. Grimshaw. 1969. *Racial Violence in the United States*. Chicago: Aldine.
23. National Advisory Commission. *Report.*: 206.
24. Ibid.: 6.
25. ''A Mixed Verdict on Howard Beach.'' 1988. *Newsweek* (January 4): 24.
26. ''Police Officers Named in Bias Suit.'' 1989. *Journal Star* (December 15): 12.
27. Ellis. ''L.A. Lawless.''
28. For an interesting discussion of the current state of affairs in this regard, see Dean DeJong. 1994. ''Civil Disorders: Preparing for the Worst.'' *FBI Law Enforcement Bulletin* 63(3): 1–7.
29. Carl S. Taylor. 1992. ''Easing Tensions Between the Police and Minorities.'' *Footprints* 4(2): 4–5.
30. Ibid.
31. Sam V. Meddis. 1992. ''Many Blacks Think Justice Not a Part of System.'' *USA Today* (May 13): 8A.
32. Linda P. Campbell. 1991. ''Police Brutality Triggers Many Complaints, Little Data.'' *Chicago Tribune* (March 24): sec. 1: 10; Hacker. *Two Nations*.

33. Roberto Rodriquez. 1993. ''Researchers Study Police Brutality Against Hispanics and Blacks.'' *Black Issues in Higher Education* 10(4): 18–19; Schaefer. *Racial and Ethnic Groups.:* 251–252.
34. Ibid.: 265.
35. Julie Stacey. 1993. ''Linguistic Diversity in the USA.'' *USA Today* (December 15): 9A.
36. Alan C. Brantley and Andrew DiRosa. 1994. ''Gangs: A National Perspective.'' *FBI Law Enforcement Bulletin* 63(5): 1–6.
37. Schaefer. *Racial and Ethnic Groups.:* 304.
38. Trojanowicz and Bucqueroux. *Community Policing.:* 61. See also, David Carter. 1985. ''Hispanic Perception of Police Performance: An Empirical Assessment.'' *Journal of Criminal Justice* 13: 487–500.
39. Livingston. *Crime and Criminology.:* 126–127.
40. Schaefer. *Racial and Ethnic Groups.:* 326.
41. Margaret L. Usdansky. 1992. ''Japanese-White Marriages Now the Norm.'' *USA Today* (December 11): 7A.
42. Kristine Donatelle. 1993. ''St. Paul Officers Gain the Trust of SE Asians.'' *Law and Order* 41(2): 50, 54.
43. Alan Harman. 1993. ''Battling Organized Asian Crime Gangs.'' *Law and Order* 41(2): 51–54.
44. John Huey-Long Song. 1992. ''Attitudes of Chinese Immigrants and Vietnamese Refugees Toward Law Enforcement in the United States.'' *Justice Quarterly* 9(4): 703–719.
45. Stephen H. Legomsky. 1993. ''An Inaccurate Image: Immigrants are More Valuable to Our Society than Many People Seem to Think.'' *Journal Star* (December 5): A7.
46. Tom Watson and Andrea Stone. 1994. ''Fighting Battles in a War That Is Over.'' *USA Today* (August 11): 1A–2A.
47. Martin N. Marger. 1994. *Race and Ethnic Relations.* Belmont, CA: Wadsworth: 54–58; Schaefer. *Racial and Ethnic Groups.:* 63–64.
48. DeWayne Wickham. 1993. ''L.A. Police Chief: Treat People Like Customers.'' *USA Today* (March 29): 13A.
49. Alex. *Black in Blue.*
50. Donatelle. ''St. Paul Officers.'': 50.
51. *U.S. News and World Report.* 1991. ''Why Brutality Persists.'' (April 1): 24–25. See also, Campbell. ''Police Brutality.''

Suggested Readings

Austin, Roy L. and Hiroko Hayama Dodge. 1992. ''Despair, Distrust, and Dissatisfaction Among Blacks and Women.'' *The Sociological Quarterly* 33(4): 579–598.
Baldwin, James. 1962. *Nobody Knows My Name.* New York: Dell.
Hacker, Andrew J. 1992. *Two Nations: Black and White, Separate, Hostile, and Unequal.* New York: Charles Scribner's Sons.
National Advisory Commission on Civil Disorders. *Report.* New York: E. P. Dutton.
Sommer, Ira, Jeffrey Fagan, and Deborah Baskin. 1994. ''The Influence of Acculturation and Familism on Puerto Rican Delinquency.'' *Justice Quarterly* 11(2): 207–228.
Song, John Huey-Long. 1992. ''Attitudes of Chinese Immigrants and Vietnamese Refugees Toward Law Enforcement in the United States.'' *Justice Quarterly* 9(4): 703–719.
Terkel, Studs. 1992. *Race: How Blacks and Whites Think and Feel About the American Obsession.* New York: The New Press.

Chapter 9

Diversity in Policing

*A*s noted earlier, some of the most problematic police public encounters occur between white male police officers and members of minority groups. Although confrontations between white police officers and black citizens are frequently challenging, blacks are not the only minority group hostile to the police as a result of racist attitudes, historical distrust, or past discrimination. Mexican Americans, American Indians, Puerto Ricans, Cubans, and Asian Americans also frequently have poor working relationships with the police. The National Advisory Commission on Civil Disorders found that poor police minority relations were an important factor in precipitating the ghetto riots of the 1960s, and recommended increased recruitment of minority officers as a partial solution to this problem.[1]

In recent years women's groups in the United States have demanded equality for women in terms of employment, promotion, and other areas. In 1972, an amendment to Title VII of the Civil Rights Act of 1964, known as the Equal Employment Opportunity Act, was passed by Congress. This amendment now applies to all government agencies with fifteen or more employees and states that it is:

> an unlawful employment practice for an employer (1) to fail or refuse to hire, or discharge any individual or otherwise to discriminate against any individual with respect to his compensation, terms, conditions, or privileges of employment, because of such individual's race, color, religion, sex, or national origin; (2) to limit, segregate, or classify his employees or applicants for employment in any way which would deprive or tend to deprive any individual of employment opportunity or otherwise adversely affect his status as an employee because of such individual's race, color, religion, sex, or national origin.[2]

The Americans with Disabilities Act (ADA) was enacted in July of 1990. The ADA makes it illegal to discriminate against persons with disabilities who are otherwise qualified for the job by blanket exclusions. It requires a selection process which deals with individuals on a case-by-case basis. It also requires that employers make reasonable accommodations to make it possible for those with disabilities to perform job-related tasks. Such accommodations might include providing access to buildings for those with disabilities, modifying workstations, or modifying work schedules. The ADA has altered the recruitment process in some police agencies by providing that medical examinations (and probably psychological testing as well) may be required only after an offer of employment has been made and by limiting the amount of information concerning medical history that can be required on application forms.[3] The extent to which the ADA will impact on policing is yet to be fully determined, but it will almost certainly lead to specifying job-related tasks more clearly and perhaps to the hiring of individuals who would previously have been excluded from police work.

The Equal Employment Opportunity Act of 1992 made an important change in the law. The change made it illegal to use statistical or other adjustments (such as adjustments to test scores) that would give minorities an advantage over majority applicants in the selection process. This will likely lead police agencies, among others, to develop a category of candidates considered ''qualified,'' rather than using rank-order eligibility lists.[4]

According to a 1971 United States Supreme Court decision, discrimination exists in employee selection procedures if a practice has an adverse impact on minority groups and if the practice cannot be shown to be directly related to successful job performance.[5] This Supreme Court decision is significant for two reasons. First, it states that an employment practice which has an adverse impact on a minority group is not necessarily a violation of the Equal Employment Opportunity Act (EEOA). An employment practice which has an adverse impact is discriminatory only if it is not directly related to the job to be performed. Thus, if a fire department eliminated from job applicants all potential fire fighters who could not carry a specified amount of weight down a ladder of specified height in a specified time period, the department might eliminate all female applicants. However, if the department could demonstrate that such activities were a normal or routine part of the fire fighter's job, no violation of the EEOA would have occurred. Second, the EEOA states that no one may be discriminated against because of his (her) ''race, color, religion, sex, or national origin.'' Thus, white males are presumably covered by the EEOA (and this was further clarified in the EEOA of 1992). As we shall see shortly, however, many white male applicants for police jobs and promotions still feel they are discriminated against as the result of the EEOA.

There is little doubt that many of the traditional selection procedures employed by police departments discriminated against minorities, women, and the disabled. It also seems probable that such discriminatory practices have seriously impaired police community relations. Let us now examine some of the practices outlawed by the EEOA, the changes which have occurred as a consequence, and the results or anticipated impact of these changes on police community relations. Because the ADA has only recently been implemented, we will not discuss its implications in detail here, but in the remainder of this

Are Women Better Cops?

In some important ways, yes, especially as the job evolves.
Cool, calm and communicative, they help put a lid on violence before it erupts.

By Jeanne McDowell

Los Angeles

Among the residents, merchants and criminals of Venice, Calif., officer Kelly Shea is as well known as the neighborhood gang leaders. The blond mane neatly tied back, slender figure and pink lipstick violate the stereotype of guardian of law and order; but Shea, 32, has managed to win the respect of street thugs who usually answer more readily to the slam of a cop's billy club. She speaks softly, raising her voice only as needed. While her record of arrests during her 10 years on patrol is comparable to those of the men in her division, she has been involved in only two street fights, a small number by any cop's standard. Faced with hulking, 6-ft. 2-in. suspects, she admits that her physical strength cannot match theirs. "Coming across aggressively doesn't work with gang members," says Shea. "If that first encounter is direct, knowledgeable and made with authority, they respond. It takes a few more words, but it works."

Hers is a far cry from the in-your-face style that has been the hallmark of mostly male police forces for years. But while women constitute only 9% of the nation's 523,262 police officers, they are bringing a distinctly different, and valuable, set of skills to the streets and the station house that may change the way the police are perceived in the community. Only on television is police work largely about high-speed heroics and gunfights in alleys. Experts estimated that 90% of an officer's day involves talking to citizens, doing paperwork and handling public relations. Many cops retire after sterling careers never having drawn their guns.

As the job description expands beyond crime fighting into community service, the growing presence of women may help burnish the tarnished image of police officers, improve community relations and foster a more flexible, and less violent, approach to keeping the peace. "Policing today requires considerable intelligence, communication, compassion and diplomacy," says Houston police chief Elizabeth Watson, the only female in the nation to head a major metropolitan force. "Women tend to rely more on intellectual than physical prowess. From that standpoint, policing is a natural match for them."

Such traits take on new value in police departments that have come under fire for the brutal treatment of suspects in their custody. The videotaped beating of motorist Rodney King by four Los Angeles cops last year threw a spotlight on the use of excessive force by police. The number of reports continues to remain high across the country after the furor that followed that attack. Female officers have been conspicuously absent from these charges: the independent Christopher commission, which investigated the L.A.P.D. in the aftermath of the King beating, found that the 120 officers with the most use-of-force reports were all men. Civilian complaints against women are also consistently lower. In San Francisco, for example, female officers account for only 5% of complaints although they make up 10% of the 1,839-person force. "And when you see a reference to a female," says Eileen Luna, former chief investigator for the San Francisco citizen review board, "it's often the positive effect she has had in taking control in a different way from male officers."

Though much of the evidence is anecdotal, experts in policing say the verbal skills many women officers possess often have a calming effect that defuses potentially explosive situations. "As a rule, they tend to be much more likely to go in and talk rather than try to get control in a way that makes everyone defensive," says Joanne Belknap, an associate professor of criminal justice at the University of Cincinnati. Women cops, she has found, perceive themselves as peacekeepers and negotiators. "We're like pacifiers in these situations," says Lieut. Helen DeWitte, a 21-year veteran of the Chicago force who was the first woman in the department to be shot in the line of duty. Having women partners for 14 years taught San Francisco sergeant Tim Foley to use a softer touch with suspects, instead of always opening with a shove. "It's nonthreatening and disarming," he says, "and in the long run, it is easier than struggling."

Such a measured style is especially effective in handling rape and domestic-violence calls, in which the victims are usually women. In 1985 a study of police officers' treatment of spousal-abuse cases by two University of Detroit professors concluded that female officers show more empathy and commitment to resolving these conflicts. While generalizations invite unfair stereotyping, male officers often tend not to take these calls as seriously, despite improved training and arrest policies in almost half of all states. "Men tend to come on with a stronger approach to quiet a recalcitrant male suspect," notes Baltimore County police chief Cornelius Behan, whose 1,580-member force includes 143 women. "It gets his macho up, and he wants to take on the cop."

Continued

Despite the research, the notion of "female" and "male" policing styles remains a controversial one. Individual temperament is more important than gender in the way cops perform, argues Edwin Delattre, author of *Character and Cops: Ethics in Policing.* Other experts contend that aggressiveness among officers is more a measure of a department's philosophy and the tone set by its top managers. "When cops are trained to think of themselves as fighters in a war against crime, they come to view the public as the enemy," observes James Fyfe, a criminal-justice professor at The American University.

Some female officers have qualms as well about highlighting gender-based differences in police work, especially women who have struggled for years to achieve equity in mostly male departments. The women fear that emphasizing their "people skills" will reinforce the charge that they don't have the heft or toughness to handle a crisis on the street. But while women generally lack upper-body strength, studies consistently show that in situations in which force is needed, they perform as effectively as their male counterparts by using alternatives, such as karate, twist locks or a baton instead of their fists.

Yet the harassment that persists in many precinct houses tempts female cops to try to blend in and be one of the boys. All too often that means enduring the lewd jokes transmitted over police-car radios and the sexist remarks in the halls. In most places it means wearing an uncomfortable uniform designed for a man, including bulletproof vests that have not been adapted to women's figures. The atmosphere is made worse because about 3% of supervisors over the rank of sergeant are women, in part owing to lack of seniority. Milwaukee police officer Kay Hanna remembers being reprimanded for going to the bathroom while on duty. Chicago Lieut. DeWitte found condoms and nude centerfolds in her mailbox when she started working patrol.

Women cops who have fought discrimination in court have fared well. Los Angeles officer Fanchon Blake settled a memorable lawsuit in 1980 that opened up the ranks above sergeant to women. Last May, New York City detective Kathleen Burke won a settlement of $85,000 and a public promotion to detective first-grade. In her suit she had alleged that her supervisor's demeaning comments about her performance and his unwillingness to give her more responsible assignments impeded her professional progress. He denied the charges. But many women still fear that complaining about such treatment carries its own risks. Beverly Harvard, deputy chief of administrative services in Atlanta, says a female officer would have to wonder "whether she would get a quick response to a call for backup later on."

Resistance toward women cops stems in part from the fact that they are still relative newcomers to the beat. In the years after 1910, when a Los Angeles social worker named Alice Stebbins Wells became the country's first full-fledged female police officer, women served mostly as radio dispatchers, matrons, and social workers for juveniles and female prison inmates. Not until 1968 did Indianapolis become the first force in the country to assign a woman to full-time field patrol. Since then, the numbers of women in policing have risen steadily, thanks largely to changes in federal antidiscrimination laws. Madison, Wis., boasts a 25% female force, the highest percentage of any department in the country.

Because female cops are still relatively few in number, a woman answering a police call often evokes a mixed response. Reno officer Judy Holloday recalls arriving at the scene of a crime and being asked, "Where's the real cop?" Detective Burke, who stands 5 ft. 2 in. and has weighed 100 lbs. for most of her 23 years on the force, says she made 2,000 felony arrests and was never handicapped by a lack of physical strength. Burke recalls subduing a 6-ft. 4-in., 240-lb. robbery suspect who was wildly ranting about Jesus Christ. She pulled out her rosary beads and told him God had sent her to make the arrest. "You use whatever you got," she says. When it looks as though a cop may be overpowered, the appropriate response for any officer—male or female—is to call for backup. "It's foolish for a cop of either sex to start dukin' it out," says Susan Martin, author of *On the Move: The Status of Women in Policing.*

A growing emphasis on other skills, especially communication, comes from a movement in many police departments away from traditional law enforcement into a community-oriented role. In major cities such as New York, Houston and Kansas City, the mark of a good officer is no longer simply responding to distress calls but working in partnership with citizens and local merchants to head off crime and improve the quality of life in neighborhoods. In Madison, which has been transformed from a traditional, call-driven department into a community-oriented operation in the past 20 years, police chief David Couper says female officers have helped usher in a "kinder, gentler organization." Says Couper: "Police cooperation and a willingness to report domestic abuse and sexual assaults are all up. If a person is arrested, there is more of a feeling that he will be treated right instead of getting beat up in the elevator."

In Los Angeles the city council is expected to pass a resolution next month that will lead to a 43% female force by the year 2000, up from 13.4% now. "We have so much to gain by achieving gender balance, we'd be nuts not to do it," says councilman Zev Yaroslavsky. Ideally, the solution in all cities and towns is a healthy mix of male and female officers that reflects the constituency they serve and the changing demands of the job.—*With reporting by Georgia Pabst/Milwaukee* chapter we will focus on police officers who are black, Hispanic, Asian American and/or female. Keep in mind that much of what we say here applies to other minority officers as well, and that changes are still forthcoming based on court decisions concerning the ADA.

Police Employment Criteria: Changing Regulations and Expectations

Height, weight, and strength requirements established by many police departments prior to 1972 served to eliminate many minority applicants and most women. Most of these requirements could not be demonstrated to be job-related, and have now been eliminated from the selection procedure.[6] In fact, the exact nature of physical requirements for the job of police officer have still to be identified in spite of numerous attempts to develop standards which apply.

A number of written examinations for entry into police work as well as for promotion have also been struck down by the courts as discriminatory.[7] In some cases background investigations, a subjective screening device employed by many police departments, have also been found to be discriminatory. Similarly, duty assignments based on race and gender have come under attack by the courts.[8]

Among the positive results of these changes in police employment criteria has been an increase in the number of minority group members and women employed. To the extent that representatives of these groups are able to perform police duties as well as their white male counterparts, the pool of qualified applicants for police work has been considerably expanded. In addition, one of the sources of poor police community relations has been modified—that of the "we-they" phenomenon based on race and gender.

Women as Police Officers

At this time reports leave little doubt that women can perform police patrol work as well as males. Block and Anderson discovered that female officers responding to calls similar to those of male police officers performed in generally similar fashion and that citizen respect for the police was also similar for the two groups.[9] Further, a study by Kerber et al. found that in eight of thirteen categories of police work, males and females were judged by citizens to be equally competent, while females were perceived as more competent in two categories (dealing with children under thirteen and dealing with rape victims).[10] In addition, 84 percent of the respondents in this study indicated that "both male and female police officers should be hired in order to improve the quality of police service."[11] And 59 percent of the respondents stated it did not matter whether they dealt officially with a male or a female officer (although 35 percent said they preferred to deal with a male officer and only 3 percent preferred dealing with a female officer).[12] Since this study was conducted in a university community, the universal validity of the results is questionable. The

authors conclude that, in general, "respondents from larger cities with higher levels of education and better jobs" have more liberal views on female police officers, but that demonstrated competence on the job is the basic criterion if policewomen are to gain acceptance.[13]

Studies by Horne,[14] Bouza,[15] Sherman,[16] and others[17] indicate that women can perform the patrol function as well as men, though sometimes in somewhat different fashion. Female officers may be somewhat less likely to resort to arrest and the use of force than their male counterparts, and more likely to defuse situations through the use of negotiating skill.

At present, women account for between 8 and 9 percent of all sworn police employees, a sizable increase in the last two decades.[18] Similarly, women now account for over 3 percent of police supervisory personnel, representing a three-fold increase from 1978.[19] Linn and Price indicate that the "role of the female police officer appears to be one in transition, with changes taking place slowly, but deliberately, as more and more women are assimilated into generalist patrol positions."[20] Although advancement to supervisory positions has been slow, this may well be due to the fact that supervisors are selected from entry level officers, often with a specified number of years of service. As time passes, the percentage of female supervisors should approach that of female sworn officers. Rich (1994) believes that mentoring is one way to help in this regard. Her research indicated that female officers with mentors were more likely to seek promotion than those without. Further, she believes mentors can help avoid "reinventing the wheel" by discussing avenues taken to overcome barriers to promotion by those who have been successful.[21]

Before concluding our discussion of women as police officers, we should note some of the less positive effects associated with female officers. Wives of male officers are frequently quite concerned about the prospect of their husbands sharing a patrol car with a female partner. This concern appears to stem from two sources. First, the wives appear to believe that female partners are less capable than male partners of protecting their husbands in violent confrontations. This is a belief shared by, and perhaps originating with, many male police officers. Second, jealousy over the possibility of extramarital sexual encounters appears to be fairly common, though perhaps less often initially verbalized than the concern with safety. The problem of lack of confidence in female partners can perhaps be alleviated by competent performance on the part of female police officers. The incidence of jealousy further complicates the already complex family life of many police officers. Some police departments invite officers' spouses to participate in stress reduction programs, and to ride along to observe the nature of police public encounters, in an attempt to deal with these two problems.

Though women in policing have made progress, there is evidence that some of their male peers and supervisors continue to be involved in discriminatory and harassing behavior.[22]

Black Police Officers

Last year residents of Cicero, a Chicago-area community notorious for its racism, called the police to report that a black man was impersonating a police officer, wearing a police uniform and driving a squad car. That was patrolman Wesley Scott, the town's first and only black policeman. Almost daily, he endures racial insults and humiliation, not only from the people he has sworn to protect but also from some of his fellow officers upon whom his life may depend.[23]

Some progress has been made in augmenting the number of blacks hired as police officers and they now comprise roughly 10 percent of local police officers.[24] Considering the fact that blacks account for approximately 12 percent of the population in the United States, this figure is relatively low. Cities like Washington, D.C., Atlanta, Detroit, and New York show increases in percentages of black officers, but even in some of these cities the proportion of blacks serving as police officers is below their numerical representation in the population of the cities. In general, other ethnic groups also remain underrepresented in police work.

As Alex points out in his perceptive analysis of black police officers in New York City, police work offers blacks civil service benefits (reasonable salary, job security, and pension) that make this profession attractive.[25] Most minority group members who become police officers apparently do so because of these perceived benefits (as is also true of most whites). Further, as Alex notes, police departments have a great deal to gain from the "protective coloration" offered by blacks in police work. Black undercover agents can collect intelligence information from the black community, information which no white agent could collect. In dealing with black protests, demonstrations, and unruly or intoxicated crowds, black police officers may be charged with brutality, but not with interracial brutality.[26] Again, similar benefits accrue to police departments when other minority officers are hired.

A third benefit to be derived from the employment of minority police officers (in addition to employment opportunities for minorities and the benefits of "protective coloration" for police departments) is a decrease in the widespread minority hostility toward the police. The available evidence, however, indicates that the extent of this benefit may have been overestimated by those doing research in the aftermath of the ghetto riots of the 1960s. Jackson and Wallach report that black citizens do not necessarily prefer black police officers to white police officers.[27] Similarly, Alex reports that black police officers sometimes have more difficulties than white police officers when dealing with the black community (particularly young, black males).[28] According to Berg: "Perhaps the single most difficult barrier to encouraging minority members to apply for police positions is the image the police have in minority communities."[29] This same situation confronts Hispanic and Asian American youth in their homes and neighborhoods.

Alex uses the concept of "double marginality" to describe the lot of the black police officer. He argues that the black police officer is sometimes viewed by his or her colleagues on the police force as being more "black" than "police officer," and that the black community may tend to focus on the police officer aspect of the role and view the officer as a traitor to his or her own race, or a turncoat. In short, neither the officer's occupational nor his or her racial peer group trusts and respects him or her.[30] According to Alex, there are considerable costs as well as rewards for blacks who select policing as a career; and the same is undoubtedly true for other minority group members. We might point out, for example, that the concept of double marginality, while questioned by some,[31] appears to apply (with appropriate modifications, of course) to women in policing as well.

Criticism may also be incurred by police administrators who actively recruit and hire minority officers. Many white male officers believe that standards of entry into policing have been lowered to accommodate minorities, that different norms are used for whites and for minorities. Other applicants may feel they are discriminated against by the "preferential treatment" clause of the EEOA which allows equally qualified minority group members to be recruited and promoted ahead of white males using a process involving consent decrees. In cases such as this, the employer consents to hire a certain number or percentage of minority group members to achieve some statistical balance in terms of race, sex, religion, or national origin. White "backlash" has created serious problems for many police administrators and this, coupled with a growing political awareness among minority police officers, has in some instances caused white and nonwhite officers to become or remain polarized. Black officers who

Police Officers Tell of Strains of Living as a 'Black in Blue'

Lena Williams

James Hargrove remembers the time he saw a robbery in progress in Manhattan. As a police officer, he wanted to jump out of his patrol car. As a black man in civilian clothes, carrying a weapon, he knew better.

So Patrolman Hargrove did what most other off-duty black police officers have been trained by instinct and by the job to do in such situations: he stayed in the car and radioed for help.

The episode, recalled recently by Mr. Hargrove, who is now an Assistant Police Commissioner in New York City, reflects some of the special problems faced by black police officer as they try to reconcile their race with their work.

Conflicts and Ambiguities

It also underscores a more complex issue: how the pervasive stereotype of criminals as young black males may influence police officers' responses. That point was illustrated in December in Prince Georges County, Md., when a black Washington police officer was shot and killed in his home by a white county police officer who mistook him for an armed burglar.

In interviews around the country, black police officers said the conflicts and ambiguities that arise from being "black in blue" can be humiliating and demoralizing.

"When the white guys finish work, they go home to their white neighborhoods and the black guys go home to the black community," said Ronald Hampton, a black Washington police officer who lives in a predominantly black section of the capital.

Another black officer in Washington said: "You may be their partner on the job, but the minute you're off duty, it's a different story. It's like you'll find a bunch of white cops hovering in the locker room snickering at something, then when you walk in they stop. Now what are you supposed to think?"

A Belief in Opportunities

Despite such problems, most of those interviewed said that their jobs were satisfying and that they believed there were opportunities to advance. The number of black police officers nationwide has more than doubled since 1972, to 42,000 from 20,000. There are 12 black police chiefs in cities, including New York, Chicago, Washington and Houston.

The black officers also overwhelmingly expressed the belief that regardless of personal likes, dislikes or prejudice, white officers would come to their aid and that they would aid white officers. All shared the view that the relationship between black police officers and the black community, where the black officer is sometimes regarded as a traitor and is often shunned, has improved in recent years, in part because of attempts by black police officers to control crime in black neighborhoods.

"We're tied to the black community by this umbilical cord," said Mr. Hampton, who is also the information director for the National Black Police Association, which has 35,000 members. "We can't sever it because we have a commonality, and that is our color. We know that if we take off our uniforms, whites would treat us the same as they do other blacks in Anacostia," a predominantly, low-income black community in the District of Columbia.

"On the one hand, we're asked to think of ourselves as being blue, not black," Sgt. Donald Jackson of the Los Angeles Police Department said in a telephone interview. "I had one fellow officer, who was white, tell me that if he calls blacks niggers it shouldn't offend me because I'm blue, not black."

But when Mr. Jackson began to speak out against such racial slurs, first to his superior officers and then to the local news media, he said he was ostracized by whites in the department.

Integration vs. Solidarity

Charles Bahn, professor of forensic psychology at the John Jay College of Criminal Justice in New York City, said the comments of these and other black officers illustrated the contradictory nature of the job.

"The police fraternity has not stretched to the point of fully embracing blacks or women." Mr. Bahn said, "It is true, in part, because black officers have segregated themselves to be a force for their own people. Self-integration interferes with the issue of solidarity, which says anyone in blue is your brother or sister."

In his book "Black in Blue: A Study of the Negro Policeman," Nicholas Alex wrote: "The black policeman can never escape his racial identity while serving in his official role. He attempts to escape his uniform as soon as possible after his tour of duty. He avoids the friends of his youth in order to avoid learning of their criminal behavior. He does not socialize with white cops after duty hours. In short, he is drawn into an enclave of black cops and becomes a member of a minority group within a minority group."

Continued

Police Officers Tell of Strains of Living
as a 'Black in Blue' *(Continued)*

Most law-enforcement officials acknowledge that racial prejudice exists in their profession, but they say it is no more pervasive than in the rest of American society. ''The police department is not much different than broader society to the extent that you have racism in the broader society,'' said Chief Lee P. Brown of the Houston police. He is black.

Shift in Training Emphasis

To combat this, nearly all the nation's 19,000 police departments are shifting some emphasis from training at the firing range to training in judgment and sensitivity. A few have brought in experts in an attempt to identify racially biased officers.

Referring to the shooting in Maryland, Sergeant Jackson of the Los Angeles police said rhetorically: ''Had an armed white man been in that house, would he have been shot? I doubt it. He would have been given the benefit of the doubt by any officer, black or white.''

That is vigorously disputed by other police organizations. ''That's garbage,'' said Buzz Sawyer, president of the Prince Georges County's Fraternal Order of Police, a social and professional organization that is the bargaining unit for the 915-member force. ''When someone turns at you with a gun, you don't sit there and determine what color he is. Color has nothing to do with the fact that a person is armed.'' Mr. Sawyer is white.

Statistics do not support the notion that race is a significant factor when police officers decide to shoot. A 1986 study by the Crime Control Institute, a nonprofit research organization in Washington, reported a sharp decline from 1971 to 1984 in killings by police officers in cities with populations over 250,000. The researchers concluded that the 39 percent reduction was ''almost entirely'' a result of fewer blacks being killed.

In 1971, the report said 353 people were killed by police officers. In 1984, 172 were killed. The number of blacks killed dropped by nearly 50 percent, from an average of 2.8 per 100,000 in 1971 to 1.4 per 100,000 in 1984.

Assignments and Promotions

Black officers frequently complain that they are treated differently from whites in assignments and promotions. In a 1981 study, Dr. James J. Fyfe, chairman of the Department of Justice, Law and Society at American University in Washington, a white former New York City police officer, concluded that black police officers were more likely to be assigned to high-crime areas in which minority groups live.

''Fewer than one in three white police officers or detectives is assigned to narcotics, street crime and A precincts,'' those where violent crime is likely, Dr. Fyfe said, ''while nearly half the blacks and more than 4 of 10 Hispanics work in these units. On the other hand, whites are more than three times as likely to work in traffic or emergency as are blacks or Hispanics.''

Some of the black officers interviewed said they preferred to work in minority communities, even with the greater potential for danger.

''We serve a dual purpose in the black community in that we are seen as protectors of the community and in some respects as role models.'' said Inspector Harold Washington of the Detroit police. He is the president of the National Organization of Black Law-Enforcement Executives.

Most black police officers say they have learned how to respond to the pressures they face on and off the job, but most also concede that constant stress may eventually begin to take its toll.

''It was destroying me as a black man,'' said Sergeant Jackson, who is 29 years old, a graduate of California Lutheran College and the son of a retired Los Angeles police officer. ''When I joined the force eight years ago I went along with the racial slurs in order to be accepted by the police fraternity. It began to turn me against my own people. I began to see fellow blacks as untrustworthy, as thieves and criminals. I began to shut myself off from my family and friends.''

Officer Jackson said he did not begin to feel better until he started to speak out against racists in the department. Three months ago he formed an organization of black police officers to address racism in the Los Angeles Police Department. Last month the department began a racial sensitivity program and established a panel to examine acts of racism and discrimination in the department.

Police officers who can understand and relate to the minority community are essential.

Photo courtesy of Galesburg Police Department, Galesburg, Illinois.

greet one another as ''brother,'' who acknowledge black citizens with black power salutes, and who openly support political and social reforms may improve the police image in the ghetto, but do little to improve the morale of their white colleagues. Pursuit of goals apparently in direct conflict with those of police administrators, such as objectives pursued by groups like the Afro-American Patrolmen's League in Chicago, has on many occasions been in the best interests of black officers, but this undoubtedly intensifies racial conflict within police departments. As Williams points out, ''The police fraternity has not stretched to the point of fully embracing blacks or women. . . . It is true, in part, because black officers have segregated themselves to be a force for their own people. Self-integration interferes with the issue of solidarity, which says anyone in blue is your brother or sister.''[32] Similarly, many white male officers would prefer to see ''best qualified'' applicants hired rather than ''fully qualified'' applicants; and many would prefer to see written tests which have been shown to be racially or culturally biased continued since, in general, whites outscore minorities on such tests. Finally, a recent Supreme Court decision which required the Alabama State Police to promote one black officer for every white officer promoted until blacks hold 25 percent of the top ranks in the department has made it clear that under some circumstances, quotas are acceptable means of redressing injustices in promotional practices, further aggravating many whites.[33]

Hispanic officers, as well as Asian American officers, are being hired in increasing numbers in some departments.[34] About 4 to 5 percent of local police officers are Hispanic, for example. While research on these minority officers is quite limited, their concerns and difficulties appear to be very similar to those of black police officers. Kozel and Tennant, for example, found that residents of Asian American communities do not generally view the job of police officer as either an appropriate or desirable one.[35]

Summary

It is evident that there are both positive and negative aspects of employing minority police officers. The EEOA and court decisions supporting it have made it possible for greater numbers of women and minorities to pursue careers in police work. On the positive side of the ledger, this provides chances for advancement to members of minority groups, increases the size of the qualified applicant pool available, and demonstrates that individuals of different physical abilities, genders, colors, and creeds can perform the police function. As more minority group members choose police work as a career, the stereotype of the big, white, male police officer may be modified, and the alienation of those without any or all of these characteristics may be reduced. To that extent police community relations would be improved.

On the negative side of the ledger, minority recruitment places stresses and strains on the police institution; these may temporarily increase instead of decrease hostility between white and black, male and female officers. Further, we should not discount the possibility that police community relations may deteriorate as increasing numbers of minorities are hired; this is implied in some of the conclusions based on the research discussed above. Still, if Sir Robert Peel was right in his assumptions when he established the first metropolitan police force, the better the police understand and respect the publics and the more the publics understand and respect the police, the better the relationship between the two. The hiring of qualified minority and female police officers can be a valuable move toward improving mutual understanding and respect. Perhaps Hubert Williams, president of the National Organization of Black Law Enforcement Executives, expressed it best:

> You are going to get better minority community support for the police if you have police officers who understand and relate to the minority communities. And in the absence of that community support, we cannot function as a democracy, and that's a problem that goes beyond the minority community to the community at large.[36]

Discussion Questions

1. Why is the recruitment, selection, and promotion of minority police officers both important and challenging to police administrators?
2. What are some of the important provisions of the Equal Employment Opportunity Act, and what impact has the EEOA had on police hiring and promotion? What impact do you think the Americans with Disabilities Act might have on police hiring practices?
3. What are some of the benefits and costs of hiring female police officers?
4. Suppose a white male and a minority male both take all required tests for employment with a police department. Suppose also that a combined score of 70 has been determined to represent a "qualified" applicant. Further, the police department in question is operating under a consent decree. The white applicant's total score is 80, the minority applicant's total score is 78. The minority applicant is hired. Present the arguments

that may be made by each applicant with respect to the fairness or unfairness of the hiring procedure.

5. Promotion of qualified minority applicants is extremely important. Why?
6. Will hiring and promoting minority officers eliminate racial tensions between the police and minority groups? Why or why not?

Endnotes

1. Report of the National Advisory Commission on Civil Disorders. 1968. Washington, D.C.: U.S. Government Printing Office.
2. Public Law 92–261, Section 703 (a) (I) (2).
3. Jeffrey Higginbottom. 1991. ''The Americans with Disabilities Act.'' *FBI Law Enforcement Bulletin* (August): 25–32; Paula N. Rubin. 1993. ''The Americans with Disabilities Act and Criminal Justice: An Overview.'' *Research in Action* (September) Washington, D.C.: National Institute of Justice.
4. Gaines, Kappeler, and Vaughn. *Policing in America.*: 73.
5. *Griggs v. Duke Power Company.* 401 U.S. 424 (1971).
6. Susan E. Martin. 1991. *On the Move: The Status of Women in Policing.* Washington, D.C.: Police Foundation; Alpert and Dunham. *Policing Urban America.*: 37; Roberg and Kuykendall. *Police and Society.*: 285.
7. See *United States v. City of Chicago.* 41 IF. Supp. 218, 228 (1976) or *Afro-American Patrolmen's League v. Duck.* 366F. Supp. 1095 (1973); 503F.2d294 (6th Cir., 1974); 538F. 2d328 (6th Cir., 1976).
8. Martin. *On the Move.*
9. Peter Block and Deborah Anderson. 1974. *Policewomen on Patrol: Final Report.* Washington, D.C.: The Police Foundation.
10. Kenneth W. Kerber, Steven M. Andes, and Michele B. Mittler. 1977. ''Citizen Attitudes Regarding the Competence of Female Police Officers.'' *Journal of Police Science and Administration* 5(3): 337–347.
11. Ibid.: 345.
12. Ibid.: 345.
13. Ibid.: 346–347.
14. Peter Horne. 1975. *Women in Law Enforcement.* Springfield, IL: Charles C Thomas.
15. Anthony V. Bouza. 1975. ''Women in Policing.'' *F.B.I. Law Enforcement Bulletin* (44): 2–7.
16. Lawrence J. Sherman. 1975. ''An Evaluation of Policewomen on Patrol in a Suburban Police Department.'' *Journal of Police Science and Administration* 3(4): 434–438.
17. See J. Balkin. 1988. ''Why Policemen Don't Like Policewomen.'' *Journal of Police Science and Administration* 16(1):29–37; or C. G. Garrison, N. Grant, and K. McCormick. 1988. ''Utilization of Policewomen.'' *Police Chief* (September): 32–72; or Martin. *On the Move.*
18. Kathleen Maguire, Ann L. Pastor, and Timothy J. Flanagan. 1993. *Sourcebook of Criminal Justice Statistics—1991.* Washington, D.C.: U.S. Government Printing Office.
19. Martin. *On the Move.*
20. E. Linn and B. R. Price. 1985. ''The Evolving Role of Women in American Policing'' in A. S. Blumberg and E. Neiderhoffer, eds. *The Ambivalent Force: Perspectives on the Police.* 3ed. New York: Holt, Rinehart and Winston: 69–80.
21. Jayne T. Rich. 1994. ''Mentoring: Its Role in the Advancement of Women in Law Enforcement.'' *Women Police* 28(1): 5.
22. Dorothy M. Schulze. 1993. ''From Policewoman to Police Officer: An Unfinished Revolution.'' *Police Studies* 16(3): 90–98; Jeanne McDowell. 1992. ''Are Women Better Cops?'' *Time* (February 17): 70–72.
23. Ted Gup. 1988. ''Racism in the Raw in Suburban Chicago.'' *Newsweek* (October 17): 25.
24. Maguire, Pastore, and Flanagan. *Sourcebook.*: 46.

25. Nicholas Alex. 1969. *Black in Blue: A Study of the Negro Policeman.* New York: Appleton-Century-Crofts: Chapter 2.

26. Ibid.: 25–31.

27. Collete C. Jackson and Irving A. Wallach. 1973. ''Perceptions of the Police in a Black Community'' in J. R. Snibbe and H. M. Snibbe, eds. *The Urban Police in Transition.* Springfield, IL: Charles C Thomas: 382–403.

28. Alex. *Black in Blue.* See also, J. L. Maghan. 1991. ''Black Police Officer Recruits: Aspects of Becoming Blue.'' *Police Forum* 2(1): 8–11.

29. Berg. *Law Enforcement.:* 164.

30. Alex. *Black in Blue.;* Lena Williams. 1988. ''Police Officers Tell Strains of Living as a 'Black in Blue'.'' *The New York Times* (February 14): 1, 26; John W. Fountain. 1991. ''Minority Cops Making Gains in the Suburbs.'' *Chicago Tribune* (October 20): sec. 2: 1–2.

31. See, for example, Valencia Campbell. 1980. ''Double Marginality of Black Policemen: A Reassessment.'' *Criminology* Vol. 17(4): 477–484.

32. Williams. ''Police Officers Tell Strains.'': 1.

33. T. Gest. 1987. ''A One-White, One-Black Quota for Promotions.'' *U.S. News and World Report* (March): 8.

34. National Archive of Criminal Justice Data Bulletin. ''National Survey of Law Enforcement Agencies, 1987.'' Ann Arbor: University of Michigan.

35. P. Kozel and W. Tennant. 1992. ''Attitudes of Asian SFPD Officers.'' Unpublished paper: Personnel Division, San Francisco Police Department.

36. Bruce Cory. 1979. ''Minority Police: Tramping Through a Racial Minefield.'' *Police Magazine* (March): 9.

Suggested Readings

Alex, Nicholas. 1969. *Black in Blue: A Study of the Negro Policeman.* New York: Appleton-Century-Crofts.

———. 1976. *New York Cops Talk Back: A Study of a Beleaguered Minority.* New York: John Wiley and Sons.

Block, Peter and Deborah Anderson. 1974. *Policewomen on Patrol: A Final Report.* Washington, D.C.: The Police Foundation.

Carter, David L. 1986. ''Hispanic Police Officers' Perception of Discrimination.'' *Police Studies* 9(4): 204–210.

Cashmore, Ellis and Eugene McLaughlin. 1991. *Out of Order? Policing Black People.* London: Routledge.

Frisby, David. 1994. ''Reasonable Force and the Smaller Officer.'' *Women Police* 28(1): 6–7.

McDowell, Jeanne. 1992. ''Are Women Better Cops?'' *Time* (February 17): 70–72.

Rich, Jayne T. 1994. ''Mentoring: Its Role in the Advancement of Women in Law Enforcement.'' *Women Police* 28(10): 5.

Training the Police in Community Relations, and Types of Police-Sponsored Community Relations Programs

Chapter

10

"Generally speaking, the key to any police community relations program is the understanding and enthusiasm brought to it by the police participants. Since these factors are not always present, they must be developed."[1] "At the present time, in any large police agency, too many officers have an unprofessional posture, but professional officers must become a conspicuous majority, for the health of the nation and for the well-being of all citizens."[2] "Things will only change when the police get rid of their code of silence and demand a code of honor."[3] "The establishment of specifically focused departmental policies and procedures for addressing hate violence is a proactive step which will send a strong message to victims and would-be perpetrators that hate crimes are not pranks and that police officials take them seriously. Every department should adopt a written policy, signed by the police chief, to respond effectively to hate violence."[4]

These quotations clearly indicate the importance of the police in initiating community relations training and programs. While it is true that police community relations are a two-way street, the burden of pursuing improved relations generally falls squarely on the police. Still, as Sparrow, Moore, and Kennedy put it, most police officers believe that community relations work is a specialty, not "real police" work. They view the work of community relations officers as relieving them of the responsibility for delivering speeches and distributing crime-prevention literature.[5]

Training and Educating the Police for Community Relations

In order to develop positive attitudes toward the community, special training and/or education are required. As Dolan points out, when it comes to community policing, we seldom recruit personnel who are adept at performing community policing tasks, usually training is required. Traditionally, officers receive a good deal of training in high-liability areas (force, firearms, motor vehicle operations), but very little training in creative problem solving, public speaking, or mental health issues. [6] While some improvement has occurred in this area, recent discussions with graduates of several midwestern police training institutes and academies revealed that many could not recall whether they had any presentations or instruction dealing with police community relations, while most others reported only cursory treatment of the subject. These reports are supported by analysis of the training curricula employed in the various states as presented in Table 10.1.

Further, in-service training in this area is often lacking as well. We have observed over the years that a significant proportion of police officers who do attend either pre- or in-service training seminars on community relations are not enthusiastic about the topic or overly attentive. It appears that many of these individuals assume either that they are already well-versed and successful in community relations or that community relations are a matter of common sense. While it is easy to assume that all of us are acquainted with the basic aspects of community relations, since we are all constantly involved in human relations, acquaintance with the basics is far from being expert or even competent. Moreover, if successful police community relations were simply a matter of common sense, seminars and texts on the subject would be unnecessary. Successful police community relations are actually the product of "uncommon sense." That is, those who understand and are good at police community relations are relatively uncommon, as are the knowledge and training required to develop such individuals. Therefore, training and/or education in community relations are necessary. Whether education or training is the best means of dispensing the required knowledge, or whether some combination of the two is preferable, are subjects of considerable discussion.

In 1967, the President's Commission on Law Enforcement and Administration of Justice noted that "psychology, culture, and problems of minority groups and the poor, the dynamics of crowd behavior, the history of the civil rights movements, and the attitudes of various segments of the public toward the police," were relevant fields of study for those interested in police community relations.[7] Even though these elements of community relations and their importance were spelled out a quarter of a century ago, there has been no amelioration of many of the community relations problems which existed at the time.

Many believe that the ideal setting for learning more about community relations problems is in college, and that exposure to the subjects outlined by the President's Commission during the college years broadens the perspective of those who attend. Some experts advocate increased hiring of college-educated police officers as a partial solution to community relations and associated police problems. Others believe that education must be supplemented (or in some cases perhaps replaced) by training which translates theory into practice. There appears to be increasing recognition that if either of these approaches is to be successful refresher courses offered on a continuing basis are a must.

Table 10.1

Requirements for Police Entry-Level Training Programs by Type of Competency Area and State, as of December 1985 (In Hours).

State	Total Number of Hours Required	Human Relations	Force and Weaponry	Commu- nications	Legal	Patrol and Criminal Investigations	Criminal Justice Systems	Adminis- tration
Hawaii	954	17	153	65	133	444	29	113
Rhode Island	661	42	65	0	48	480	0	26
Vermont	553	4	80	30	74	330	3	32
Maine	504	27	62	17	73	277	21	27
West Virginia	495	14	98	20	120	195	36	12
Pennsylvania	480	76	88	10	94	196	16	0
Maryland	471	0	0	0	73	366	0	32
Massachusetts	460	35	132	28	90	167	8	0
Utah	450	19	73	27	49	247	15	20
Connecticut	443	23	48	8	64	284	11	5
Indiana	440	21	73	4	83	192	32	35
Michigan	440	9	105	8	48	244	0	26
Washington	440	34	152	24	85	145	0	0
New Hampshire	426	20	75	8	60	205	8	50
New Mexico	421	30	69.5	18	56	238.5	9	0
Arizona	400	24	110	16	78	135	12	25
California	400	15	80	15	60	185	10	35
Iowa	400	33	75	12	44	175	13	48
Kentucky	400	6.5	84.5	3.5	75.5	182.5	6	41.5
South Carolina	382	18	77	12	72	178	2	23
Texas	381	14	48	18	68	233	0	0
North Carolina	369	28	64	20	72	170	0	15
Delaware	362	12	64	17	87	174	6	2
Montana	346	22	77.5	14	19.5	183.5	15	14.5
Nebraska	341	36	58	10	62	158	2	15
Colorado	334	19	55	22	79	141	18	0
Florida	320	24	39	18	54	158	9	18
Kansas	320	34	42	20	45	170	1	8
Mississippi	320	8	70	20	50	153	7	12
Wyoming	320	10	71	14	53	119	33	20
North Dakota	313	10	23	20	84	139	16	21
Idaho	310	0	47	9	51	169	16	18
New Jersey	310	26	40	13	49	116	17	49
Arkansas	304	14	60	6	19	190	0	15
New York	285	9	38	7	44	169	10	8
Alabama	280	14	49	8	48	138	3	20
Ohio	280	16	42	10	76	111	20	5
Oregon	280	14	64	12	62	104	8	16
Alaska	276	1	20	7	74	139	13	22
Georgia	240	18	45	5	47	110	2	13
Louisiana	240	16	57	8	36	78	5	40
Tennessee	240	2	50	7	31	136	8	6
Wisconsin	240	18	30	9	16	121	10	36
Nevada	200	8	28	11	46	96	2	9
South Dakota	200	17	32	8	22	109	6	6
Missouri	120	3	23	10	28	55	1	0

Notes: These data were obtained through a mail survey of law enforcement training directors. Oklahoma, Illinois, Virginia, and Minnesota were omitted from the study due to incomplete data regarding their curriculum content. Each State mandates the minimum hourly requirements reported above, but police agencies within each State may establish entry-level training in addition to State requirements.

"Human relations" training stresses the development of the whole person in dealing with the problems of society. Training involves subjects such as human relations, crisis intervention, and stresses awareness. "Force and weaponry" involves the development of skills in the use of firearms, chemical agents, hand to hand combat, and other measures of physical force. "Communications" is the development of interpersonal skills for conducting interviews and interrogations; included in this category are report writing, basic training in grammar, spelling, and body language. "Legal" training encompasses criminal law, rules of evidence, basic Constitutional law, laws of arrest, search and seizure, civil rights, and liability. "Patrol and criminal investigations" training focuses on patrol techniques and procedures, defensive driving, basic criminal investigation, emergency medical aid, traffic control, physical fitness, accident investigation, jail/custody procedures, and other technical competencies. "Criminal justice systems" training stresses the knowledge needed for understanding the criminal justice system; included in this area are corrections and courts, and professional conduct and ethics. "Administration" covers training matters related to the use of equipment, basic orientation to the training program, and diagnostic testing and/or examination time. (Source, pp. 8 10).

Source: Robert J. Meadows, "An Assessment of Police Entry Level Training in the United States: Conformity or Conflict with the Police Role?" Boone, NC: Appalachian State University, 1985. (Mimeographed.) Table 11. Reproduced in Sourcebook of criminal justice statistics 1986. Table adapted by SOURCEBOOK staff.

These courses should be as dynamic as possible in order to avert boredom or negative reactions. Participation in such courses is crucial so that problems confronting the students can be discussed and possible solutions examined. Further, such courses should not be limited to patrol officers, but should also be required of police supervisory and administrative personnel, whose support and understanding are needed if patrol officers are to view community relations as an important part of police work. Training which concentrates on the dual aspects of community relations—human relations and public relations—is likely to be most effective. Throughout, training should provide participating officers with a framework for analyzing human encounters (such as the one provided in Chapter Three), as well as strategies for developing and evaluating new programs (as described in Chapter Four).

Community Policing Strategies

In 1970, the Los Angeles Police Department initiated the "Basic Car Plan."[8] The idea of this plan was to make police officers responsible for a certain geographical area in order to develop more effective working relationships and improved communication and acquaintanceships between officers and the citizens who resided in their territories. Eventually the concept expanded to team or neighborhood policing, and in Los Angeles at least, included meetings held in private residences during which officers and residents discussed local problems.[9]

In other cities, like New York, Cincinnati, and Syracuse, team policing was also experimented with as early as the 1960s. In most of these programs the traditional military chain of command was replaced by more decentralized control. In New York, for example, the teams were organized around a sergeant and a specific group of officers. In some programs, the officers perform general patrol functions, but each officer is also specifically trained in some area (such as handling domestic disputes). The intent is to offer a full range of police services to the neighborhood and to provide these services through police officers who are well-known in and identified with the neighborhood, thereby removing some of the anonymity associated with the use of patrol cars and centralized police dispatch. In many ways, team policing is an attempt to restore the individual contact between officer and citizen which was possible when police officers walked assigned beats, but at the same time to take advantage of advances in police technology and expertise.

Recognizing that neighborhood-based policing clearly has many potential advantages, we should remember that this localized form of organizing the delivery of police services is accompanied by certain significant risks. While there were, no doubt, many other more important reasons for almost universal abandonment of the neighborhood beat a few decades ago, one factor often cited was the propensity of familiarity to breed, in this case not contempt, but favoritism in the application of police powers, with resulting inequity in the enforcement of the law, because of personal acquaintance or the bias of an individual officer (which is the most pernicious exercise of police discretion).

Another factor often cited as a disadvantage of neighborhood-based policing was the susceptibility of the beat officer to corruption in the form of bribes, graft, and other payoffs for overlooking certain offenses and actively participating in others. Also, the more localized a police jurisdiction, the more likely it is to fall exclusively within the boundaries of a small political jurisdiction, often under the political leadership of one or two persons (wards, districts, precincts, etc.). Elected officials depend in large measure on their ability to influence persons and their activities in "their" district. Thus police activity is often the object of the local politician's efforts to demonstrate his or her power and influence because the police have frequent and direct impact on individual citizens. Organizing police services in a way that cuts across small political unit boundaries and/or puts the general supervision of police activity in the hands of a larger group of elected officials (e.g., a city council or board of supervisors) provides some insulation between the individual police officer and the undue influence of powerful individuals in the community. As a result of some of these difficulties, coupled with a lack of strong support from most police administrators (including many who gave lip service to the neighborhood policing concept), team and neighborhood policing became less popular in the late 1970s and early 1980s. Out of them grew perhaps the most intriguing concept in police community relations in the latter half of the twentieth century—community-oriented policing.

As we have noted earlier, in many ways community-oriented policing is an old idea, traceable to Sir Robert Peel and others. The concept is based on the premise that the police and the public work as a team in order to maintain order and enforce the law, as were team and neighborhood policing. Indeed the ideas of foot patrol, relatively permanent geographic assignment of officers, and decentralization that were part and parcel of team and neighborhood policing are the cornerstones of community-oriented policing as well. Perhaps the major difference is the extent of the partnership between the police and other citizens. Ideally, community-oriented policing makes the two partners equal, although there is some doubt that such equality exists in practice.[10] Further, community-oriented policing is intended to be proactive rather than reactive and involves a good deal of "civilianization" (hiring of civilian employees by police departments), in addition to areal decentralization.[11] In cities such as Newark, Houston, Oakland, Detroit, Denver, and Santa Ana, California, research has indicated that community-oriented policing, while not a panacea for police community relations problems, has made positive contributions in this area. Further, community-oriented policing calls upon us to reconsider the way in which we evaluate the police. As Skolnick and Bayley (1986) put it:

> While the fundamental objective of policing should remain the protection of the public, crime and arrest rates are much too crude and elusive measures to nail down the dynamic relationship between the police and public safety. The efficacy of the police must also be considered in terms of elicitation of cooperation from the public, the understanding police develop of particular areas and social circumstances, the anxiety of the police themselves, the changing composition of calls for police service, the effectiveness with which

noncrime requests are handled, the enthusiasm of the public for working preventively with the police, and the strength of the ''we-they'' dichotomy felt mutually by police and public.[12]

There are some problems with community-oriented policing as we have noted. It remains unclear what the overall budgetary implications are. For example, it is probably considerably more expensive to engage in community-oriented policing, especially if the beats are sufficiently small to gain some of the advantages associated with this style of policing. There may also be some problems associated with the administration of such programs, especially in providing adequate supervision of the beat officers and in utilizing in the neighborhood the special skills available from experts in the modern police department. Yet both police officers and other citizens who are involved appear to have positive feelings about this approach to policing. At the present time, there is little evidence that these positive feelings have resulted in or from lower crime and/or victimization rates, so we must conclude that they are the result of other factors—perhaps the increased interaction between officers and other citizens which may result in the latter feeling safer even though the incidence of crime remains about the same. This, too, could lead to negative consequences if such feelings lead citizens to inappropriately throw caution to the winds, but if the partnership is solid this is perhaps unlikely to occur.[13]

It is well to remember, then, that neighborhood beats have and continue to encounter significant obstacles and risks. Many of the departments which have been experimenting with updated versions of these styles of policing have come to recognize that in a time of limited funds, it is difficult to afford such programs or to sell them on the basis that they are more cost-effective than traditional programs. New administrative and supervisory procedures are necessary. Perhaps most important, in the long run and probably in the short run as well, if the potential for corruption of the police that is apparently inherent in neighborhood policing cannot be counteracted, police community relations will suffer. Components of programs designed to maximize the benefits and to minimize the risks of community-oriented policing have been identified by Cooksey and by Trojanowicz and emphasize supervisory vigilance and the role of the police officer as a partner, one who is highly visible to those whom he/she serves.[14]

Police-Sponsored Citizen Crime Prevention Programs

While it is still too early to accurately assess the impact of community policing, it does represent an attempt to provide a workable alternative to the traditional police model, a program based upon the fundamental principle we have repeated throughout this book: police community cooperation is an essential ingredient of effective policing. While we recognize the distinction, discussed in Chapter Seven, between police community relations and community policing, it is important to note that successful community relations programs contribute

Police and other citizens engage in a cooperative effort to prevent crime.

© James L. Shaffer

to the community policing goals, and that community policing, by definition, seeks to improve relationships between the police and other citizens. Some of the efforts discussed here were initiated as specific community relations programs, others as components of community policing, but all share the goal of developing better working relationships between the police and other citizens in the interest of improving quality of life.

Along these lines, numerous cities have experimented with neighborhood "walk-in centers" which are staffed by the police. Often located in storefront buildings, these centers are intended to bring the police and citizens closer together by making it convenient for citizens to talk with a police officer about problems of all types.

In Columbia, South Carolina, a Police Home Loan program has been instituted to encourage police officers to buy homes in troubled neighborhoods, providing low-interest, fixed-rate mortgages and no down payment as incentives.[15]

Perhaps as a logical outgrowth of various community-oriented policing programs, a number of citizen crime prevention groups sponsored by the police have been organized throughout the country. In cooperation with law enforcement agencies, many citizen organizations sponsor special areawide campaigns to educate and motivate the public to report (1) crimes in the process of being committed, (2) information that would help police solve or prevent crimes, and, (3) persons and events considered suspicious. Various names have been attached to these campaigns such as Operation Cul-De-Sac, Operation Clean, Neighborhood Oriented Policing, Crime Stoppers, the South Seattle Crime Prevention Council, and so on.[16]

While these programs are too numerous to describe in detail, an example will illustrate more clearly their bases and acceptance. In the spring of 1992, the Neighborhood Oriented Policing program (NOP) was implemented in Joliet, Illinois. Initially, police officers who had volunteered to participate in the program went door-to-door in their neighborhoods, identifying themselves and passing out literature explaining the program which was designed to accomplish three main objectives: deal with problems of crime and violence in neighborhoods most affected by these problems; build better relationships with local citizens, businesspersons, and community leaders; and modify the Joliet Police Department's organizational structure in such a way that NOP could be sustained.[17] By the winter of 1992, there had been a decrease in complaints against the police, an increase in support from the local media, a decrease in service requests from the area involved, and a decrease in the crime rate.[18] Evaluations disclosed improved citizen support and positive attitude changes toward the police. Whether or not these positive changes will continue, only time will tell, but so far the effort seems to be paying off.

Citizen volunteer programs have become quite numerous and several hundred thousand citizens are involved in county and municipal programs. Jobs range from crime analysis to clerical work and from crime prevention to victim assistance. Although they are often scorned by police unions, volunteers are typically accepted by police officers with whom they work once their ability to do the job has been demonstrated.[19]

Other programs sponsored by the police for citizens include Operation Identification programs—engraving identifying numbers on valuables and/or displaying decals on windows announcing that the house is equipped with an alarm or has participated in an identification program. "Turn in a Pusher" (TIPS) and "Crime Stopper" programs also exist in many communities. These programs encourage citizens to report drug and other crimes to the police. Callers need not identify themselves immediately, but are assigned a number and if the information they provide leads to arrest and conviction, they are eligible for rewards. "Block Watcher" programs are another variation of citizen prevention programs. Mass media campaigns, such as the "Take a Bite Out of Crime" ads in newspapers and magazines and on television provide a variety of suggestions for citizens who are determined to make themselves and their communities less vulnerable to crime. All these programs potentially contribute not only to reduced crime rates and/or greater apprehension rates, but also to improved communication and understanding between the police and the citizens they serve.

Police Programs for the Elderly

Recognizing that fear of crime is a major problem among the elderly, many police administrators are involved in attempting to establish working relations with senior citizens (those over sixty-five years of age). While most police departments do not have ''senior-citizen officers'' as such, most law enforcement administrators and researchers remain convinced that special programs for the elderly are desirable for a variety of reasons. We have discovered that in many cases the elderly have difficulty even reading the small print on brochures and pamphlets developed for use in police community relations programs. Some may also have difficulty digesting the information provided through such programs. For example, during a program on proper utilization of 9-1-1, one senior citizen who had heard the emergency number referred to as ''9-11,'' was concerned that he could not use the system because his phone did not have the number ''11'' on the dial. The officer presenting the program explained to him the misunderstanding, but this was only possible because the individual in question spoke up. Were there others in the group with similar concerns? In addition, we know that senior citizens are less likely than younger citizens to leave their residences to attend police-sponsored programs. Also, as Gross reports, the elderly often appear to be more comfortable when addressed as part of a small group of citizens of the same age, or individually:

> Careful planning must precede the implementation of a new crime prevention program for senior citizens. To ensure that new efforts respond to the needs of the community's senior citizens, the planning process should include input from the local or state Office of Aging, from members of the senior community, and from other appropriate community organizations—such as representatives from a local university's gerontology program. This group effort will help to avoid the pitfalls common to those programs which are designed in accordance with the needs as perceived by the police rather than in accordance with the needs as perceived by the elderly.[20]

At this time, senior-citizen crime prevention programs include educational programs, crime-prevention assistance programs, victim assistance programs, and senior volunteer programs. Specifically, the police in many communities are using programs similar to the ''Elderwatch'' program in Tulsa, Oklahoma, to help senior citizens prevent residential burglaries, purse-snatchings, and check-snatchings, as well as fraudulent home repairs and bank schemes.[21] The relationship between senior citizens and the police has, in general, been perceived by both groups as positive and it is to the advantage of both groups to continue to improve on that relationship.

Police Juvenile Programs

Since the youth of today will become the leaders of tomorrow, many police officers and administrators feel that programs oriented toward youth are among the most important community relations efforts that police departments can

sponsor. As a result, there are juvenile programs of every conceivable type and description. Without claiming to present an exhaustive list of such programs, we will discuss a number of different types of youth-oriented programs in which the police frequently participate.

Athletic activities sponsored by the police have long been a key part of police juvenile relations. These activities include, among others, Silver and Golden Gloves boxing, baseball and football leagues, and summer camps. The basic goals of these programs include teaching youth athletic skills and good sportsmanship, while encouraging both the juveniles and the officers involved to view one another as individuals deserving of respect. In addition, programs like the "Midnight Basketball League" in Chicago also provide youth with alternatives to street life.[22]

School-related activities (besides athletic programs) are quite popular with police administrators. "Officer Friendly" and "Meet Your Policeman" programs (and their numerous offshoots) provide opportunities for youngsters in school to see, talk to, and learn about police officers, their equipment, and some of their functions. Often elementary school children tour police facilities and/or examine police vehicles and equipment with "Officer Friendly." The intent of all these programs is to encourage young children to view police officers as friends by getting to know one, or more, specific officer(s). Extensions of the "Officer Friendly" concept include police officers assigned to junior and senior high schools as liaison officers. These officers are not primarily law

Police Officer Enters Classroom to Warn Students of Drugs

Critical Issue

By Geri Reynolds

Staff Writer

GALESBURG—Once a week a uniformed Galesburg Police Department officer tells it like it is about drugs and their effects to sixth graders at Lombard Junior High School.

Patrolman Ed Barragan teaches the Drug Abuse Resistance Education (DARE) program at Lombard. He will be at Churchill in the spring.

DARE is a preventative program in which uniformed police officers teach a 17-week curriculum. Its aim is to equip young people with the skills to resist peer pressure to experiment with and use harmful drugs.

Barragan believes in DARE and what it is accomplishing, not only in Galesburg but in other schools across the country. He volunteered to teach the course when the Illinois State Police, who started the pilot Galesburg program two years ago, stepped aside this fall.

He attended the DARE training school in November at the Illinois State Police Academy in Springfield and stepped into the classroom in January to start an abbreviated 10-week DARE program. It will be the full 17-week program next year, he said.

"I am at Lombard all day each Thursday and, beginning in March, will be at Churchill. I like kids and I like teaching this program. We focus on feelings the kids have relating to self-esteem, interpersonal and communication skills, decision-making and positive alternatives to drug abuse behavior," he said.

There are a variety of techniques he uses to encourage the students to respond to problem-solving situations. "I have a DARE box on the desk where the students can drop in their questions—unsigned—relating to drugs or anything," he said.

"I really go into the consequences of drugs quite deeply. I tell them about the effects alcohol, pills, heroin, cocaine, PCPs, LSD, and smack have on their minds and bodies. I've seen these effects on people as a police officer and I can get this information across to the students," Barragan said.

He shows a movie on drug use and then discusses it with the students. "I keep reinforcing that drugs will affect them both mentally and physically."

Barragan said the students admit peer pressure to try drugs and alcohol is greater than pressure from other sources.

"We do role playing in which one student will try to get another to try pills

or alcohol. They learn a lot from doing this."

He also stays around school after classes. "Sometimes a kid needs to talk to you outside the classroom. Also, this provides me with an opportunity to meet students from the other grades. Many come up and introduce themselves or join the group talking with me.

"This provides a great opportunity for the students to get to know a police officer on a more personal level. Hopefully, they will learn we are not out to bust them for any small infraction but that we are people, too, and that we care about the citizens for whom we are responsible."

It is this sense of responsibility for self and others that Barragan is trying to instill in the students in his DARE classes.

"At the very least, I am laying the groundwork and the students can continue building on this, using the knowledge they have gained from the DARE program," he said.

"If just one kid does not turn to drugs or alcohol because of the DARE program, then I will feel I have been successful," he said.

© Register Mail, *Galesburg, Ill. Reprinted by permission.*

---

enforcers, but are available to discuss problems with youth on an informal basis. In addition, some high schools now offer courses in law enforcement, taught by police officers. These courses furnish basic information about police functions, police careers, and crime and criminality. They also provide the opportunity for interaction between students and the officer on a continuing basis.[23]

Among the more popular programs today are the Drug Abuse and Resistance Education programs (DARE) taught by police officers to fifth and sixth grade students. Officers attend a training program to prepare them to teach the seventeen-week course and, as the Critical Issue article indicates, the programs have been well-received, even though the long-term effects of the program in reducing drug usage remain to be demonstrated.

Bike safety, right to say no, and police cadet programs are other youth activities sponsored by the police. Some departments run "Big Brother/Sister" programs, some sponsor Boy Scout troops, and still others have ride-along programs for youth. Whatever the type of activity, the underlying goals are to prevent youth from engaging in delinquent activities and to encourage interaction between the police and the individuals with whom future generations of police officers will be working.

Community Service Officer Programs

Maximizing the efficiency of existing police resources while providing the best possible service at the lowest possible cost have become the goals of police administrators in the United States. During the past decade, more and more departments have worked to reach these goals by instituting Community Service Officer (CSO) or Police Assistant (PA) programs. Individuals occupying CSO or PA positions are non-sworn personnel assigned to handle service requests that do not require special police training. In many instances, better services are provided to the public at reduced cost. This is particularly true when CSOs and PAs have education, training, and/or experience in handling domestic disputes or dealing with minority groups. (For example, CSOs or PAs with bilingual capability may be able to relate to minority group members more comfortably than sworn officers under the same conditions, for reasons discussed elsewhere in this text.) In addition, problems involving the police may come to the attention of the CSO or PA when they might be concealed from a sworn officer. Finally, the police department benefits by having more resources to assign to crime-related activities.

Police-Media Programs

Local radio and television shows in many communities present call-in programs or roundtable discussions featuring police officers and other concerned citizens. These programs cover a wide variety of topics, ranging from interpretations and questions concerning new laws, to discussions about the need for new police facilities and the value of citizen participation for effective law enforcement.

Police departments, large and small, in cities across the country have worked with local television stations to encourage citizen participation in solving crimes. In what might be described as an extension of citizen awareness programs, participating television stations are given information by the police concerning selected unsolved crimes. Using this information, operators of the television station dramatize the crimes (using actors, actresses, and appropriate props) in order to attract public attention. Viewers are given a phone number to call if they have information concerning the crime. In addition, they are offered rewards, provided by the police, for information leading to the arrest

The Community Feedback Program

By Assistant Sheriff Dennis W. LaDucer

Orange County Sheriff's Department, Santa Ana, California

The critical link between police effectiveness and community support cannot be overstated. Yet, few law enforcement agencies include instruments that measure community support on a regular basis as part of any internal evaluative component.

The Orange County Sheriff's Department began its Community Feedback Program to gather citizens' perceptions about patrol services in the unincorporated areas of Orange County. While the department had routinely collected data about personnel complaints, such data failed to explain in specific behavioral terms the methods by which police/citizen communication techniques could be enhanced. These data also failed to record a representative sample of the service population, as they focused only on complainants.

A very simple, inexpensive survey instrument was developed to randomly solicit from victims and informants their perceptions of our performance. (See questionnaire.) Approximately 10 percent of calls for service in which the informant or victim could be identified were targeted, and questionnaires were mailed along with a short letter of explanation from the sheriff.

Each questionnaire was marked as to the type of crime or request for service, the name of the primary officer responsible for handling the call and the area in which the call occurred. Questions were designed to elicit respondents' impressions of the officer's friendliness, helpfulness, promptness and effort, as well as their perceptions of telephone contacts with the department when applicable.

Perhaps from the standpoint of formal research methodology, the method is flawed. But from a practical standpoint, consumers were asked very simple, straightforward questions about the service provider's effectiveness, and not many public agencies do that. In such circumstances, the police administrator is looking not only for a research program but rather a method by which community support can be measured. . . .

Completed questionnaires are returned to the officer who handled the call. This is one of the most important components of the program, since it provides timely feedback to the officer, who can then use the information to reinforce or reevaluate his behavior. Of course, one negative response may not be significant, but officers are asked to watch for recurring perceptions in the questionnaires they receive. . . .

While the project is an assessment of community perceptions, it is also therapeutic in nature. Knowing that their individual performance may be evaluated in this manner may cause some officers to use more appropriate behavior with informants and victims, and may even transfer their general behavior with all field contacts. Usually, the beginning of a community feedback program will be the first time a police agency routinely solicits information from the community about officers' performance.

Continued

and conviction of the offenders involved. Programs of this type are extensions of more general information-for-rewards programs sponsored by the police and have become so popular that several now appear on national television on a weekly basis. Finally, most large cities have ''Bear in the Sky'' or similar radio programs during which a traffic officer in a helicopter gives timely traffic information to rush-hour drivers.

Other Police-Sponsored Programs

Police departments routinely provide officers to speak on timely topics to civic groups. ''Rap sessions'' between officers and representatives of the community are another means of increasing police-citizen interaction. In the former case,

The Community Feedback Program *(Continued)*

The key to success in this type of program is the return of the questionnaires to the officers through their supervisors. This not only provides the supervisor with some insight into other people's views of officer performance, but it allows direct feedback to the officer. While it can be argued that insight alone does not lead to change, it can provide direction for the agency, the supervisors and most importantly, the officers. . . .

Patrol Community Feedback Questionnaire

1. Was this your first formal contact with law enforcement?
    □ Yes
    □ No

2. Did the deputy explain what was going to happen with this incident?
    □ Yes
    □ No

3. How friendly was the deputy?
    □ Extremely friendly
    □ Friendly
    □ Didn't notice
    □ Unfriendly
    □ Very unfriendly

4. How hard did the deputy try to help you?
    □ Tried very hard to help
    □ Tried hard to help
    □ Did what he/she had to do
    □ Did not try hard to help
    □ Did not try at all to help

5. How effectively did the deputy handle your call?
    □ Exceptionally well
    □ Well
    □ Did what he/she was supposed to do
    □ Not well
    □ Poorly

6. What would best describe the time it took the deputy to arrive at the location of the incident?
    □ Very prompt
    □ Prompt
    □ Did not notice
    □ Slow
    □ Very slow

7. What would best describe the deputy who took your telephone request for service?
    □ Very friendly and helpful
    □ Friendly and helpful
    □ Okay
    □ Somewhat rude and unhelpful
    □ Very rude and unhelpful

the officer needs to be well-versed in the subject he is presenting, since the image which is projected helps determine the audience's impression of the department represented. In the latter case, officers should be able to express themselves calmly and logically, even when being severely criticized. Ride-along programs are popular with some police departments. This activity allows citizens to observe firsthand the nature of police work. While observing, the rider also has an opportunity to become acquainted with the police officer he/she rides with as an individual. Some law enforcement administrators tend to avoid ride-along programs because they feel too many riders of questionable intent appear. Others feel the benefits are positive even though an occasional rider has questionable motives. Obviously, departments in which ride-along programs operate are led by administrators who have confidence in their personnel and who believe that police operations should be as open to public view as possible.

Tours of police facilities, exhibitions of police equipment, and open houses are other means of encouraging police contact with citizens of the community on an other-than-official basis.

The Orange County Sheriff's Department has developed a Community Feedback Program. The program is based on a simple survey instrument administered on a more or less random basis to victims and informants in order to elicit comments concerning police performance. The Critical Issue article describes the program in more detail.

As you can see from the great variety of police-sponsored community relations programs now in operation, the scope of such activities is limited only by the ingenuity of the police officers involved in their planning and implementation. Most police-sponsored community relations activities are based on the assumption that positive personal contacts (human relations) lead to a positive image of the police (public relations).

Summary

Although many police officers are not interested in learning about community relations, there is ample evidence that education and/or training in community relations are essential for all law enforcement personnel. We are all familiar with human interaction, but we are not all experts in analyzing these interactions or in understanding the attitudes and beliefs of others. In-service training, a belief that community relations are a vital part of every police officer's duties and responsibilities, and well-planned programs are all required for positive interaction with citizens.

Projects sponsored by the police range from media-oriented efforts to programs for special groups such as youth and the elderly. Athletic activities, school projects, ride-along programs, and public speaking engagements are typical activities sponsored by the police. Community-oriented policing, citizen crime watch programs, and walk-in centers represent other police community relations efforts.

Whatever the particular nature of the project, the ultimate goals are to increase police interaction with other citizens, to improve communication between the two groups, and to eliminate negative stereotypes by encouraging individual interaction. Innovation and experimentation are valuable assets in any police-sponsored community relations program.

Discussion Questions

1. What is the relative importance of education and training in community relations? How might we arouse more enthusiasm and encourage participation among police officers involved in community relations workshops?

2. What types of police-sponsored community relations programs exist in your community? How effective are these programs? Does your local police department engage in community policing? If so, what if any changes have you noticed in public response to the police?

3. In Chapter Four we discussed the critical role of policy and action for police public relations. How important are these two factors for police-sponsored community relations programs? Give some specific examples to justify your answer.

4. Design what you consider to be a good community relations program for your local police department. How would you go about implementing such a program if you were a police administrator?

5. What are some of the strengths and weaknesses of community-oriented policing? Of Community Service Officer and Police Assistant programs? Of school liaison programs?

Endnotes

1. Paul M. Whisenand and R. Fred Ferguson. 1978. 2ed. *The Managing of Police Organizations.* Englewood Cliffs, N.J.: Prentice-Hall: 524.

2. A. C. Germann. 1993. ''Changing the Police: An Impossible Dream?'' *Law Enforcement News* 19(383): 6.

3. Rodriquez. ''Researchers Study.'': 19.

4. Michael Liberman. 1993. ''Giving the Green Light for Vigorous Enforcement of Hate-Crime Laws.'' *Law Enforcement News* 19(385): 10.

5. Malcolm K. Sparrow, Mark H. Moore, and David M. Kennedy. 1990. *Beyond 911.*

6. Harry P. Dolan. 1994. ''Coping with Internal Backlash.'' *The Police Chief* 61(3): 28–32.

7. The President's Commission on Law Enforcement and Administration of Justice. 1967. *Task Force Report: The Police.* Washington, D.C.: U.S. Government Printing Office: 156.

8. Edward Davis. *Staff One: A Perspective on Effective Police Management.* Englewood-Cliffs, NJ: Prentice-Hall: 226.

9. Ibid.

10. Jack R. Greene. 1993. ''Civic Accountability and the Police: Lessons Learned from Police and Community Relations'' in Dunham and Alpert, eds. *Policing Urban America.*: 369–394.

11. Jerome H. Skolnick and David H. Bayley. 1986. *The New Blue Line: Police Innovation in Six American Cities.* New York: Free Press.

12. Ibid.: 227.

13. For further discussion, see Jacob R. Clark. 1994. ''Does Community Policing Add Up?'' *Law Enforcement News* 20(399): 1, 8.

14. Otis E. Cooksey. 1991. ''Corruption: A Continuing Challenge for Law Enforcement.'' *FBI Law Enforcement Bulletin* (September): 5–9; Robert Trojanowicz. 1992. ''Preventing Individual and Systemic Corruption.'' *Footprints* 4(1): 1–3.

15. Tina McLanus. 1992. ''Columbia, South Carolina: Officers Become Neighbors Through Police Home Loan Program.'' *Footprints* 4(2): 10–12.

16. Robert L. Vernon and James R. Lasley. 1992. ''Police/Citizen Partnerships in the Inner City.'' *FBI Law Enforcement Bulletin* (May): 22; Richard W. Hatler. 1990. ''Operation CLEAN: Reclaiming City Neighborhoods.'' *FBI Law Enforcement Bulletin* (October): 22–25; Teresa Vlasak. 1992. ''Walking the Beat in Joliet, Illinois.'' *The Compiler* 11(4): 13–15; *National Institute of Justice Journal.* 1992. ''Community Policing in Seattle: A Model Partnership Between Police and Citizens.'' (225): 9–18.

17. Vlasak. ''Walking the Beat.''

18. Ibid.: 15.

19. Ordway P. Burden. 1988. ''Volunteers: The Wave of the Future?'' *The Police Chief* (July): 25–26.

20. Philip J. Gross. 1979. ''Crime Prevention and the Elderly'' in Arnold P. Goldstein, William J. Hayer, and Phillip J. Monti, eds. *Police and the Elderly.* New York: Pergamon Press: 43.

21. Bob Chance. 1990. ''Law Enforcement Innovation: Elderwatch.'' *FBI Law Enforcement Bulletin* 59(5): 9–10.

22. See, for example, Albert R. Roberts. 1989. *Juvenile Justice: Policies, Programs, Services.* Chicago: Dorsey Press: 100–106; Wayne C. Torok and Kenneth S. Trump. 1994. ''Gang Intervention.'' *FBI Law Enforcement Bulletin* 63(5): 13–17; or Jill Smolowe. 1994. ''Out of the Line of Fire.'' *Time* (July 25): 25.

23. Anthony Moriarty and Patrick Fitzgerald. 1992. ''A Rationale for Police-School Collaboration.'' *Law and Order* (May): 47–51.

Suggested Readings

Bowers, W. and J. Hirsch. 1987. ''The Impact of Foot Patrol Staffing on Crime and Disorder in Boston: An Unmet Promise.'' *American Journal of the Police: Special Issue on Foot Patrol and Community Policing* 4(1): 17–44.

Dolan, Harry P. 1994. ''Community Policing: Coping with Internal Backlash.'' *The Police Chief* 61(3): 28–32.

Eck, J. and W. Spellman. 1987. ''Who Ya Gonna Call: The Police as Problem Busters.'' *Crime and Delinquency* 33(1): 31–52.

Sherman, Lawrence W., Catherine H. Milton, and Thomas Kelley. 1973. *Team Policing: Seven Case Studies.* Washington, D.C.: Police Foundation.

Skogan, Wesley G. 1994. ''The Impact of Community Policing on Neighborhood Residents: A Cross-Site Analysis'' in Rosenbaum. *The Challenge of Community Policing.* 167–181.

Skolnick, Jerome H. and David H. Bayley. 1986. *The New Blue Line: Police Innovation in Six American Cities.* New York: Free Press.

Sorrentino, Anthony and David Whittaker. 1994. ''The Chicago Area Project.'' *FBI Law Enforcement Bulletin* 63(5): 8–12.

Wilson, J. Q. and G. L. Kelling. 1982. ''Broken Windows: Police and Neighborhood Safety.'' *Atlantic Monthly* 249(March): 29–38.

Chapter 11

The Role of the Community in Police Community Relations

L et us begin by reminding the reader that most police activity is a response to requests for assistance by citizens. It is the community, as Reiss remarks, which in most instances determines when the police act, about what the police act, and on whom the police act.[1]

Because the personnel and equipment available to the police are limited and the ratio of police officers to offenses against the law and community order is small, the police could not possibly do their jobs without substantial cooperation and support from other citizens. In this sense, the community itself represents a vital resource to the police. The availability of this resource depends significantly on the state of police community relations in a particular locality.

As was stated in the last chapter there are a number of special community relations oriented programs and activities that police departments may initiate and/or sponsor. These are highly visible signs of a department's concern to maintain and improve relations with the community. Replacing specialized police community relations units and programs with an emphasis on community relations as an aspect of all police activities, has been the trend in recent years.[2] This is a risky strategy to the extent that accountability for policy implementation is diluted, but is worth the effort if joint accountability (police and public) is the outcome. No matter how diligent the efforts or what particular form they assume, police-initiated programs can succeed only if citizens are willing to cooperate in the effort.

In this chapter, we will focus on some particular dimensions of police and community activities which reflect the general principle that the community plays an essential role in the establishment and maintenance of positive police community relations. We will also discuss some particular roles which citizens may assume in relation to the police, and the implications of these roles for police community relations. In this context it is necessary to keep in mind those principles of police accountability and responsiveness (discussed in the following chapter) which citizens may legitimately demand of their police (and, in community policing at least, vice versa).

Social Approval and Compliance with Norms

Police behavior is shaped by the same rewards and punishments that influence human behavior in general.[3] While the effects of rewards and punishments may be less direct and more complex in humans than in other animal species, two general principles still hold. First, behavior which is rewarded tends to be repeated, and behavior which is punished tends to be avoided. Public criticism of illegal or inappropriate police behavior tends to discourage such behavior. On the other hand, public approval and praise of exemplary behavior tends to encourage repetition of such desirable conduct. Second, rewards for desirable behavior influence behavior more than do punishments for undesirable behavior. In short, the most effective approach to getting people to behave in a desirable way is to reward them for meritorious conduct. Applied in the context of the role played by the community in police community relations, this precept means that a community that fails to reward its police when they have performed well misses the best opportunity to influence most effectively the behavior of its police.

Rewards take several different forms. Advancement within the department, reasonable pay incentives, improved working conditions, and better equipment are meaningful rewards. So also is the simple, but too often neglected verbal expression of appreciation and support expressed by an individual citizen to an individual officer, or by a community to its police department.

Social approval, irrespective of its particular form, is a powerful incentive. When people receive social approval for a job well done, they are likely to work harder. As a rule they will also feel better about themselves and others, be more committed to the community of which they are a part, and abide by the norms of the community they serve. There is no reason to believe that the police are any different from the rest of us in this regard. A police force that receives the recognition and support of the community when it deserves it is much more likely to respond by providing that community with exemplary police services. Constant complaints can produce withdrawal, resentment, and a siege mentality among the police. Police isolationism, discussed earlier in this book as inherent to some degree in the role of the police in our society, can only be exacerbated by the feeling of alienation of the police resulting from unrelenting public criticism. Individuals or groups can hardly be expected to show much respect for or appreciation of a community that they feel rejects and isolates them. When the police are subjected to extreme rejection and isolation, their willingness to abide by the rules of the larger community is eroded. Police corruption and misconduct are likely to be encouraged by such conditions. Looked at from this point of view, community support for the police when they deserve it is indispensable, if positive relations between community and police are to be maintained or enhanced.

Citizens' blind, unquestioning support of their police is not appropriate in a democracy. But neither is unthinking, comprehensive condemnation. The interests of positive police community relations would be best served by a community that provides just, informed, and accurate evaluation of its police. To provide such evaluations, citizens must have access to and familiarize themselves with facts about departmental policy and practice. The police may supply some of this information directly to the public by means of their public relations efforts, some will be exchanged between police officers and citizens who view themselves as partners in community policing, and some will be obtained through the mass media—newspapers, magazines, radio, and television. The media, therefore, as the communicating link between the police and the public, have a compelling obligation to furnish reasonably balanced coverage of police policy and practice, carefully distinguishing between reporting and editorializing in presenting subjects involving the police. When they are properly informed, American citizens have an obligation to their police to try to understand the dilemmas that often confront the police in a modern, industrialized society, and then to judge their conduct fairly, conferring both praise and blame as they are merited.

The Roles of Other Citizens in Interaction with the Police

Individual citizens interact directly with the police in a variety of different roles, including those which we shall call the tattler, the crime victim, the eyewitness, the informant, the suspect, the supporter, and the observer/bystander. These roles are not mutually exclusive, of course; for example, a tattler can at the same time be a victim, a witness, an informant, and a suspect. It should be remembered that here we are discussing roles, not persons, and that various roles may be played by the same individual on different occasions. Usually, however, a citizen plays only one of these roles during any given encounter, and they will be treated here as if they were always separate. In this section, each of the roles identified above will be discussed, and the implications for police community relations will be noted.

Citizens sometimes complain to the police about the behavior of others. This may occur even in circumstances where the person complaining is not directly involved in or harmed by the situation about which the citizen is complaining. In these cases, the person may be said to be playing the part of **tattler**.

Tattlers often, though not always, wish to remain anonymous. This may stem from several different concerns, but the predominant one would seem to be a desire for self-protection. Tattlers may be sufficiently concerned about a matter to want to call it to the attention of the authorities but not sufficiently concerned, or actually afraid, to risk being drawn into the role of an informant or an eyewitness. Were this to happen the citizen might be entangled in a more or less complex legal situation; thus he or she would be identified, not only by the police but also by those about whom the tattler is complaining.

All of this assumes that the complaint is real. Occasionally, tattlers wish to remain anonymous because they are using a fake or exaggerated complaint in the expectation that the police will respond and create trouble for others, (perhaps to avenge some insult to the tattler). Regardless of the motives of tattlers, however, most of them expect the police to respond to the complaint.

Tattlers are often regarded as "busybodies" and nuisances by the police. Usually the information provided is sparse and the content of the complaint is of relatively low priority. Moreover, the tattler's desire not to become involved significantly decreases the likelihood that formal action can be taken, should the police, in fact, act on the complaint. As a result, the police often ignore tattlers.

Occasionally, however, tattlers provide significant or valuable information. Police ordinarily welcome assistance from any quarter, in any guise, and in some situations they specifically invite anonymous, "no-questions-asked" tips. The most useful technique is to encourage helpful talk about "real" problems, but to discourage citizens' efforts to bring in the police simply to meddle in the affairs of others. One solution to the problem is to make the tattler aware at the time of the call that there are limits to police resources and power. Another approach is to inform citizens about these limits through a community education program. In any event, one phase of establishing constructive police community relations is responding to tattlers' complaints whenever this is possible and appropriate, and explaining why they do not respond when such is not the case.[4]

The role of **crime victim** is especially significant in police community relations. The citizen in the role of victim has been directly harmed by the activities reported and often interacts face-to-face with the police. This individual's identity is usually revealed to the police, and he or she has a very direct interest in successful police intervention, perhaps to recover property or to derive the personal satisfaction which comes from seeing the perpetrator of the offense brought to justice.

Obviously, the police also have a high stake in these interactions with victims, since in the mind of the public, crime solving is the primary activity of the police. Although in theory the police are recognized as public servants, it is in their relationships with crime victims that their public service assumes its most visible and concrete form; in such situations the police can accomplish a great deal to reinforce or to undermine good police public relations.

An especially critical aspect of encounters between the police and crime victims is the difference or contrast in the definitions of the situation formulated by the police and the citizen victim. On the one hand, the victim is likely to define what has happened as a personal crisis. Personal crises are characterized by high tension, excitement, emotion, some confusion, ambivalence, and a sense of urgency. The police, on the other hand, tend to treat such encounters as "routine." In most instances the officers who deal with the victim are, or appear to be, emotionally neutral, and they proceed at a slow, methodical pace. The skepticism of the police sometimes contributes to this impression. As a result, the police are often perceived by the victim as cold, unsympathetic, and insufficiently concerned about what has happened.

It is probable that the police understand the behavior and feelings of the victim better than most victims understand the behavior and feelings of the police, since officers have often observed personal crises, while citizens rarely have had the experiences of the police officers. It seems also to be the case, however, that the police often fail to communicate this understanding to citizens. Officers could make significant advances in police community relations were they to express sympathy and concern for the victim and provide an honest assessment of the prospects and the difficulties involved in pursuing the case to a successful conclusion. In this connection they might impress upon the victim the valuable role he or she can play in assisting the police in their efforts and, where resources permit, by reporting periodically to the victim the progress being made in the investigation.

The citizen as **eyewitness** is also appreciated by the police. Eyewitness accounts of criminal activities (particularly those of victims or others very close to the scene), however, are often inaccurate in many respects.[5] Firsthand observations of an offense can be extremely valuable in the investigation. When the eyewitnesses are relatives or close associates of the victim, however, they may interpret the routine response of the police as inappropriate or unconcerned. As with the victim, expressions of sympathy, support, and gratitude for the witness's assistance, with some explanation of police procedures, can bring real benefits to police community relations.

The role of the **informant** differs from that of the tattler and the eyewitness, in that the informant ordinarily receives direct compensation in the form of favors or money in return for the information furnished. Despite its importance in many cases we shall not here discuss this role in detail. But two interrelated comments are in order. First, the informant ordinarily enters into relationships with the police primarily for personal compensation and gain; as a result, this person's relationship with the police takes on a businesslike tone, with occasional bargaining over the value of the information. Second, although the use of informants may be necessary in some circumstances, in most situations it is not in the general interest of the police or the public to encourage citizens to expect material compensation for assisting the police.

The citizen in the role of **suspect** is also closely associated with police community relations. In Chapter Three we have already discussed some aspects of police-suspect encounters. A few additional comments are appropriate here. First, ordinarily citizens do not assume the role of suspect voluntarily. Rather, they are forced into the role by the police. Second, the police almost always seem convinced that persons they have identified as ''suspects'' are, in fact, guilty. This is as we might expect. Presumably, the police do not make a practice of pursuing and arresting persons they believe to be innocent. It is also true, however, that some citizens who may find themselves in the role of suspect are, in fact, innocent; and many others claim to be either innocent, or unfairly singled out for attention.

Thus, from one point of view, one might say that the police never arrest an innocent person, or looked at another way, the person arrested never deserves to be. Evidently there are many considerations when an officer is interacting with a suspect; for example, when apprehending a suspect, the officer is concerned about his or her own safety as well as the protection of the suspect and bystanders. Moreover, in many instances, it is possible to consider various interpretations of an encounter, and some of these may make the situation very dangerous for all involved. Any action on the part of police or citizens that reduces the threat to face in such encounters also contributes to constructive police community relations.

As discussed earlier in this chapter, the role of the citizen as **supporter** is also significant in police community relations. Members of official or semi-official organizations like the auxiliary police may be counted as supporters; so too are citizens who express in private and in public their support for the police when the subjects of law enforcement, maintenance of order, or related issues arise. Both organized and informed public support can be a valuable asset to the police force.

It should be noted, however, that in some circumstances such support entails risks for both the police and the public. From the point of view of some citizens, there is little distinction between the official police and vigilante groups which claim to be supporting and assisting the local police in law enforcement and the maintenance of public order. Some very real police community relations problems may be created by these groups. Such problems involve the possibility of extralegal behavior on the part of those who belong to ''neighborhood protection groups.'' Furthermore, the very existence of such groups may reflect unfavorably on the police force, because it implies that the latter are unable to do their job satisfactorily. To the extent that this view prevails it may impair police community relations. In the following section of this chapter we shall have more to say about citizen support groups of various kinds.

The citizen in the role of **observer/bystander** was also mentioned in Chapter Three. Here it need only be stressed once more that citizens who observe police behavior form impressions of the police as a result of such observations. A citizen who observes a police officer treat another citizen with as much dignity and respect as the situation permits is much less likely to interfere in the situation on behalf of that citizen and is much more inclined to feel at least grudging sympathy for the officer and her performance of duty. It is conceivable that such behavior may induce the bystander to help the officer, for example, by assuming the role of eyewitness.

Since this book is addressed primarily to law enforcement officers rather than to the public, much of the discussion in this chapter is directed to a police audience. Thus attention is focused upon the impact of police behavior on citizens. It would be inappropriate, however, to conclude this section without some remarks addressed more to the public than to the police.

If we are consistent with the interactionist perspective employed in this book, we must recognize that insofar as police community relations are concerned, the behavior of citizens in police-public encounters is as critical as that of the police officer. Furthermore, the citizen incurs some responsibility for the nature and quality of police community relations, especially when involved in community policing efforts. Citizens who, by word or deed, threaten the face or reputation of a police officer invite identical derogatory responses from the officer, and they should not be surprised when the officer so reacts. Police officers are not *supposed* to respond in kind, but the temptation is very real. Citizens who make little or no effort to understand the role of the police in their community and to consider the problems which the police confront daily have slight basis for complaint about the quality of police services in their community. Citizens who, in most situations, treat the police as aliens have little reason to expect sympathetic treatment when they ask for police assistance. There is, in short, some truth in the old adage (slightly amended for present purposes) that a community gets the sort of police force it deserves. As the Critical Issue article indicates, positive steps on the part of a police officer may well result in positive responses from the public.

Unfortunately, the majority of citizens pay little attention to the police, their problems, and their potential until some personal or community crisis occurs. This means that for all practical purposes the police must assume the initiative in efforts designed to increase community awareness and to improve police community relations. Thus the police in a particular community will bear the largest share of responsibility for the quality of police community relations in that community.

The Community and Their Police: Teamwork Is the Key

Without the police, most communities would be far more vulnerable to crime and general mayhem. For communities to survive, other civic agencies undoubtedly would have to assume law enforcement and peace-keeping functions. Furthermore, communities would be compelled to find other ways to furnish those general service functions now provided by the police. It is axiomatic that communities *need* their police. It is just as evident that the police certainly cannot do their job well, in fact they cannot do much of their job at all, without at least minimal understanding, cooperation, and support from the community. It is apparent, then, that when a community and their police find ways of working together, both parties benefit.

Community involvement in crime prevention and detection assumes many forms and cooperation with the police in these efforts exists in different degrees. In addition to the transition to community policing, which we have already discussed in some detail, let us consider several examples.

The Crime Prevention Through Environmental Design (CPTED) movement brings city planners, business executives, architects, and law enforcement officials together to design public as well as private space and structures. The guiding philosophy of this initiative (sometimes referred to as defensible space theory)[6] is that factors such as lighting, landscaping, and physical layout can significantly influence the attitudes and behavior of occupants or users (e.g., by creating a greater sense of community), thereby both directly and indirectly serving as a deterrent to criminal activity.

Chicago Children Want Cop to Stay

Budget Moves Don't Sit Well with 7th-Graders

By Bob Secter

of the Los Angeles Times

CHICAGO—It's 2:30 in the afternoon, the dismissal bell has just rung, and the kids at Kosciuszko Elementary School explode out the front door in a burst of pent up energy and anxious delight.

Kilroy is here.

That is officer Howard Kilroy, the big, smiling Chicago policeman who has planted himself reassuringly in the center of the schoolyard like a guardian angel. He is as much a fixture in the gang-plagued, drug-infested North Side Puerto Rican neighborhood as Kosciuszko's chipped and shopworn turn-of-the-century brown brick facade.

"Hi, amigo, hi, amigo," the youngsters shout, mobbing the gray-haired man in blue, pulling on his pants legs, hugging him, kissing him, filling his arms with Christmas cards made by hand out of construction paper, crayons and love. "Are you coming back?"

Maybe not. For 17 years, the mild-mannered, 58-year-old Kilroy has been the soul, the conscience of Kosciuszko, a throwback to a bygone era when cops walked beats, knew everybody by name and were seen by children as role models, not objects of hate or fear.

Because of budget cuts and a hiring freeze, Kilroy has been reassigned indefinitely from his familiar foot patrol near the school to a squad car. As of next week, he will no longer be around each day to watch over the students at Kosciuszko as they head home through one of Chicago's rougher neighborhoods.

The story, however, doesn't stop there. In a city where police brutality charges make frequent headlines and ethnic strife can be as regular and bitter as the winter winds, a bunch of Latino kids have launched a major battle on behalf of a German-Irish cop who can't speak a word of Spanish.

"I don't want him to leave 'cause he's part of the cause," explained eighth-grader Waldy Gonzalez. "He's straight. He's a cool dude, bro."

On Thursday, a delegation of sixth-, seventh- and eighth-graders lobbied Ronald Garcia, Kilroy's commander at the Shakespeare District precinct house, for Kilroy's return. They have been promised meetings with Police Superintendent Leroy Martin and Chicago Mayor Richard M. Daley, and have gathered "keep Kilroy" petition signatures from 1,104 Kosciuszko students as well as 900 of their parents.

Walls in the school auditorium are plastered with hand-drawn posters of sad-faced youngsters crying, in both English and Spanish, "Where's Kilroy?" and "We want Kilroy." Dozens of youngsters have also scrawled impassioned letters on his behalf, many illustrated with bright crayon pictures of happy stick-figure children holding hands with a smiling stick figure policeman.

"Dear Mr. Martin," Kateri Barreto wrote to the Chicago police chief. "I go to Kosciuszko school. We need officer Kilroy to come back to our school. He keeps our school protected from gang members who come around and drug dealers. We miss him very much. Will you please bring him back to our school? The end."

"Everybody knows him, it's unbelievable," said Jim Bailey, Kosciuszko's principal. "It's like something out of the past where the neighborhood policeman is a respected figure and not an object of scorn and derision."

Kilroy, however, insisted that he had done nothing out of the ordinary. "I'll walk the streets and these kids will say I'm their father, their grandfather, their godfather, even their mother," he said. "They're just starving for someone, anyone, to look up to . . . I've always liked kids. I just think it's our job to win friends. We have enough enemies already."

Modest disclaimers aside, students, teachers and parents at Kosciuszko insist that Kilroy is something rare: a genuinely nice, unpretentious guy who walks kids home from school, sponsors neighborhood ball teams with money from his own pocket and stands in for Santa Claus at the school Christmas pageant.

Don Greczyk, the assistant principal at Kosciuszko, said that Kilroy was one of the few authority figures respected by local gangs.

Friedman reports on the Chicago Alliance for Neighborhood Safety (CANS) and its efforts to encourage and cooperate in the Chicago Police Department's community policing effort. The Alliance has recommended to the police department more ''neighborhood-oriented alternatives'' through the use of informal pilot projects and liaison agreements. At least some of these projects have been successful as a result of cooperation between the police and the citizens involved.[7]

The community policing initiative discussed in Chapter Seven clearly holds some promise for increasing constructive police community cooperation. The approach encourages citizens to exercise significant influence over police priorities and activities in their neighborhoods. Specially trained officers assigned more or less permanently to particular neighborhoods, develop personal relationships with residents, identify community problems, work with citizens in resolving the problems, and provide liaison with other police personnel and functions.

The ''Take a Bite Out of Crime'' national media campaign features the trench-coated cartoon crime dog, ''McGruff,'' whose gravelly voice and no-nonsense style match his name. Among other things, McGruff advises readers or viewers concerning actions citizens should take when they witness criminal activity. The media spots are prepared in consultation with crime control experts and underwritten by the National Advertising Council.

The increasingly popular ''Crime Stoppers'' program offers rewards for information about unsolved crimes. The volunteer boards overseeing the independently operated community chapters include police officers, business people, and other citizens. Funds for rewards are donated by businesses and individuals.

In some larger cities, volunteer neighborhood citizen boards have been established to mediate disputes among residents. Relatively minor conflicts that might otherwise wind up in police and court hands are dealt with informally by the disputing parties themselves, with the assistance and advice of the dispute resolution board. The agreements arrived at are not backed up by the force of law, but are, nevertheless, often effective in diffusing interpersonal tensions.[8]

There are thousands of block or neighborhood watch areas scattered throughout both urban and rural communities across the nation. Two basically sound ideas underlie these programs: (1) among the more effective deterrents to criminal activity is visibility; and (2) those in the best position to notice unusual goings-on in a neighborhood are those who live there. With the encouragement and assistance of the police, area residents organize themselves into a volunteer watch group, dedicating themselves to increased vigilance and prompt reporting of suspicious activities. Street signs declaring the neighborhood as a watch area are erected. In some cases, members patrol the neighborhood, but even in these instances, the volunteers act only as informants, relying on the police for any necessary intervention. Specially trained police officers provide moral support and crime prevention information (through brochures and presentations at group meetings). Police personnel also respond as quickly as possible to area residents' requests for service. In a few cases, where special training has been provided, neighborhood watch groups have extended their activities into other arenas, such as counseling victims and informing them about criminal justice system operations as well as encouraging them to testify in court.[9]

The effectiveness of national media campaigns, such as "Take a Bite Out of Crime," is difficult to assess in part because of the necessarily general nature of the message and target audiences. Programs operating in local arenas are easier to evaluate. In a recent review of evaluation studies on both national and local programs, Lab indicates that public awareness of the national media efforts is widespread, but whether changes in the behavior of citizens occurs is difficult to determine. The news on local programs is quite encouraging. Many studies show reductions in crime rates when neighborhood citizens become informed and involved in crime prevention efforts, though displacement of criminal activity to other areas lacking citizen organization appears to be common. There is also some evidence that citizens' fear of crime is alleviated, confidence in avoiding victimization is enhanced, and the frequency of precautionary behavior is increased.[10]

Our discussion of community involvement in crime control would be incomplete without some consideration of independent and occasionally renegade "neighborhood protection committees." These committees differ from neighborhood watch and similar groups in three important ways: (1) they are created without the approval or guidance (and sometimes in the face of overt opposition) from local law enforcement agencies; (2) they sometimes do intervene directly in suspected criminal activity; and (3) they tend to focus on violent rather than property offenses.[11]

The Guardian Angels are perhaps the best known of these groups, having achieved national publicity and established local chapters in a number of urban areas. More recently, anti-drug efforts have resulted in the formation of citizen groups who march through their neighborhoods warning drug dealers to take their business elsewhere and, occasionally, physically evicting suspected drug dealers or burning crack houses. The proactive interventionist practices of these groups make them at once appealing and dangerous. In many respects, they are modern versions of an old American tradition of vigilantism.[12] While most contemporary groups of this genre (including the Guardian Angels) turn alleged offenders over to the police and profess no desire to become judge, jury, and executioner, whenever citizens (especially well-organized groups) take the law into their own hands, fundamental democratic values are at risk.

The controversy surrounding the emergence and spread of autonomous neighborhood protection committees is not likely to go away soon, because their presence and activities force us to confront some very difficult and significant questions. Those issues include: (a) the reality of crime and the prevalence of violence in our society; (b) the vulnerability and fears of many citizens, especially the elderly and the poor; (c) the rights of citizens to organize, to protect, and to defend themselves; (d) the limited financial and human

Leaders Praise Accreditation for Quality Assurance

Spokespersons from the fifteen agencies accredited during the Columbus, Ohio, Commission meeting, July 29, 1989, voice pride in their achievement. In addition, they believe accreditation is a commitment to future quality service. Following are their comments:

ANN ARBOR, MICHIGAN, POLICE DEPARTMENT—

Chief William J. Corbett:

''We have always believed we are a progressive, professional law enforcement agency. However, we will be an even better organization after having compared ourselves to these nationally recognized standards and made the improvements necessary to meet them.''

Deputy Chief William J. Hoover:

''Accreditation is a major step toward improvement of the image of law enforcement. It is a method we . . . can use to convince ourselves, and those we serve, that real professionalism takes more than just doing a good job.''

Mayor Gerald D. Jernigan:

''. . . Ann Arbor Police Department has an outstanding record of effectively and professionally handling a wide range of difficult situations associated with a university community . . . now the rest of the nation will know of our officers'

dedication to the laws of this land and their commitment to the people they protect.''

City Administrator Del D. Borgsdorf:

''Accreditation is more than a process and a set of standards—it is a statement of the importance of public service and the approach to the delivery of those services. The Ann Arbor Police Department's accreditation reflects well on the quality of its management, the performance of its employees, and reinforces the importance of serving the community in an effective, professional, competent manner.''

BOCA RATON, FLORIDA, POLICE DEPARTMENT—

Chief Peter A. Petracco:

''I would like to paraphrase a statement made about 20 years ago regarding 'one small step.' I think it (accreditation) was one large step for the Boca Raton Police Department and one giant step for criminal justice and law enforcement.''

JACKSON, TENNESSEE, POLICE DEPARTMENT—

Chief E. B. Alderson:

''. . . as I close out a career spanning some 40 years of service, I have seen a

lot of things come and go down the track in law enforcement . . . and accreditation is probably the greatest . . .''

HARRISBURG, PENNSYLVANIA, POLICE DEPARTMENT—

Chief Alexander Whitlock:

''. . . for a law enforcement agency to identify with the community it is serving and to gain the interest and trust of the community it serves, accreditation is the only way to go.'' Chief Whitlock also said, ''We also learned that in order to succeed, we had to put the best team together that we could and that is what we did . . .''

JAMES CITY COUNTY, VIRGINIA, POLICE DEPARTMENT—

Chief Robert C. Key:

''The accreditation effort . . . was a team effort. It involved the police department, the county administration, county personnel and other county and community organizations. Before the process started, we felt like we were a good service oriented police department. But accreditation was an opportunity to test ourselves against national standards, to be looked at and reviewed by outsiders . . . an impartial group.''

resources available to the police; (e) the impossibility that any police force, regardless of its resources, can meet all the citizens' needs for protection and other services; (f) the threat which vigilante-like groups pose to presumption of innocence and protection of due process for the accused, which are so essential to the preservation of freedom in a democracy; and (g) the control and accountability of privately organized and funded ''security forces'' operating in a public arena.

LAS VEGAS, NEVADA, METROPOLITAN POLICE DEPARTMENT—

Sheriff John Morgan:

"We have always thought of ourselves as being somewhat unique . . . unique or not, we basically have the same kinds of policing responsibilities as other agencies across the country. We have found out, as others have before us, that we could meet the challenge of accreditation with a conscientious effort and be recognized nationally . . . I realize that becoming accredited is not the final step. Rather, we must now, with a commitment to continued excellence, strive to maintain these high standards of performance."

Deputy Chief Tom Crawford:

"Constant and consistent self-inspection of every facet of the agency to insure substantial compliance with the standards—that's the name of the game in gaining accreditation. And, certainly it's the better method of remaining accredited for the years to come."

MT. LEBANON, PENNSYLVANIA, POLICE DEPARTMENT—

Chief David A. Varrelman:

"I think a community has respect for the fact that accreditation brings to it the state of the art in terms of police management, operations, and administration." He adds: "The reason we went into it in the beginning is we feel that accreditation is a natural evolution of a good law enforcement agency."

NEW BRIGHTON, MINNESOTA, POLICE DEPARTMENT—

Chief John C. Kelley:

"The accreditation process is the best thing that has happened to our profession for the 23 years I've been in it . . . I would like to make a special point that as far as I'm concerned, there is absolutely no reason that a B or A-sized agency cannot get involved and successfully complete the accreditation process."

NORTH DAKOTA HIGHWAY PATROL—

Colonel Brian C. Berg:

"Accreditation causes us to look at ourselves and recognize our mission in the true light of trust. I mean that from the public's standpoint—they put a lot of trust in law enforcement. (With accreditation), we are taking a look at our organization and our delivery of that type of service. . . ."

ST. CHARLES, ILLINOIS, POLICE DEPARTMENT—

Chief James L. Roche:

". . . as newly developed procedures began to take effect during the self-assessment phase, noticeable improvements began to occur, especially in the areas of training, career development, and management operations . . . I suspect that as an organization, we have experienced only a 'sampling' of the benefits of professional growth and development. . . ."

*Accreditation Manager
Lieutenant Darryl Rogers:*

"Improvements in administration, operating procedures, staff functions, morale and professionalism are just the beginning of a long list of rewards gained from the accreditation process. . . . The liaison and communications that it (accreditation) has fostered between city departments has not only improved our performance but theirs as well. Improvements in personnel policies, budgeting practices and finance procedures have been an added benefit for the entire city and its employees.

Reprinted from Commission Update, Fall 1989. © Commission on Accreditation for Law Enforcement Agencies.

In spite of these issues, there is certainly a role for citizen patrols in high crime areas—especially where the citizens are patrolling their own neighborhoods. The nature of the crimes involved and the environment in which they are being committed make it extremely difficult not to have a strategy of intervention when the group encounters a crime in progress. It would be possible for groups like the Angels to limit themselves to carefully observing an alleged crime and the alleged perpetrator, filing reports with the police about these

Watchful Guardian Angels on patrol in Little Tokyo, L.A. The Angels and their supporters maintain that they provide a psychological boost to people who must walk the city's most dangerous streets and ride its subways—and that this primarily black and Hispanic group provides role models for teenagers who too often see only criminals to look up to.

© Alon Reininger/Unicorn Stock Photos

offenses, and assisting the police in identifying and locating the alleged perpetrator. But to do so would mean standing by while citizens were beaten, stabbed, shot, raped, or murdered. Such violence occurs regularly in many places and adopting a mere spectator role while it happens does not seem a very realistic alternative for those who care about their fellow humans. So long as the human resources of the police department are severely limited (as they certainly will be), and while those human resources which are available are distributed in a way that leaves particular neighborhoods and areas especially vulnerable to crime, the periodic emergence of citizen groups who endeavor to protect their neighborhoods and themselves from victimization seems inevitable.[13]

There are, to be sure, many other situations and different ways in which citizens and their police can and do work together. In many communities, for example, volunteer ''emergency police'' assist regular police with traffic control during events that attract large crowds, and provide emergency service following a natural disaster like a tornado or an earthquake. This cooperation not only provides real and valuable services to the community, but also gives citizens an opportunity to give concrete expression to their support of the police. Furthermore, through their association with the police, they acquire a better understanding of the role of the police in the community.

In addition, the police and community residents often work together in developing special programs for dealing with community problems and individual offenders. Programs that divert first-time juvenile offenders from the formal processing of the juvenile court to special community-supported work and counseling programs, are examples of such cooperation. So also are arrangements between the police and community-supported rehabilitation programs like Alcoholics Anonymous. National accreditation also requires police involvement with those they serve (see Criticle Issue on p. 198).

Whatever the particular context, on those occasions when citizens and their police find ways of joining forces and working together to solve some community problems, the community becomes a better place to live, the task of the police is easier, and police community relations are almost always improved. In short, teamwork is the key to building positive police community relations.

Summary

The role of the community in crime prevention and police community relations encompasses a number of critical dimensions. One way of making the community's contributions more visible is to emphasize the role of citizens as recipients of police services. Citizens, after all, initiate most police action and are favorably impressed by police responsiveness to their needs. Also, as with any service agency, citizen clients expect their police to be accountable to them for the quality of services rendered.

In a more direct way, the community may exercise a very positive influence on its police by providing overt and explicit support for the police when such reinforcement is merited. Offering constructive criticism of those police actions of which the community disapproves is also an essential community function. Negative criticism of their police seems to come easier to Americans; but public approval of satisfactory services probably has a more powerful influence on police conduct.

Citizens' efforts to protect themselves and to assist the police may take many forms. A willingness to request services from the police when appropriate is a minimum level of citizen support for them. Supplying information and, in some instances, furnishing testimony, are also important. National anti-crime media campaigns, crime newsletters, DARE, and Crime Stoppers are among the programs linking law enforcement and community resources. Neighborhood watch programs represent an effort on the part of citizen groups to increase the safety and security of their own living areas, and can furnish valuable assistance to the police. The emergence of groups like the ''Guardian Angels'' has created far-reaching discussions concerning the limits of police resources in meeting the community's demand for protection, as well as the scope of activities that, in a democracy, are conceded to privately organized, funded, and controlled security forces working in the public arena.

When the community and its police join forces and work cooperatively toward common goals, communities improve. So also do police community relations.

Discussion Questions

1. Does the public support the police in your community? Why or why not? How might community support be increased?
2. What are the basic obligations of a police force to its community? Of a community to its police force?
3. Identify the community-based crime prevention programs operating in your community. Are they effective? How do you know? How could you find out?
4. Are the police in your community rewarded for exemplary conduct? How? Are the police punished for unsatisfactory service? How? Are rewards more effective than punishment in shaping police behavior?
5. What are the limits, if any, to citizen involvement in law enforcement? Would you support the formation of a ''Guardian Angels'' group in your community? Why or why not?

Endnotes

1. Reiss. ''Police Brutality.'': 70–80.
2. See Chris Offer. 1993. ''C-OP Fads and Emperors Without Clothes.'' *Law Enforcement News* 19(376): 8; Rosenbaum. *Community Crime Prevention.*; Trojanowicz and Bucqueroux. *Community Policing.*; Sparrow, Moore, and Kennedy. *Beyond 911.*
3. Although there are many more recent statements, we believe the best general discussion of the role of rewards and punishments in influencing human conduct is B. F. Skinner. 1953. *Science and Human Behavior.* New York: The Macmillan Company. See especially Chapter V ''Operant Behavior,'' Chapter XII, ''Punishment,'' and Chapter XIX, ''Social Behavior.''
4. See Reiss' similar discussion of persons he calls informants and complainants in Reiss. ''Police Brutality.'': 84–88.
5. Gary L. Wells and John W. Turtle. 1987. ''Eyewitness Testimony Research: Current Knowledge and Emerging Controversies.'' *Canadian Journal of Behavioral Science* 19(4): 363–388.
6. See Oscar Newman. 1972. *Defensible Space.* New York: Macmillan; M. D. Maltz, A. C. Gordon, and W. Friedman. 1991. *Mapping Crime In Its Community Setting: Event Geography Analysis.* New York: Springer-Verlag; Ellen K. Coughlin. 1992. ''Violence and America's Young: Psychologists' Panel Urges Research on Combating Aggressive Behavior.'' *The Chronicle of Higher Education.* 39(2): 7–8.
7. Warren Friedman. 1994. ''The Community Role in Community Policing'' in Rosenbaum. *Community Crime Prevention.*: 263–269.
8. Kennedy, Sparrow, and Moore. *Beyond 911.*: 102; Mark H. Moore. 1992. ''Problem-Solving and Community Policing'' in Michael Tonry and Norval Morris, eds. *Modern Policing.* Chicago: University of Chicago Press: 102–103.
9. See, for example, Peter Finn. 1986. ''Block Watches Help Crime Victims in Philadelphia.'' *NIJ Reports.* U.S. Department of Justice. Washington, D.C.: U.S. Government Printing Office (November/December): 2–8.
10. Steven A. Lab. 1988. *Crime Prevention: Approaches, Practices and Evaluations.* Cincinnati: Anderson. See also Dennis P. Rosenbaum, ed. 1986. *Community Crime Prevention: Does It Work?* Beverly Hills, CA: Sage; and Aaron Podolefsky. 1983. *Case Studies in Community Crime Prevention.* Springfield, IL: Charles C Thomas.
11. See, for instance, Thomas R. Windham and Randy P. Ely. 1994. ''Code Blue: Citizens on Patrol.'' *The Police Chief* 61(5): 52–54.
12. William Tucker. 1985. *Vigilante: The Backlash Against Crime in America.* New York: Stein and Day.

13. For a good discussion of the need for citizen involvement in high-crime areas, see Lee P. Brown. 1992. ''Violent Crime and Community Involvement.'' *FBI Law Enforcement Bulletin* (May): 2–5.

Suggested Readings

Bursik, R. J. and H. G. Grasmick. 1993. *Neighborhoods and Crime: The Dimensions of Effective Community Control.* New York: Lexington.

Lab, Steven A. 1988. *Crime Prevention: Approaches, Practices and Evaluations.* Cincinnati: Anderson.

Nash, Doreen. 1991. ''Miami's Ethnic Sharing Program.'' *FBI Law Enforcement Bulletin* (August): 8–9.

Shapland, Joanna and Jon Vagg. 1988. *Policing by the Public.* London: Routledge.

Skogan, Wesley. 1990. *Disorder and Decline: Crime and the Spiral of Decay in American Cities.* New York: Free Press.

The Role of the Police in Community Relations: Summary

W hile the expression ''police community relations'' is often used, as in this book, it has some unfortunate implications. In one sense, these words reflect what is all too often the actual way in which many police officers and many other citizens perceive the relationship between a community and its police force. In short, there develops, as we have noted, a ''we-they'' attitude, as if the police and the rest of the community were two separate entities, two separate communities.

In some respects, of course, this is true. Thus, the literature on the police frequently refers to a tendency on the part of many citizens, especially those who belong to minority groups, to regard the police as unwelcome intruders representing ''the establishment,'' and prone to persecute the underdogs. As noted in the second chapter, there is, in fact, historical substantiation for this view. On the other hand, the police literature is filled with the cynicism and contempt which police officers sometimes feel for those whom they serve.[1] The tendency of police officers to ''stick together'' both on and off duty has also been frequently noted. Therefore, the idea that the police and the community sometimes view themselves as separate entities is not new, and has some foundation in fact.[2]

In spite of the fact that the police sometimes feel separate from and in conflict with other citizens, while other citizens sometimes view the police and the public as adversaries, it is nevertheless also a fact that police and public are, in another and more fundamental sense, members of the same community. The literature relating to police community relations which typically focuses on difficult and conflicting relationships, often seems to ignore the basic common interests which they share. The point is easily overlooked or ignored by both police and public during their day-to-day interactions. Yet, both the police and the public are subject to the same government; both pay taxes which support the police and other public services sponsored by the government. The children of both attend the same community schools; members of both groups belong to the same churches and other community organizations; both have

Cops Are Community Leaders

Critical Issue

Commander's Commentary

Darwin R. Odom
Patrolman

Kirby, Texas

This century has seen many changes in how a community regards its police officers and law enforcement. The time of the gun-toting, baddest man in town has long since past. The role of police officers in community life has taken on new meaning. The cop as *Public Servant* is at the pinnacle of this concept.

A police officer, with few exceptions, is an employee of the community he serves. One might postulate that in this capacity, an officer has limited ability to project leadership or influence community perceptions or actions. This quite simply is not true.

There are some underlying principles which have application in the total spectrum of the police endeavor. First and foremost: an officer must know his trade and his mandate and align civilian leadership and the citizenry with trust in his operational competence, sound judgment and ethical decisions.

Responsibilities
A leader's most fundamental responsibility is to those that constitute the wherewithal to carry out his function as a police officer and to those which he is entrusted to serve. Police officers, in a community leadership role, are expected to provide direction, security, example, and both ethical and moral leadership.

Direction
Direction comprises those activities such as guidance, decision-making, motivation, encouragement, and supervision—which a police leader employs to focus his resources to address sometimes very difficult situations. Effective direction demands an appreciation for the relative importance of any activity undertaken by the officer or his department and the ability to communicate both verbally and nonverbally the significance of this activity to the public and the civilian leadership.

Security
Security is both a reality and an emotional benefit derived from police leadership, organization and activity. Security (emotional or real) is at the crux of police responsibility. Officers and their departments foster a sense of security for members of the community. An officer's leadership skills in community relations, program management (such as neighborhood watch), and education provides fertile groundwork for crime suppression and communication between police, community, and civilian leadership.

Example
Setting an example is a police responsibility frequently overlooked. A true leader always sets an example for others to follow. A simple event, like rolling a stop sign instead of executing a proper stop, is certainly an example to the public, however a bad one. Examples a department and its individual officers set are inevitably the standard by which the community responds.

Continued

extensive interests in and inevitably share in the fate of the community as a whole. It should also be recalled that the police are recruited from, hired by, and sworn to serve the community. Many other examples could be cited, but these should suffice to demonstrate the extent to which the police and the public are fundamentally members of the same community, as the Critical Issue article indicates. In fact, current community policing efforts are based on that very premise.

In what sense, then, are the police and the public different? The police are different from the public in the sense that the former have work and duties which are different from those of the other citizens in the community. The functions of the police are essential to the welfare of the community, but they

Cops Are Community Leaders *(Continued)*

The public will always have a reaction to any police contact, positive or negative. Establishing the proper example can set the stage for these encounters, the result of these encounters, and for future encounters.

Ethical Leadership

Ethics is as essential to police leadership as the ethics required of a physician or lawyer. The issue of *Ethical Leadership* suggested is the framework within which an officer is expected to function and carry out his enforcement role. Ethical leadership demonstrates a set of values.

A frequently asked question is, How can my department implement an ethical leadership program? A better question is, What ethical framework do my officers function under? Ethical considerations should be the basis of any policy or regulation. In sensitive situations not specifically covered by policy or regulations, the ethical ''grass roots''

become the standard for police action, providing an expanded support base and framework from which to work. The policies and regulations of any agency should be a functional subset of the ethical framework from which they were derived. Ethical leadership will reduce negative public relations, enhance decisive actions and standardize police response in a given situation.

Moral Leadership

Moral leadership is less well-defined in terms of law enforcement. The most likely reason is that morality and moral issues remain an individual consideration, and are therefore seldom a departmental issue. Moral leadership is a set of individual values not normally taught in the educational setting and not easily evaluated. It is easier to evaluate a lack of moral excellence than to dictate the parameters of the subject.

It is true that the policies can be established to address these issues. However, infractions of such policies are normally a consequence after-the-fact, and any damage has already been done. The agency and the individual officer must suffer the consequences in the public eye. Moral leadership is therefore a major component of the cop as a community leader.

The law enforcement community can make an impact on the future of our communities, reduce risks and, at the same time, suppress crime with appropriate consideration given to our role as a community leader. We are obligated to abide by the concepts of direction, security, example, and ethical and moral leadership, for we are, in every respect, *Community Leaders.*

© *LAW and ORDER, November 1989. Reprinted by permission.*

---

are neither more nor less important than the tasks of many other citizens in that regard. Like other occupations, the police officer's job has characteristics which make it more or less unique, confronting the person who is trying to do the job with special problems and special opportunities for satisfaction. It has been the purpose of this book to explore some of these more or less unique characteristics and their implications for police community relations. The central thesis here presented, however, is that the community consists of many different people performing many different assignments or functions, yet all sharing and contributing to the same community life.

In our judgment, good police community relations depend upon emphasizing the common community membership which police and other citizens share, irrespective of the vocation which they have chosen. If the police expect a trusting public, if the police wish the public to advise them, if the police depend upon the willingness of citizens to help them in the prevention and detection of crime and in the apprehension of criminals, they cannot allow the public to regard them as an alien force. If the public expects to be protected from crime and criminals, if they hope to be reasonably safe and secure in their homes and on the streets, if they look for the police to come to their aid when an emergency exists, then that same public cannot afford to treat the police as an alien force in their midst. If the police and the public would perceive each other as members of the same community, many of the problems in police community relations could be mitigated and others could be solved. This, of course, is the basis upon which community policing rests today, and the basis upon which Sir Robert Peel developed the London Metropolitan Police more than 150 years ago.

Of course, recommending that the police and other citizens view one another as members of the same community is much easier than actually creating a situation in which the perception of their interrelated, interdependent membership in the community predominates. As frequently noted in previous chapters, there are special features of the police role which create tensions between the police and the community. Because of the complexity of modern industrial society and its cultural diversity, conflicts between the police and some segments of the community are inevitable. It is essential, therefore, that both the police and the public be reminded from time to time that they are interdependent members of the same community. To accomplish this there are a number of measures that police departments can initiate in order to emphasize their foundation in the community. Some of these will be discussed below.

Critical Aspects of the Police Community Connection

The distinctive characteristics of the police role in the community, and the tensions which this role inevitably produces in their relationships, require discerning efforts on the part of both so that each will view the police as part of the community. A critical component of these efforts is to insure that the police reflect the community in several basic ways.

First, the police department should recognize and express the ethnic composition of the community. A great deal has been written about ethnic discrimination in the hiring practices of police departments. Most of this discussion has centered on the moral, philosophical, and legal injustices involved in these practices. Although we agree with the general thrust of these arguments, it appears to us that too little attention has been directed to the practical implications for police community relations. In fact, these are closely related to eliminating discriminatory hiring in police departments. It is necessary to help the public to realize that the police, as part of the community, should form a police force which reflects the community's ethnic composition. Furthermore, departments should express the community's ethnic composition, not only in simple numerical percentages of the entire force, but also at the various ranks of the police force.

What are the practical implications of such a "representative" police department for police community relations? It is a well-known principle in the social sciences that people tend to differentiate themselves from others. They do so in a number of ways, one of which is to focus attention on the more obvious differences in height, gender, color of skin, dress, hair length, physical abilities, speech patterns, and so on. It is also well-known that people tend to generalize these differences by assuming that persons who are different from themselves in some readily noticeable way are also different in many other, less visible ways. An all-white police force provides nonwhite members of the community a ready argument for the ''differentness'' of the police; this provides a convenient basis for making invidious assumptions about the motives of the police and the ''real'' community which the police serve. That argument and those assumptions can be refuted by organizing a police force composed in part of persons from those ethnic groups. A multiethnic police force will certainly not solve all of the problems which arise among ethnic minorities in communities; in fact it sometimes creates serious problems for minority persons who join the police force. Nevertheless, a police department whose ethnic composition reflects that of the community will be in a much better position to build constructive police community relations, than one that does not represent the diverse ethnic blend.

The argument regarding ethnic composition applies also to the representation of women on the police force. Women are asserting their individuality and rights more overtly; and recent reports indicate that they are becoming more actively involved in juvenile and adult crime. In the course of their duties, members of the police force are interacting more frequently with women. Thus, the presence of women on the police force can help others of their sex to view the police as a part of the community. It may thus serve to refute the argument that the police do not understand or are insensitive to the needs of women. Furthermore, insofar as women possess special skills and are more experienced in certain aspects of life, they bring much needed expertise to the department.[3]

Although there are qualities of maturity and competence which clearly take precedence, within the limits of these characteristics age is also an important factor. Since a community comprises persons of different ages, age differences often become the focus of conflicts and discriminatory practices. When a police force reflects the adult age composition of the community it serves, the department is more likely to be recognized and accepted as part of that social group.

Obviously, one would not want the police to reflect the community in all respects. We would hope, for example, that there would be proportionately fewer criminals on the police force than in the larger community. We would also expect that the police force would be better educated in the social sciences, more adequately trained in the law, in better physical condition, more skilled in the use of firearms, and better equipped to deal with crises and emergency situations than are the vast majority of citizens. These are differences directly related to the competence of the police; the perception of differences in these qualifications between police officers and the public contributes to good police community relations. But in the basic qualities of ethnicity, gender, and age composition it is manifestly in the interests of both police and public that the police force reflect the community. If the public views the police as ''one of us'' in these fundamental ways, they are more likely to assist the police when the occasion arises. Also, public confidence in and respect for the law, which underlies the enforcement of law and the maintenance of order, are reinforced.

As you have undoubtedly concluded by now, we believe that community relations should be recognized as a central, if not *the* central component of any police agency. Without sound community relations, police administrators have a difficult time attracting, paying, equipping, and retaining the type of police officers they desire. Efficient police performance, whether in terms of crime prevention, arrest and conviction rates, or other services, is highly unlikely when police community relations are unsatisfactory. It is imperative that police administrators, police officers, and members of the public should stop considering community relations as an auxiliary service to be developed last and reduced first. Though many progressive police officials reached this conclusion long ago, others still view community relations as something less than essential police work. We believe that every police department would profit in one way or another from innovative community relations programs. In order to improve police community relations, police administrators and community leaders have a responsibility to develop and promote training which is more than mere "window dressing." In the 1960s it was not uncommon to hear police chiefs talking about "taking the heat off" by sending officers to sensitivity training sessions or confrontation study groups. In many instances, the officers who received this training were ill-prepared to understand the material presented, and/or disinterested. They were like sacrificial lambs offered up to pacify citizen groups intent on compelling the police to accept training in community relations. Although a great deal of money was spent on such training, much of it was wasted, and in many instances, the benefits derived by police and citizens did not meet the expectations of either group. To some extent, this remains the case today.

We have pointed out repeatedly that police community relations are a two-way street. Nonetheless, the police may have to assume the leadership, since it is possible to require them to become familiar with community relations theory and practice. For they are, in fact, public servants, and their livelihoods depend to some extent upon their ability to convince the public that they are effective public servants. Police-sponsored community relations programs, therefore, can pay big dividends to both the police and the public.

In order to develop favorable community relations, police administrators will have to convince their personnel to view participation in community relations as a crucial phase of police work. This can be accomplished by allocating resources to training in community relations and by significant recognition of those officers who demonstrate concern for improving relationships with the community. It is essential to emphasize that positive human relations are prerequisites for establishing good relations with the community. The one-on-one encounters that occur routinely between police officers and other citizens not only influence those directly involved; many others may witness or hear about these encounters. An essential criterion for employment as a police officer, then, is basic respect for the dignity and worth of all people, regardless of age, gender, race, ethnic group, religion, or social class. Officers who thus respect others can be trained to anticipate, analyze, evaluate, and control many encounters which might otherwise be frustrating. In the process, they demonstrate to citizens that they are individuals with human concerns. No police officer who routinely shows lack of consideration or respect for others should be retained, since the actions of one such officer tends to create or perpetuate negative stereotypes.

Every police officer, then, is responsible for treating those with whom he or she comes into contact with respect and concern. Similarly, every supervisor is accountable for ensuring that those whom he or she supervises are aware of and practice good human relations.

Once this attitude becomes habitual, positive public relations can be promoted. Consistently effective public relations campaigns involve continuing analyses of public opinion in order to formulate and implement relevant public relations policy. Personnel, equipment, facilities, and the media can all be used to convey to the public a positive image of the police. However, this image will not be formed by chance. It requires constant planning, evaluation, revision, and reimplementation.

Combining positive human and public relations programs will lead to positive community relations. Neither one alone is enough, and both must be coordinated in planning and implementation. The resultant community relations programs will necessarily, of course, differ according to time, place, and audience. Thus, community relations programs which work in rural areas may be inappropriate in urban centers; programs designed for youth may fail when used with the elderly; techniques which are successful with conservative rural residents may be totally unacceptable when dealing with urban minority groups. Nevertheless, the basic components—human relations and public relations—are equally essential in all these situations.

Although police community relations depend upon the actions of both groups, success is most likely when each group feels compelled to take the first step toward winning the other group over. To the extent that the police feel an obligation to convince the public that they are sincere in their intention to develop cooperative, civil relationships, and to the degree that they take advantage of available resources to attain this goal, police community relations will be improved. Although it will not be easy to change the attitudes of some groups, and though it is unrealistic to think that police community relations will ever be problem-free, improvements can be made. To the extent that such improvements occur, each of us, police and other citizens alike, will benefit.

Accountability and Responsiveness: Prerequisites for Successful Community Relations

Sometimes as a matter of departmental philosophy, and almost always in times of monetary restrictions, when the careful allocation of financial and human resources is severely limited, specially designed and explicitly detailed community relations programs are assigned a relatively low priority in police department budgets. When community relations programs are severely curtailed or completely eliminated, there may be a tendency on the part of both community and police to conclude that police community relations have been assigned a correspondingly low priority. If this impression does, in fact, exist, certainly it may have negative impact on the police or the community. But the absence of explicitly designated community relations programs and personnel may simply take a police force and its community back to the basic building blocks of police community relations. This means renewed recognition of police accountability to the community which they serve, together with alert responsiveness to the needs of the community's citizens.

In exploring the police role in police community relations, it is appropriate to begin by emphasizing the role of the community as a recipient of services provided by the police. Fighting crime through investigative work, supplemented by pursuit and capture of suspects, creates the dominant image which the public associates with the police; this is also the picture of their work which many police officers have formed. These activities convey the thrill and glamour of police work which attracts many to the law enforcement profession. Most citizens will readily acknowledge that their communities need police officers to carry out these functions and to provide these law enforcement services. It is also relatively easy for most citizens to recognize that the police are rendering valuable services to the community through such activities.

As we have seen, however, on the average, police officers devote much less than 50 percent of their time to law enforcement activities, per se. The greater share of an officer's time is spent in much less glamorous but no less essential service functions such as traffic control, routine patrol, responding to health or other personal emergencies of community citizens, summoning help for stranded motorists, picking drunks up off the streets, and the countless other tasks which the community expects its police to perform from day to day. Furthermore, as we have also seen, most police activity represents reaction rather than initiatory action, that is, responding to requests for service from the public accounts for 80 to 90 percent of police activity.

There is a tendency, as police departments have grown larger and more differentiated (i.e., divided into more specialized divisions, each with its own duties and responsibilities), for police officers and administrators to overlook a very basic truth concerning any public service institution, including the police. A public agency like the police finds it difficult indeed to enjoy a good reputation among its clients if the agency does a bad job of meeting the clients' needs. Expressed quite simply, if citizens recognize that police officers do their jobs with knowledge, skill, discipline, and courtesy, they are likely to respect their police. It is extremely difficult, in fact, almost impossible for any police community relations program to offset the negative effects of uninformed, sloppy, discourteous performances of duty on the part of the police.

One critical dimension of good work in situations where public services are provided, is *responsiveness*. By responsiveness, we mean: (1) where the service requested is one the police can provide, it is furnished as promptly and as competently as possible, and (2) where the service requested cannot be provided, a satisfactory explanation is offered and, when possible, an appropriate referral is made.

Some time ago, the home of one of the authors was broken into and burglarized. When the break-in was discovered, a call was made to the local police department. Within ten minutes an officer arrived at the door, looked through the house to be sure the burglar had, in fact, left the premises, asked pertinent questions, dusted a few items for fingerprints, gave appropriate advice to contact the bank about some blank checks which, among other items, were believed to be missing, made some observations about the amateurish appearances of the burglary, and promised a follow-up if the investigation turned up anything important. It was an impressive piece of police work. There was no police-initiated follow-up contact, but the teenage burglar was eventually taken into custody because he used his own name to cash one of the blank checks. (The officer was not wrong in his judgment that the burglar was an amateur!) Even if nothing else had characterized this particular incident, this citizen derived a very good impression of the city's police department, since the department was almost 100 percent responsive. Yet all that actually happened was that an officer did his job well. If all police departments were half as responsive in their contacts with citizens, they would certainly create a broad and powerful base of appreciation and support in the community.

It should be recognized, of course, that many police departments, especially those serving larger cities, do not possess the resources to respond satisfactorily to all citizens' requests for services. When the allocation of funds and personnel is low and the demand for police services is high, departments must, in conjunction with city or county administrators, establish policies concerning the assignment of monetary and human resources. This requires stipulating priorities as to the various kinds of police services, and identifying the level of response the department will make to citizen requests; these responses will correspond to the department's own perceived need for certain decisions and actions. In many cases, for example, an officer is not dispatched to the scene of a minor burglary; but a written record will be made of the citizen's report of the crime. By establishing policies, assigning priorities, and identifying appropriate responses, the available resources are allocated in the most efficient way.

When such apportionment of police resources is necessary, it is essential that the community be informed of the established policies and procedures, the reasons why they were decided on, and how a particular citizen's request is to be handled according to those policy and procedural guidelines. In this way many potentially negative reactions to apparent failure to respond to a citizen's request for services can be avoided. Often, in fact, citizens may be impressed by the concern of the department for keeping costs at a minimum and using their tax dollars most effectively.

Failure to inform the public about policies and procedures can be very detrimental to police community relations. The same author whose house was burglarized was visiting in Oakland, California, a few years ago. One night, while staying at a motel, his car was broken into and a pair of binoculars, together with a camera of some considerable value, were stolen. When the theft was discovered the following morning, a call was made to the Oakland Police Department to report the theft and establish a record of the theft for insurance claim purposes. When asked if an officer would be dispatched, the officer on the phone laughed, said "No" and hung up the phone. The author did not really anticipate that an officer would be sent, but a much better impression of the department would have been made if a brief, simple explanation had been given concerning the scarcity of resources available to the police and the need to concentrate on problems or incidents assigned a higher priority.

The fact that most police actions are responses or reactions, rather than positive moves initiated by them, indicates still another aspect of responsiveness and its relation to the community's share in police community relations. The community initiates a great deal of police activity simply by asking for services. A request for services may be viewed as a statement of need on the part of the person requesting the service. At the very minimum, citizens must have sufficient confidence in the police department to request help in a variety of situations. The development and maintenance of that confidence and trust are essential to creating the right attitude toward the police.

The community, too, has an obligation to perceive and be responsive to the needs of the police. Citizens who are willing to provide the police with information that may help the police in solving a crime or who are willing to testify in court, either for the prosecution or the defense, are demonstrating cooperation with the police and with the criminal justice system.

Another way the community's desires and the obligations of the police to meet those needs are expressed is in the *accountability* of the police to their community. In the broadest and most fundamental sense, police officers are both servants of the law and employees of the communities they serve. Like all employees, the police are accountable to their employer, the citizens of the community, for their performance on the job. Furthermore, because the powers entrusted to the police are so great, the citizens of a democracy will be vigilant in monitoring the actions of the police, and aware of their right to demand that the police account for their actions.

Police accountability can be assured in a variety of ways and through various police and community agencies and institutions.[4] Among the basic procedures for achieving accountability are periodic reports to the community concerning police activity. Some of these activities are reported daily in the news media, either as feature stories or in "police report" columns. The reporters, as well as the stories and reports they file, are valuable because they assure that police actions are continually visible to the community. Visibility in this context has a double significance: citizens have regular reminders of the services provided by the police; and police actions are subject to the critical scrutiny of reporters as well as observers and readers. This provides some deterrence to police misconduct as well as recognition of exemplary police behavior.

Because daily reports are necessarily specific and detailed, however, they may not be very useful in forming a general picture of the priorities of a police department, its effectiveness as a law enforcement agency, or its efficiency in dealing with requests for other services. A more suitable instrument for these purposes is the police department's annual report, usually submitted directly to the community's principal governing body (e.g., city council or county board of supervisors). Unfortunately, in some respects, crime rates and percentages of crimes solved are emphasized not only in the media coverage of these departmental reports but also in the departmental reports themselves. These are important data, of course, but as a rule they cover less than half, often as little as 20 percent of police activities. It would be very useful, indeed, not only to the police themselves but to the community as a whole, to compile and present a more complete report which provides some information about the frequency of other service activities furnished by the police. (Often, of course, data are not even gathered about these other activities; this gives some indication of their value as perceived by the police.) If more attention were paid to these services, the community might develop a better understanding and appreciation of the complete range of essential community services delivered by the police.

Another forum for the expression of police accountability is the internal affairs or internal investigative division of the police department. The existence and activities of such a division or process within a department are significant because, in this way, it acknowledges the possibility of police misconduct and of the necessity of reporting and explaining to the public the conduct of its members. With this purpose of accountability in mind, a policy recently adopted in many police departments requires the temporary reassignment of officers who, in the course of duty, have fired a gun or used other "deadly force," until the department has examined and justified the conduct of the officers. Despite the inevitable skepticism of the public about a police department's willingness to accuse one of its own members, an internal investigation and the findings of such an investigation are a significant first step in the department's efforts to account to the public for its actions. This is especially true since internal investigations often deal with precisely those actions which tend to undermine public confidence in the police (e.g., corruption), and which involve the special powers given to the police (e.g., the use of deadly force).

Another way in which communities may obtain an accounting from their police departments is through "civilian police review boards." These are groups of citizens specifically established, usually by local governing bodies, to investigate community complaints about police conduct; they are also set up to facilitate dialogue between the police and representative citizens concerning community needs and police responsiveness. Police review boards have not been uniformly successful as vehicles for ensuring police accountability or for productive dialogue between citizens and the police. This may be due, in part, to their being complaint-oriented, rather than dialogue-oriented. Nevertheless, regular, informal dialogue between citizens and the police is one means of assuring police accountability to citizens.

Police Tell Their Side of Problem

Critical Issue

By Norma Cunningham

Associate Editor

GALESBURG—A representative of the Galesburg Police Department presented case histories of the department's contacts with mentally disturbed people at a Tuesday meeting of a mayor's advisory committee.

The committee was appointed after a welfare supervisor for Galesburg Township several months ago contended there were people who had been released after treatment who were on the streets without money for food and shelter.

John Schlaf of GPD outlined nine case histories of how police handled people who were disturbed. The case histories deleted any identifying references and referred to the person only by gender and age.

Schlaf said the department is in a unique position because while representatives of other groups and organizations on the advisory committee have an interest in "target groups," police come in contact with the overall group.

The cases presented represented problem areas, he said, and shows what short-term assistance could be provided by police. Without some long-term solution, however, the department sees the same person as a repeater, according to Schlaf.

Schlaf said legal restrictions, privacy and security regulations create a division between what police can actually do in dealing with the disturbed person and what the public believes police can do. That creates a frustration with the "bulkiness" of the system, he said, and is a valid concern of police.

JoAnn Harris, chairman of Tuesday's meeting, said she has seen police deal with such problems with "much patience and understanding."

Richard Ponzer, committee member, questioned whether one of the frustrations with the situation was the time away from other duties that is required to deal with the disturbed person.

"That's part of it. But any time you devote a lot of time and there's a happy ending, that's worth it. It's when you devote a lot of time and there is no happy ending that the frustration sets in," Schlaf replied.

Dr. Martin Cohen, superintendent of Galesburg Mental Hospital and a committee member, said that workers in his field share that frustration. "We don't have that many happy endings, either, but there's no way to avoid that frustration. . . . We have to learn to live with the frustration and realize we don't have all the answers," Cohen said. He suggested that perhaps more sharing by those involved in dealing with disturbed persons may help.

Referring to an earlier suggestion to form another agency to fill the voids in present service, Schlaf said he did not believe such an agency is needed. He said each agency which deals with the problem should "do its job and take up the slack so everyone would know where to go with a problem. The resources are

Continued

Still another criterion of police accountability is that provided by the victims of crime or other persons in need of police services. It is in this very personal and specific context that accountability is perhaps most essential. The very best efforts of the police department should be dedicated to the victim of rape or mugging, or to the relatives of a murder victim.

Police departments which are responsive to the needs of a community and which recognize that they are accountable to that community for providing high-quality services, have laid the most basic foundation possible for successful police community relations. One example of an attempt to improve the quality of services provided by the police by engaging in a cooperative program is "Operation Bootstrap." This program is designed to bring together corporate leaders with leaders from the public sector, in this case police administrators, in order to help the latter upgrade management skills so they can better address the complex, ever-changing demands of society.

right here in this room. The answers to most of the questions are right here,'' he said.

Harris said if an agency receives a call for help from another person in the system, they should take for granted that it is a critical situation and not say ''see us next Wednesday.''

Ned Hippensteel, executive director of Knox County Council for Developmental Disabilities (KCCDD) and a member of the committee, said he may be in the minority, but he believes there may be a need for a whole new agency to ''do this sort of thing.'' He said it was asking a lot of such agencies as Spoon River Community Health Center and KCCDD to ''drop everything and respond.''

James H. Frakes, Galesburg police chief and a committee member, said the problem is not the person who is ''down and out'' but the person with a mental problem for whom seemingly nothing can be done to help. Frakes, who was smoking a cigar, said, ''But asking for a

new agency in this day and age—you're not smoking cigars, you're smoking something else.'' He said all agencies involved in the committee are supported by taxpayers and the solution to the problem is to get them all cooperating and working together, so problems don't have to be dealt with on the street.

Ponzer explained SRCMHC's 24-hour emergency service. He said there is a toll-free number which will reach a professional in the Cottage Hospital inpatient unit maintained by the organization.

Betty Barnstead, a member of the committee, said the police case histories did not ''bear out that it's that simple.'' She said the case histories seemed to show that police pick up a person with a problem, take him to an agency or hospital, but if the patient decides he does not want to stay, he is back out on the street.

Schlaf agreed, saying, ''It all reverts back to the guy who was picked up in the first place and his decision. . . .

That's the silliness of it all. The decision rests with the person who has the problem.''

Frakes said the ''fly in the ointment'' is that if there is a decision that the person needs help, he is moved along until he decides that he does not want help. He asked if there were not cases where doctors said a patient needs help but a court refuses to commit him for treatment.

''Oh yes, we see that every Friday,'' Cohen replied. He said there may be two competent persons who have decided the person needs help, but a judge may decide he should not be deprived of his liberty.

Frakes said the committee could recommend going to the General Assembly to seek a change in the law if such a decision were part of the final recommendation.

The next meeting of the committee was set for March 9.

Reprinted from the Galesburg Register Mail, *February 10, 1982, with permission.*

Law enforcement has become the most important ''frontline'' provider of social services in our society. Police deal not just with criminal behavior, but with the homeless, the mentally ill, abused children, battered spouses, and a host of other issues that confront our citizens. Their responsibility is not only to help solve crimes but to help manage these complex social issues. Partnerships with corporate America can help maximize our limited resources to help communities.[5]

The nature of the relationship which exists between a police force and the community it serves influences every aspect of that department's operations. A negative or unsatisfactory relationship makes the job of every police officer, from the patrol officer in the squad car to the chief or commissioner, more difficult. It undermines the department's position in the discussion of the allocation of a city's or a county's limited financial resources. Misunderstanding or enmity poisons relationships with those other elements of the criminal justice system, such as the courts, upon which the police, like other citizens, depend for the satisfactory operation of law enforcement and for the maintenance of order. A negative police community relationship makes the department a vulnerable target for politicians attempting to demonstrate their zeal. It distorts the opinions of ordinary citizens about the police and often sours the relationships within the department as well.

In contrast, positive police community relationships affect the same spheres of police and community activity and influence, but with generally beneficial results for both the police and the community. One of the best illustrations of attempts by the police to encourage good working relationships with the public is the Orlando, Florida, Citizens' Police Academy (CPA). The academy has been in existence for a number of years and resulted from an officer's suggestion to the Orlando police chief, William Kolezar, who was concerned about the negative attitude he perceived toward the police on the part of the public. Citizens enroll for a three-month time period, attending classes free of charge and participating in actual patrol duty. There is now a waiting list of some 150 citizens wishing to participate in the academy program which is offered twice a year. CPA coordinator officer Hona Edwards indicates that alumni have raised money for bulletproof vests for the police, helped defray some of the expenses of the mounted patrol unit, and provided additional funding for incentive classes for police officers seeking specialized training. Edwards' observations contain a message for police and other citizens across the country.

> Maybe through this program we're trying to earn respect, to get people to understand what kind of self-control the officer must have, and to show them that many times there's just not a single thing we can do to resolve a problem. Police work a lot in the gray area and most of the time we get it right. We would just like the citizens to know.[6]

Numerous other citizen-police academies now exist around the country.

We would like to conclude by noting the extreme importance of police administrative personnel, particularly the police chief, in promoting good community relations. "Administrators must find the courage to challenge not only themselves but all personnel to commit to change, be sensitive to resultant effects, respond to challenges and demonstrate that success involves risk."[7] Police leaders must have a clear vision of the importance of community relations, a personal commitment to improving these relations, and a method of developing and rewarding people whose performance helps achieve these goals.[8] Police chiefs who foster, encourage, or tolerate attitudes of disrespect toward citizens on behalf of their officers are unacceptable. As Bouza (1990) correctly points out: "The approach and competence of the chief executive officer set the mood and atmosphere of the agency. . . . The employees tend to respond to the value system transmitted in the daily actions of the hierarchy rather than to written policy. . . . A police department's first order of business is to get its internal house in order through the creation of an organizational climate that fosters integrity and effective performance."[9] Both the public and the officers in the department note whether the chief takes issues such as community relations, minority relations, and community policing seriously. Does he or she set the example by attending training sessions dealing with these subjects? Are minorities recruited? Does the chief meet with and listen to the views of various public groups? Do his or her words and deeds show fairness and integrity? Police leaders must be trusted by citizens and taken seriously by the rank-and-file.[10] When they are, and when they support positive community relations by word and deed, opportunities for developing and improving police community relations are maximized.

Endnotes

1. Gordon Pitter. 1994. "Police Cynicism in the 1990s." *The Police Chief* 61(5): 57–59.
2. On what are often the mutually antagonistic views of the police and other citizens see, for example, Reiss. "Police Brutality."; Jack Preiss and Howard Ehrlich. 1978. *An Examination of Role Theory: The Case of the State Police.* 2ed. St. Paul, MN.: West Publishing Co.; James Hernandez, Jr. 1989. *The Custer Syndrome.* Salem, WI: Sheffield Publishing; or Sparrow, Moore, and Kennedy. *Beyond 911.*
3. Cathryn H. House. 1993. "The Changing Role of Women in Law Enforcement." *The Police Chief* 60(10): 139–144.
4. Sparrow, Moore, and Kennedy. *Beyond 911.*: chapter 6.
5. Bill Bruns. 1989. "Operation Bootstrap: Opening Corporate Classrooms to Police Managers." *NIJ Reports.* National Institute of Justice. 217 (November): 2–6.
6. Sara Roen. 1990. "A Class Act." *Police: The Law Officer's Magazine* 14(1): 28–67.
7. Carl Dobbs and Mark W. Field. 1993. "Rational Risk: Leadership Success or Failure?" *The Police Chief* 60(12): 64–66.
8. David Couper and Sabine Lobitz. 1993. "Leadership for Change: A National Agenda." *The Police Chief* 60(12): 15–19.
9. Bouza. *The Police Mystique.*: 47–49.
10. Kenneth A. Betsalel. 1990. "Police Leadership and the Reconciliation of Police-Minority Relations." *American Journal of the Police* 9(2): 63–77.

Suggested Readings

Bennett, Charles W., Jr. 1993. "The Last Taboo of Community Policing." *The Police Chief* 60(8): 86.

Berger, William B., Linda Mertes, and Alan Graham. 1994. "A Blueprint for Police-Community Partnerships." *The Police Chief* 61(5): 20–25.

Danner, Morgan L. 1992. "Dial-A-Cop Brings Officers Closer to the Community." *Law and Order* 40(6): 43–44.

Krieble, James H. 1994. "Community-Oriented Policing: Selection, Training and Evaluation Ensure Success." *The Police Chief* 61(5): 26–29.

Overman, Richard. 1994. "The Case for Community Policing." *The Police Chief* (March): 20–23.

Skolnick, Jerome H. and James J. Fyfe. 1993. *Above the Law: Police and the Excessive Use of Force.* New York: Free Press.

Police-Media Relations Policy, Police Department Burlington, Iowa

306.00 News Media Relations

306.01 **Role of News Media:** The public has the right to be aware of current events and government happenings. They acquire this information through various news media sources. Crime, its results and police actions are regularly the center of news articles and it is the news media's responsibility to supply the public with this information.

306.02 **Role of the Department:** Although various Department rules and state laws restrict information available to news personnel, it is the Department's policy to explain why information is withheld when this must occur. The Department seeks a cooperative climate in which the news media may obtain information in a manner which does not hamper police operations, abridge constitutional rights or interfere with Departmental investigations.

306.03 **News Releases:** The day shift Patrol Commander maintains daily liaison with members of the news media and makes most news releases on routine police matters. This includes traffic accident and enforcement information, crime and arrest data, malicious damage and lost and found information. In this regard, full cooperation is expected of the Patrol Commander in charge of the day shift.

    The Public Information/Crime Prevention Officer, who reports directly to the Chief of Police, frequently represents the Department through the news media for the purpose of informing and educating the public on matters of public safety and progress of various departmental crime prevention programs.

    The Chief of Police is available to authorized representatives of the news media to assist in solving problems of mutual concern, release information relative to plans and organization of the Department and to personally make news releases on selected major crime investigations. This is done to centrally coordinate information about case development and avoid confusion in dealing with several agencies and personnel.

306.04 **Limit of Information Released:** Since patrol officers must devote their full time to the investigation of a crime when so assigned, they frequently are unable to answer media inquiries at the scene. Normally the duty command officer will provide information concerning the case either at the scene or at police headquarters. When possible, without interfering with the investigation, patrol officers or detectives may also provide certain information. In any event the following guidelines apply for release of information with due regard for the victim's and witness's safety.

Information Concerning Crime Before Arrest:
a. Nature of the crime (burglary, assault, etc.)
b. Location of the crime (unless unsafe to do so)
c. Victim(s) of the crime (unless unsafe to do so)
d. Time the crime occurred
e. Items taken or injuries sustained, if any
f. Whether or not there are suspects

Information After Arrest is Made:
a. Accused's name, age, residence, employment, marital status and similar background information
b. Charges filed and identity (where appropriate, of complainant and/or witness)
c. Identity of the investigating and arresting agency(s) and length of investigation
d. Circumstances immediately surrounding the arrest, including time and place of arrest, resistance, pursuit, possession and use of weapons and a description of items seized at the time of the arrest

Note: The above information may be made available without diminishing the accused's right to fair trial.

Information Detrimental/Prejudicial—Not Released:
a. Statements as to character or reputation of an accused person or prospective witness
b. Admissions, confessions, or the contents of a statement made by the accused
c. Administration, performance or results of tests or the refusal of the accused to take a test
d. Statements concerning the credibility or anticipated testimony of prospective witnesses
e. The possibility or probability of a plea of guilty or other disposition of a case
f. Opinions concerning evidence or argument in the case, whether or not it is anticipated that such evidence or argument will be used at trial.

306.05 **Entering Dangerous Area:** Whenever a situation arises which involves great potential danger to the life and safety of people, a Police Officer or Officer in Charge may close off that area in the interest of public safety. Members of the news media, recognized as such by the Officer in Charge, may be admitted to the area at their own risk. It is not the responsibility of Officers to provide for the safety of news media members who voluntarily choose to subject themselves to danger. The decision to allow entry or not is at the discretion of the Officer in Charge.

306.06 **Entering Crime Scene:** Members of the news media will be prohibited from entering a crime scene or area which has been secured to preserve evidence or at any location where his or her presence jeopardizes police operations.

306.07 **Compliance with Laws:** All members of the news media must comply with the law. No news media member is exempt from any municipal, state or federal statute, although the Department recognizes the need for news and photograph collection and Officers should not unnecessarily obstruct a reporter in the performance of his or her duty.

306.08 **Criminal Records:** Prior criminal convictions are matters of public records and are available to the press through the office of the Clerk of the District Court. Records maintained by the Police Department contain confidential information, arrest information in which defendants have not been convicted and intelligence data, the public disclosure of which is prohibited by law. It should be recognized that publication of a prior criminal record, without a significant public need to know, could result in being highly prejudicial to the fair adjudication of a case.

306.09 **Photographs of Accused/Suspected Persons:** The decision to photograph a suspect or defendant in a public place must be made by the individual news agency. Under no circumstances, however, should police personnel allow the accused to be posed.

306.10 **Withhold Publication:** Withholding publication of sensitive information is dependent upon a cooperative media, not upon censorship by the Department. When sensitive information is obtained by a member of the news media, it is the Department member's obligation to advise the news member or their supervisors of the possible consequences of publication; however, the Department member may not interfere with lawful acts.

306.11 **Requests for Information:** Authority for granting a member of the news media permission to interview or otherwise obtain information concerning Departmental operations rests with the Chief of Police. Under extreme circumstances involving major crime or involvement of multiple investigative agencies, the Chief of Police may temporarily suspend the authority granted to patrol and command level officers under section 306.04 of this policy.

306.12 **Contingency News Media Plans During Disasters:** In the event of a natural or manmade disaster, the heads of all departments performing emergency services form a command post near the scene or in a strategic location to coordinate the efforts of the various agencies. The Chief of Police or his designated representative is located at this command post and is available to news media representatives. Members of the news media desiring to enter a disaster area may do so under the provisions of sections 306.05, 306.06 and 306.07 of this policy.

Index

Trojanowicz, R., 3, 13–14,
  57–58, 75, 124, 134–35,
  156, 176, 186, 202
Trump, K., 187
Tucker, W., 202
Turn in a Pusher, 178
Turtle, J., 202

U

underclass, 144, 152
uniforms, 46, 48–50, 60, 67, 110
unions. *See* police unions
United States v. City of Chicago,
  169
Usdansky, M., 156
U.S. Community Relations
  Service, 118
U.S. Department of Justice, 39,
  95

V

Vagg, J., 203
values, 4, 15–17, 23, 44, 77, 79,
  82, 85–86, 102–5, 141
Van Maanen, J., 39, 58
Vaughn, J., 14, 39, 97, 155, 169
Vernon, R., 186
victims, 47, 185, 191–92, 197
video camera/tape, 2, 54, 73
vigilantism, 3, 197–98
violence, 77, 88, 91, 98, 100,
  143–44, 146, 171, 197, 200
Vlasak, T., 186
Vollmer, A., 134
Vrij, A., 50, 57–58

W

Wadman, R., 58, 74–75
Walker, S., 13, 59
walk-in centers, 177

Wallach, I., 164, 170
Walters, P., 135
Wambaugh, J., 39
Ward, D., 40
Ward, S., 135
Wasserman, R., 3, 13, 57
watch and ward system, 18–19
watchman style departments, 128,
  130
Watson, T., 156
weapons, 30, 52, 109, 130, 172,
  208
Webber, A., 75, 134
Weinblatt, R., 71, 75
Weiner, N., 96–97
Wells, G., 202
Westley, W., 57–58
Whisenand, P., 186
Whitaker, D., 187
Wickham, D., 156
Wiley, M., 58

Williams, H., 168
Williams, L., 170
Williams, W., 2, 148, 167
Wilson, J., 36, 40, 127, 134, 187
Wilson, O., 57
Windham, T., 202
Winkel, F., 58
witchcraft. *See* satanic cults
Wolfgang, M., 75, 96–97
women
  as police officers, 33, 158–63,
    208
  treatment of by police, 44
Worden, R., 40

Y

youth, 76–95, 106, 140
Yuille, J., 59

Z

Ziman, S., 58, 74–75